THE MUMMY
THE RISE AND FALL OF
XANGO'S AX

IDW Publishing • San Diego, CA

Special thanks:
Justin Eisinger, Denton J. Tipton and all at IDW Publishing, Lisa Jackson (for providing the spectacular colors), Dallas Mayr, Scott Tipton, Paul Schober, Chuck Palahniuk, Dennis Widmyer, Phil Nutman, Rod Lott, Derek Burgan, Boris Karloff, Lon Chaney Jr., Charles, Erma, & Chuckie Wilkening, the Brave Men & Women of the U.S. Armed Forces.

Much Respect:
The tireless efforts of artist extraordinaire Stephen Mooney.

Without Whom:
Chris Ryall, James & Elaine Jabcuga

This one is for my wife.

Filmed on location:
Southeast Asia, Burma, Washington, D.C., San Diego, Dublin, & Buffalo, NY.

Josh Jabcuga
May 23, 2008

IDW Publishing
Operations:
Moshe Berger, Chairman
Ted Adams, President
Clifford Meth, EVP of Strategies
Matthew Ruzicka, CPA, Controller
Alan Payne, VP of Sales
Lorelei Bunjes, Dir. of Digital Services
Marci Hubbard, Executive Assistant
Alonzo Simon, Shipping Manager

Editorial:
Chris Ryall, Publisher/Editor-in-Chief
Scott Dunbier, Editor, Special Projects
Justin Eisinger, Editor
Kris Oprisko, Editor/Foreign Lic.
Denton J. Tipton, Editor
Tom Waltz, Editor

Design:
Robbie Robbins, EVP/Sr. Graphic Artist
Ben Templesmith, Artist/Designer
Neil Uyetake, Art Director
Chris Mowry, Graphic Artist
Amauri Osorio, Graphic Artist

ISBN #: 978-1-60010-252-3
11 10 09 08   1 2 3 4
www.idwpublishing.com
SPECIAL THANKS TO CINDY CHANG, BOB DUCSAY, AND MATT STUECKEN FOR THEIR INVALUABLE ASSISTANCE.

THE MUMMY™

THE RISE & FALL OF XANGO'S AX

STORY BY **JOSHUA JABCUGA**

ART BY **STEPHEN MOONEY**

COLORS BY **LISA JACKSON**

LETTERS BY **ROBBIE ROBBINS**
NEIL UYETAKE
CHRIS MOWRY
AMAURI OSORIO

ORIGINAL SERIES EDITS BY **DENTON J. TIPTON**
CHRIS RYALL

COLLECTION EDITS BY **JUSTIN EISINGER**

COLLECTION DESIGN BY **NEIL UYETAKE**

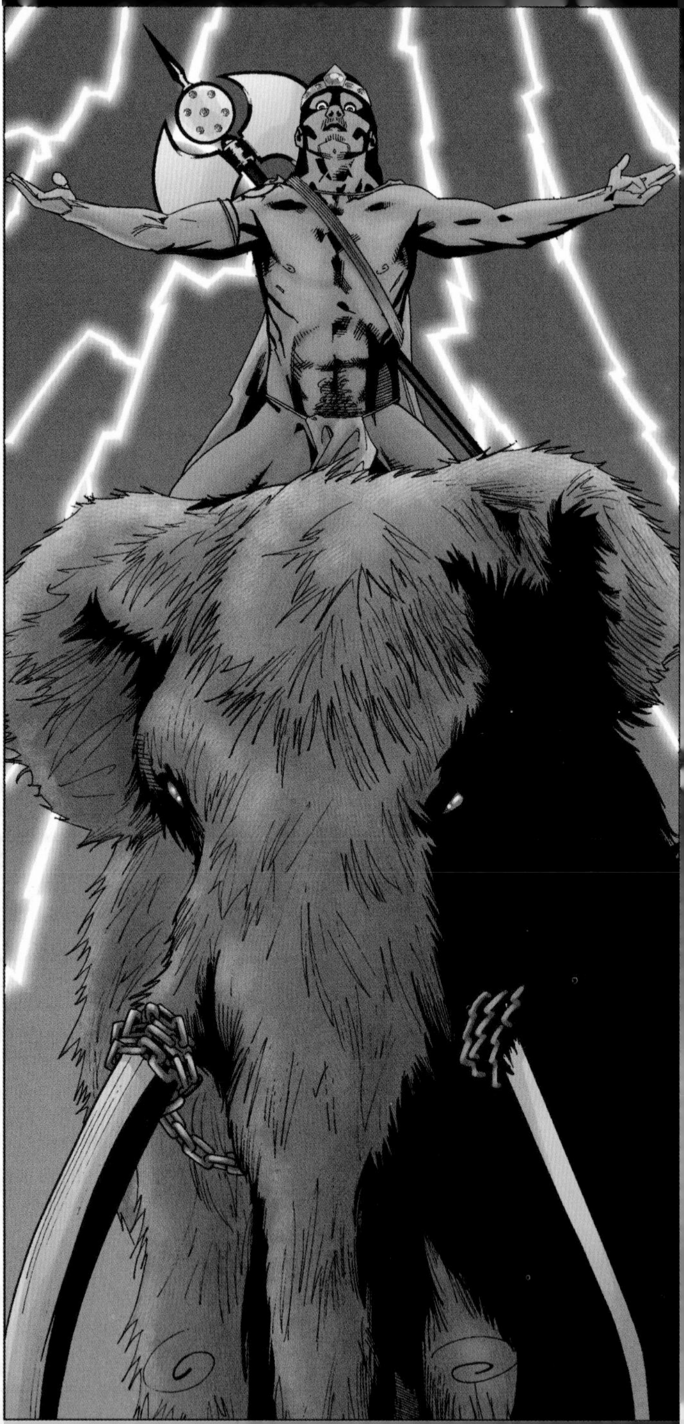

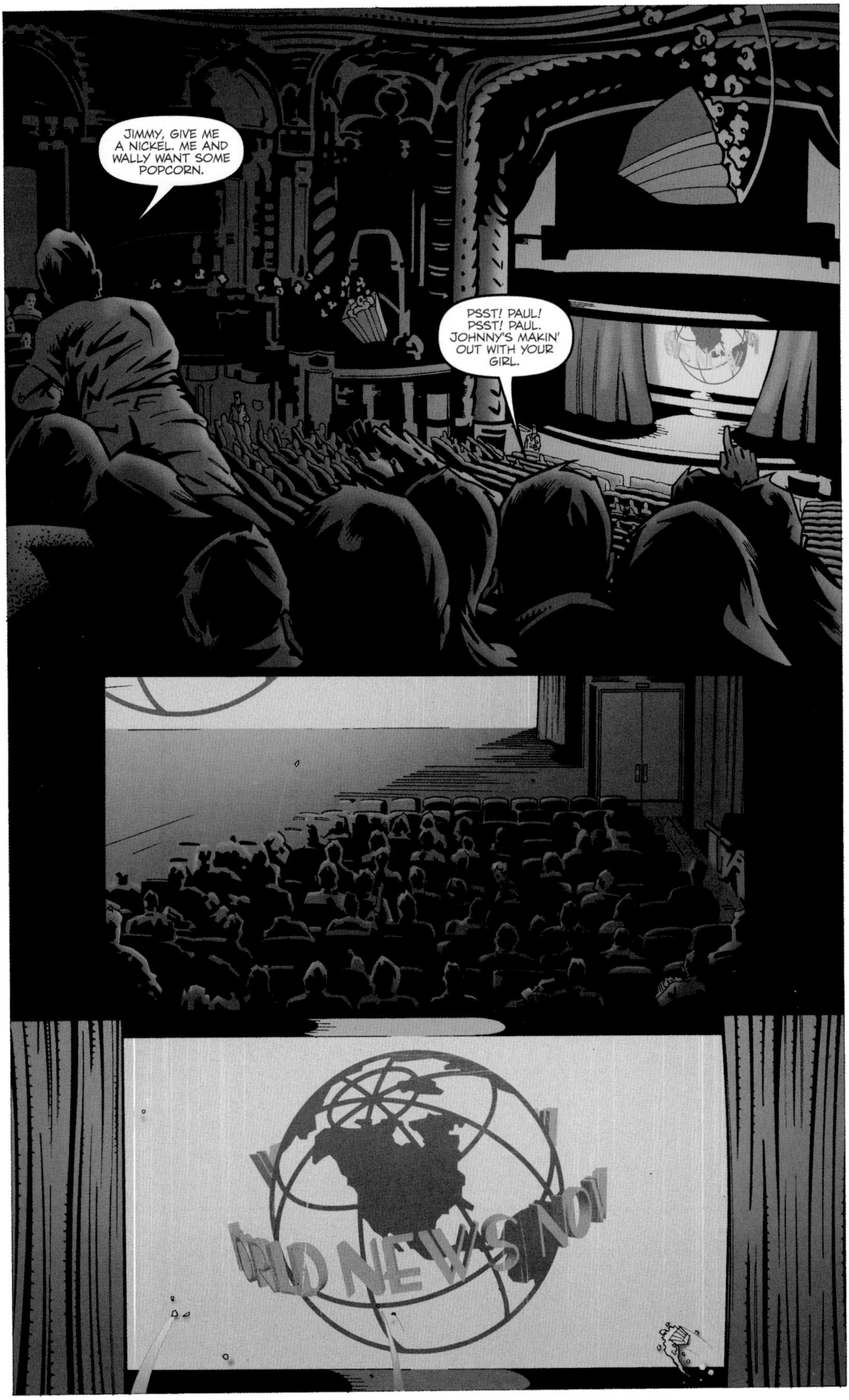
JIMMY, GIVE ME A NICKEL. ME AND WALLY WANT SOME POPCORN.
PSST! PAUL! PSST! PAUL. JOHNNY'S MAKIN' OUT WITH YOUR GIRL.

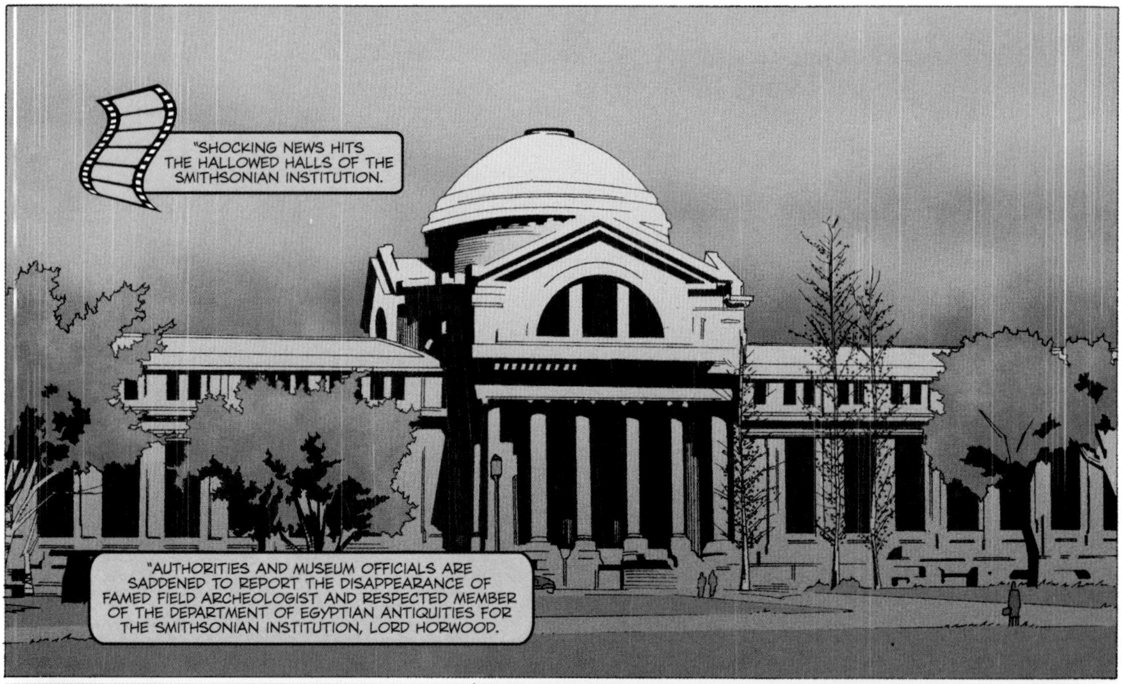
"SHOCKING NEWS HITS THE HALLOWED HALLS OF THE SMITHSONIAN INSTITUTION.
"AUTHORITIES AND MUSEUM OFFICIALS ARE SADDENED TO REPORT THE DISAPPEARANCE OF FAMED FIELD ARCHEOLOGIST AND RESPECTED MEMBER OF THE DEPARTMENT OF EGYPTIAN ANTIQUITIES FOR THE SMITHSONIAN INSTITUTION, LORD HORWOOD.

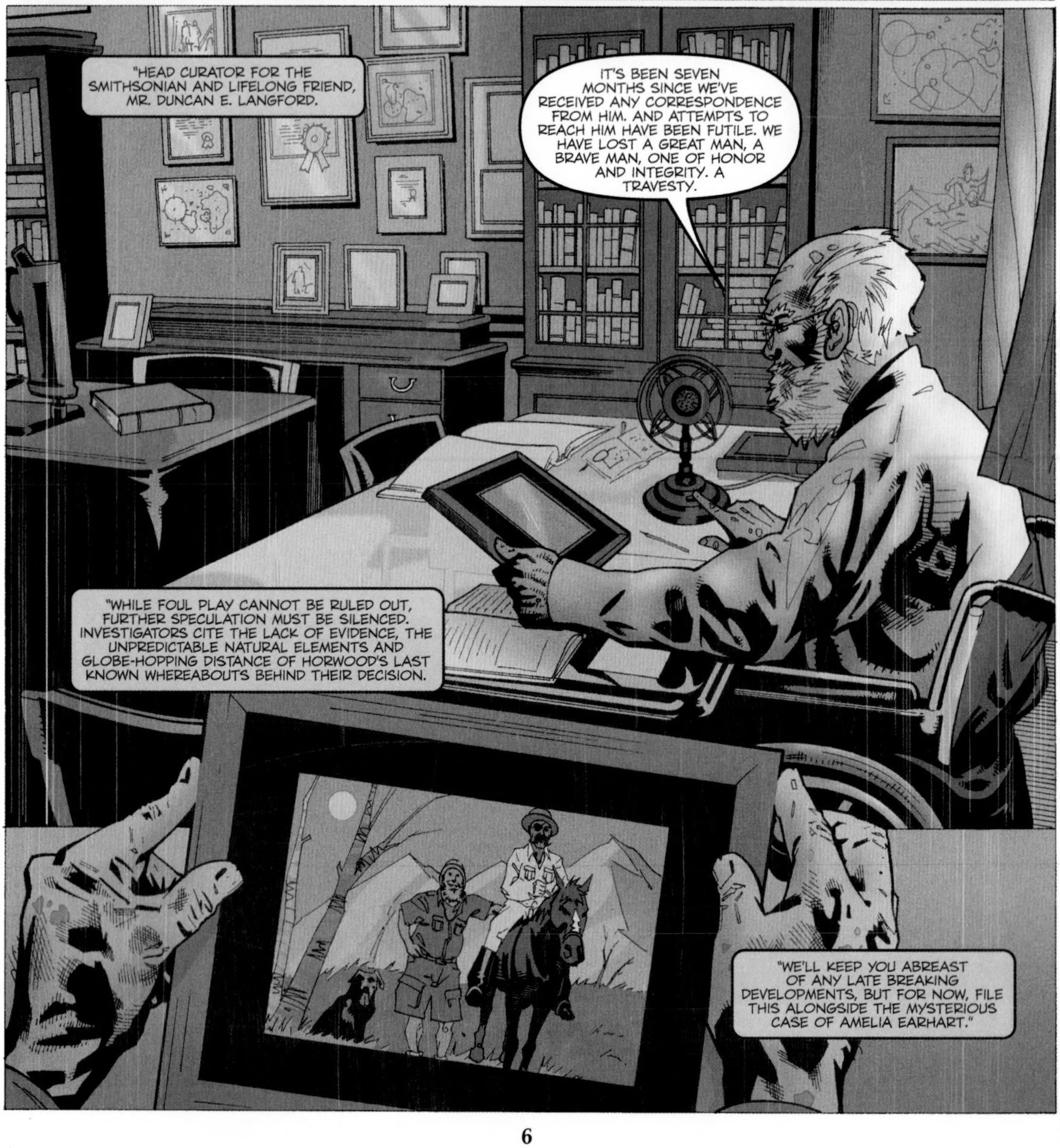
"HEAD CURATOR FOR THE SMITHSONIAN AND LIFELONG FRIEND, MR. DUNCAN E. LANGFORD.
IT'S BEEN SEVEN MONTHS SINCE WE'VE RECEIVED ANY CORRESPONDENCE FROM HIM. AND ATTEMPTS TO REACH HIM HAVE BEEN FUTILE. WE HAVE LOST A GREAT MAN, A BRAVE MAN, ONE OF HONOR AND INTEGRITY. A TRAVESTY.
"WHILE FOUL PLAY CANNOT BE RULED OUT, FURTHER SPECULATION MUST BE SILENCED. INVESTIGATORS CITE THE LACK OF EVIDENCE, THE UNPREDICTABLE NATURAL ELEMENTS AND GLOBE-HOPPING DISTANCE OF HORWOOD'S LAST KNOWN WHEREABOUTS BEHIND THEIR DECISION.
"WE'LL KEEP YOU ABREAST OF ANY LATE BREAKING DEVELOPMENTS, BUT FOR NOW, FILE THIS ALONGSIDE THE MYSTERIOUS CASE OF AMELIA EARHART."

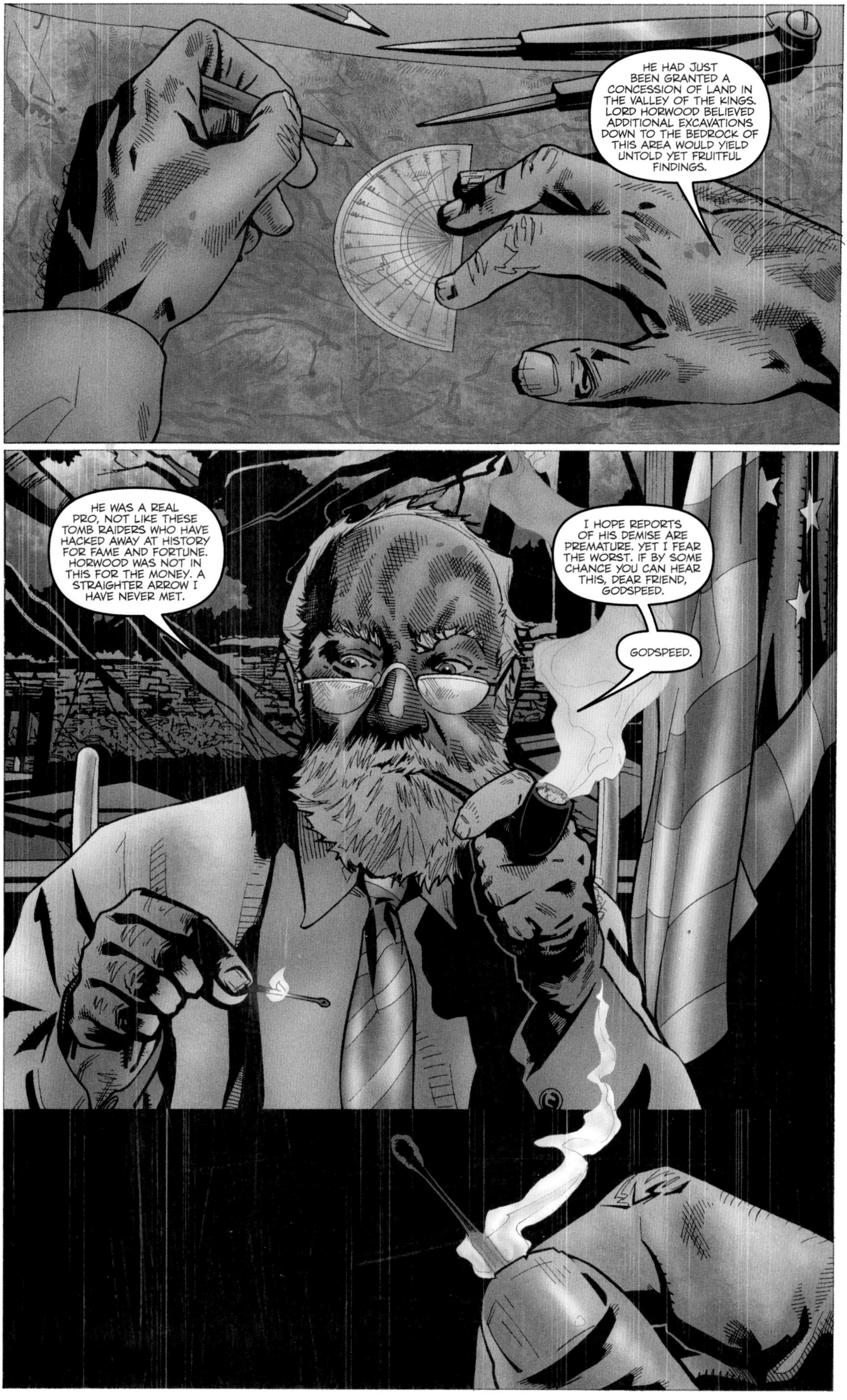
HE HAD JUST BEEN GRANTED A CONCESSION OF LAND IN THE VALLEY OF THE KINGS. LORD HORWOOD BELIEVED ADDITIONAL EXCAVATIONS DOWN TO THE BEDROCK OF THIS AREA WOULD YIELD UNTOLD YET FRUITFUL FINDINGS.
HE WAS A REAL PRO, NOT LIKE THESE TOMB RAIDERS WHO HAVE HACKED AWAY AT HISTORY FOR FAME AND FORTUNE. HORWOOD WAS NOT IN THIS FOR THE MONEY. A STRAIGHTER ARROW I HAVE NEVER MET.
I HOPE REPORTS OF HIS DEMISE ARE PREMATURE. YET I FEAR THE WORST. IF BY SOME CHANCE YOU CAN HEAR THIS, DEAR FRIEND, GODSPEED.
GODSPEED.

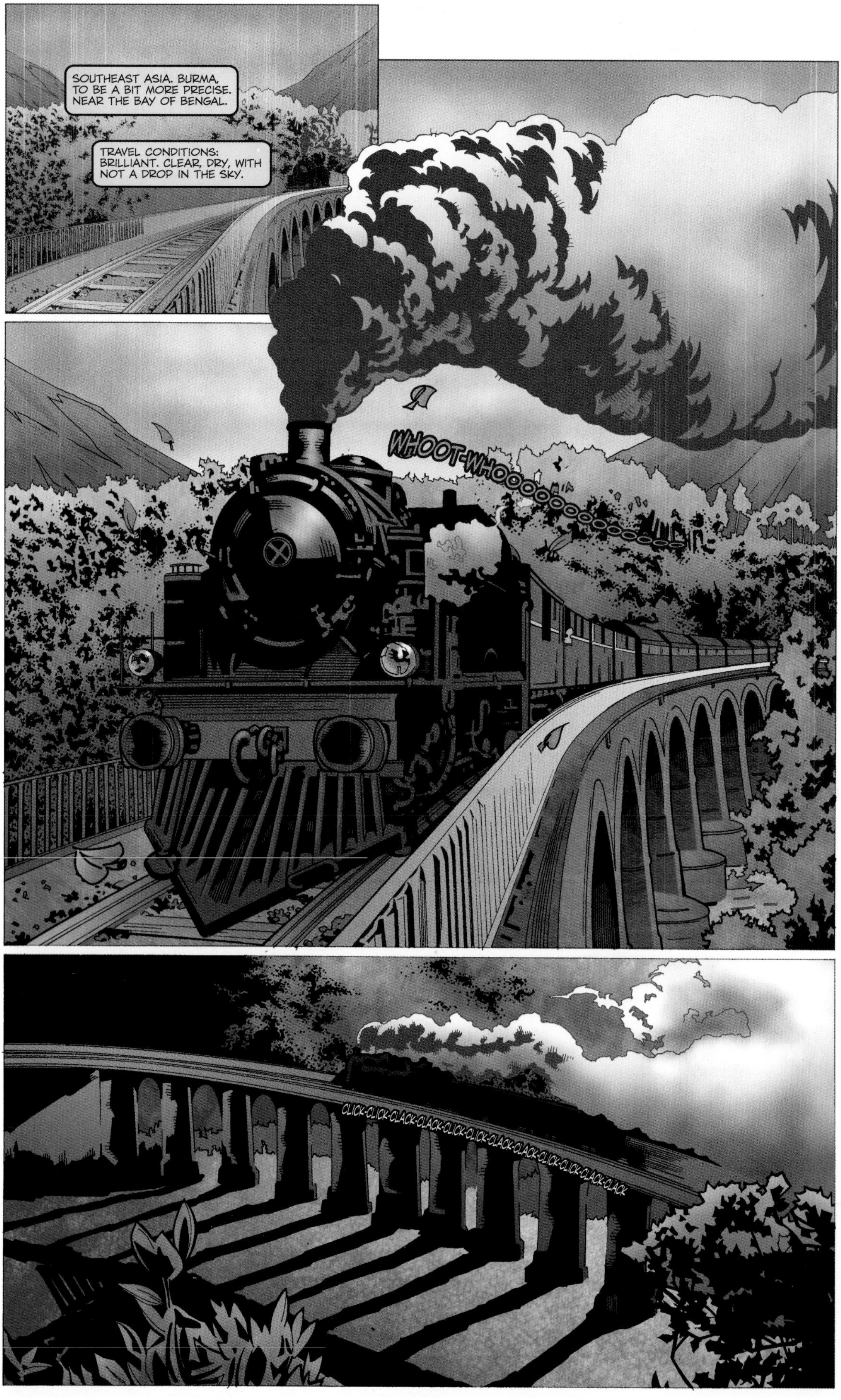
SOUTHEAST ASIA. BURMA, TO BE A BIT MORE PRECISE. NEAR THE BAY OF BENGAL.
TRAVEL CONDITIONS: BRILLIANT. CLEAR, DRY, WITH NOT A DROP IN THE SKY.
WHOOT-WHOOOOOOOOOOOOO
CLICK-CLICK-CLACK-CLACK-CLICK-CLICK-CLACK-CLACK-CLICK-CLICK-CLACK-CLACK

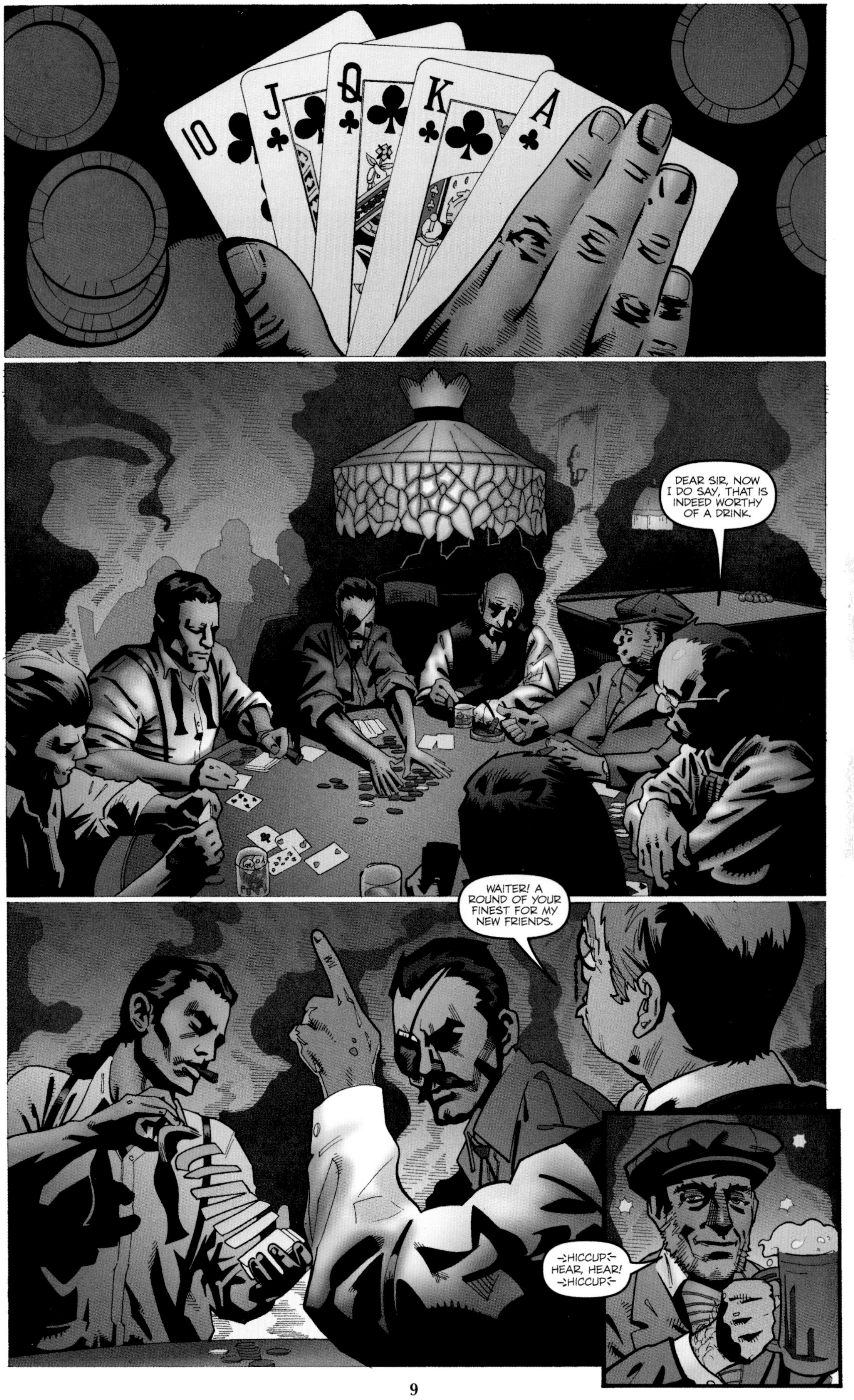
10
J
Q
K
A
DEAR SIR, NOW I DO SAY, THAT IS INDEED WORTHY OF A DRINK.
WAITER! A ROUND OF YOUR FINEST FOR MY NEW FRIENDS.
-HICCUP- HEAR, HEAR! -HICCUP-

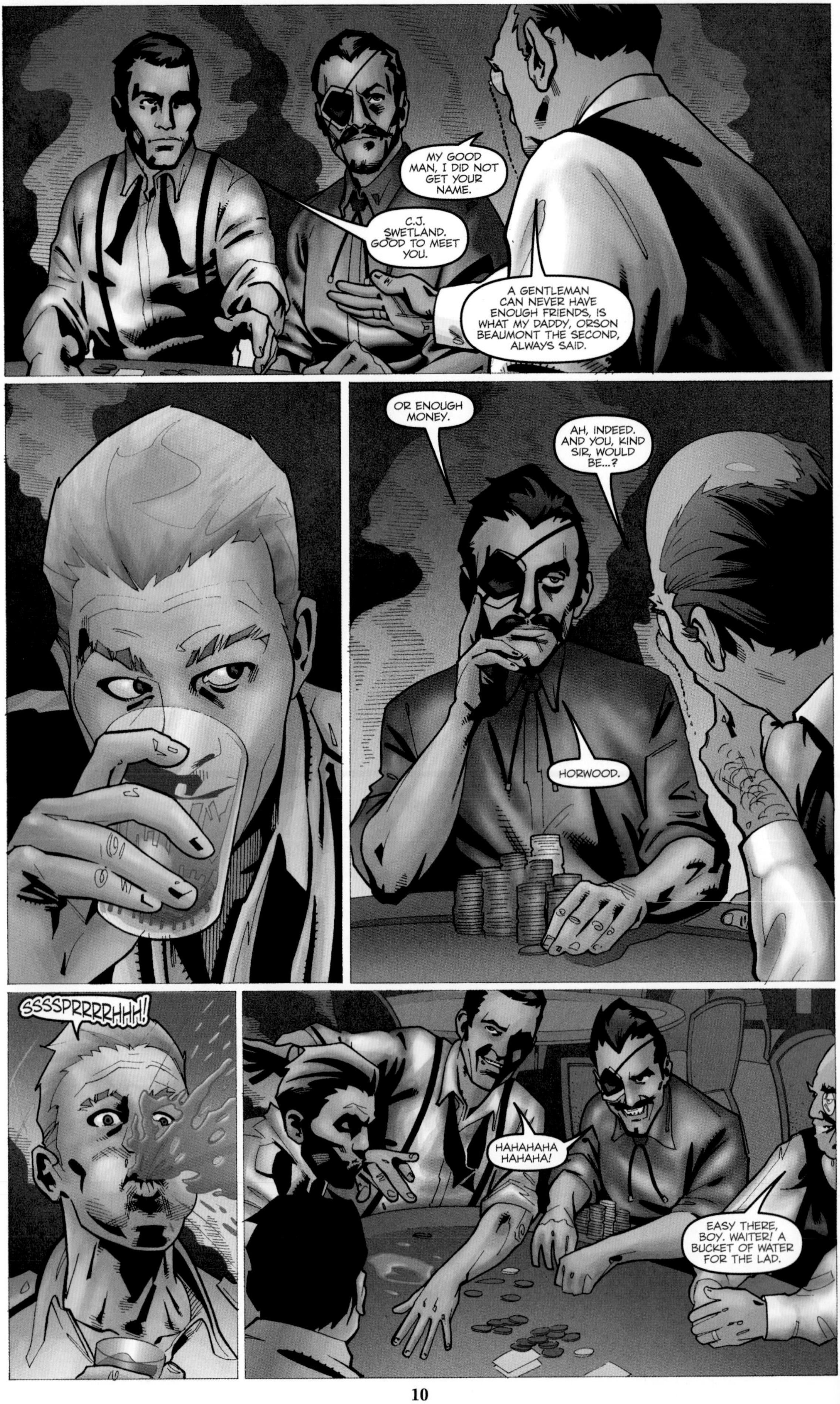
MY GOOD MAN, I DID NOT GET YOUR NAME.
C.J. SWETLAND. GOOD TO MEET YOU.
A GENTLEMAN CAN NEVER HAVE ENOUGH FRIENDS, IS WHAT MY DADDY, ORSON BEAUMONT THE SECOND, ALWAYS SAID.
OR ENOUGH MONEY.
AH, INDEED. AND YOU, KIND SIR, WOULD BE...?
HORWOOD.
SSSSPRRRRHHH!
HAHAHAHA HAHAHA!
EASY THERE, BOY. WAITER! A BUCKET OF WATER FOR THE LAD.

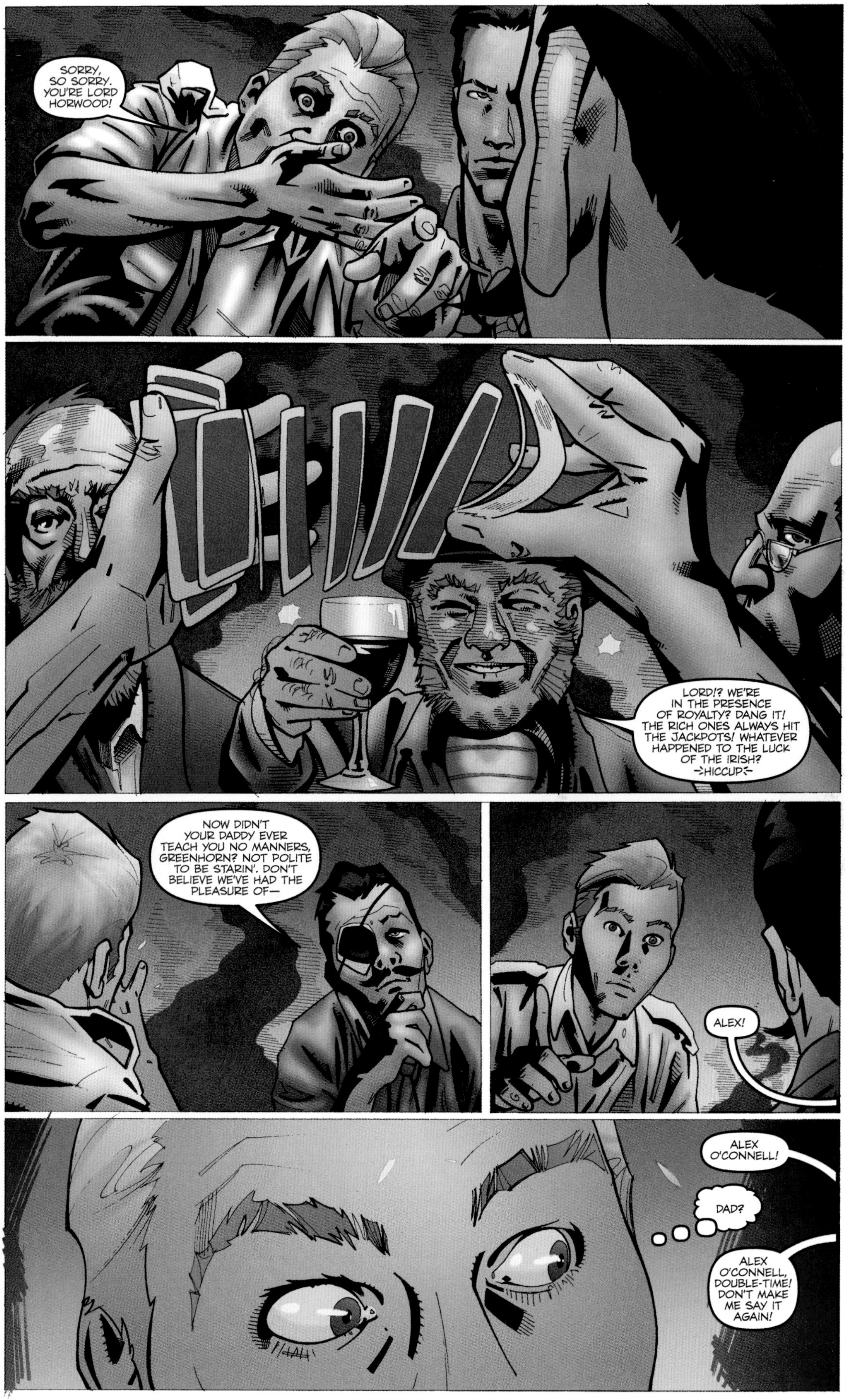
SORRY, SO SORRY. YOU'RE LORD HORWOOD!
LORD!? WE'RE IN THE PRESENCE OF ROYALTY? DANG IT! THE RICH ONES ALWAYS HIT THE JACKPOTS! WHATEVER HAPPENED TO THE LUCK OF THE IRISH? -HICCUP-
NOW DIDN'T YOUR DADDY EVER TEACH YOU NO MANNERS, GREENHORN? NOT POLITE TO BE STARIN'. DON'T BELIEVE WE'VE HAD THE PLEASURE OF—
ALEX!
ALEX O'CONNELL!
DAD?
ALEX O'CONNELL, DOUBLE-TIME! DON'T MAKE ME SAY IT AGAIN!

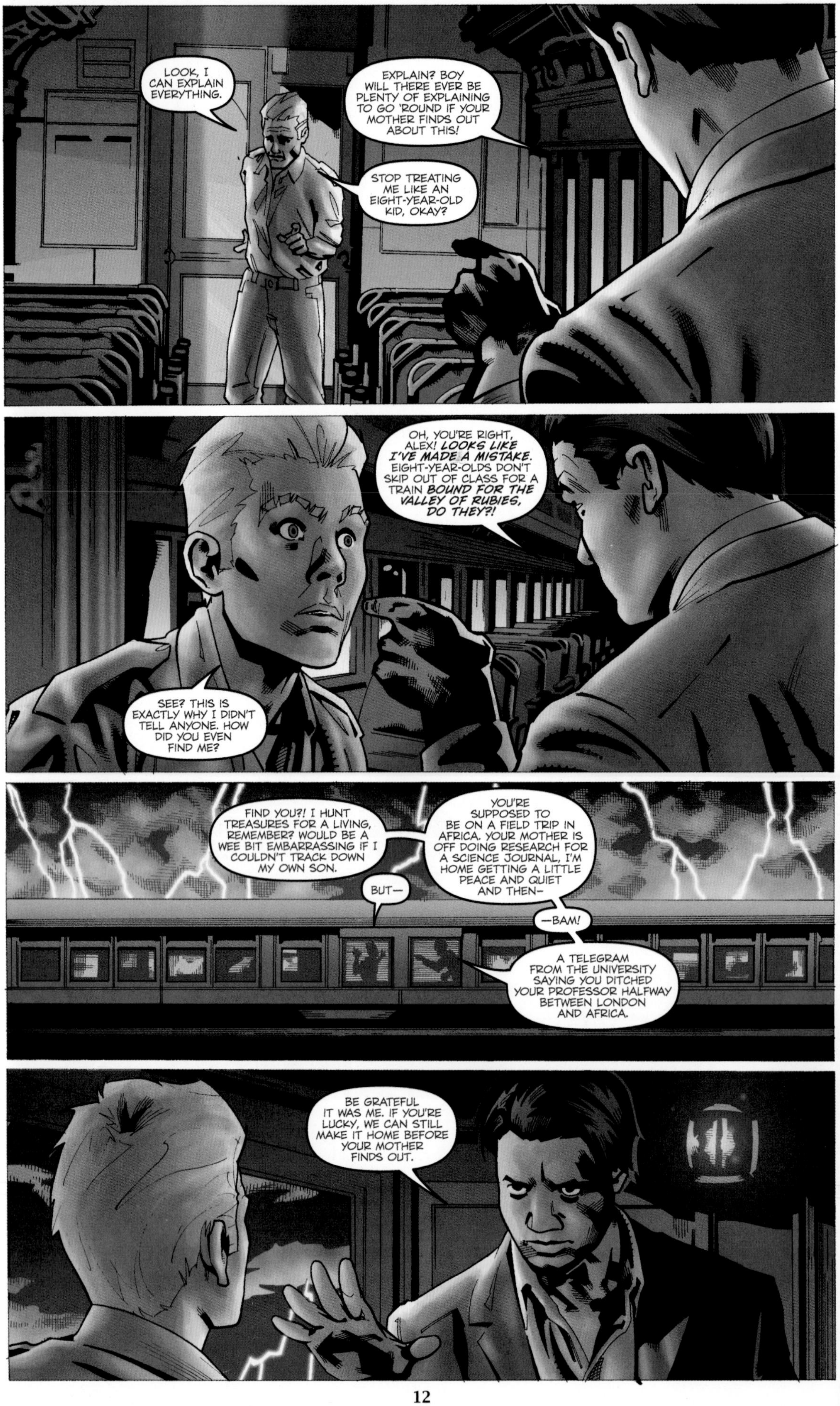
LOOK, I CAN EXPLAIN EVERYTHING.
EXPLAIN? BOY WILL THERE EVER BE PLENTY OF EXPLAINING TO GO 'ROUND IF YOUR MOTHER FINDS OUT ABOUT THIS!
STOP TREATING ME LIKE AN EIGHT-YEAR-OLD KID, OKAY?
OH, YOU'RE RIGHT, ALEX! ***LOOKS LIKE I'VE MADE A MISTAKE.*** EIGHT-YEAR-OLDS DON'T SKIP OUT OF CLASS FOR A TRAIN ***BOUND FOR THE VALLEY OF RUBIES, DO THEY?!***
SEE? THIS IS EXACTLY WHY I DIDN'T TELL ANYONE. HOW DID YOU EVEN FIND ME?
FIND YOU?! I HUNT TREASURES FOR A LIVING, REMEMBER? WOULD BE A WEE BIT EMBARRASSING IF I COULDN'T TRACK DOWN MY OWN SON.
YOU'RE SUPPOSED TO BE ON A FIELD TRIP IN AFRICA. YOUR MOTHER IS OFF DOING RESEARCH FOR A SCIENCE JOURNAL, I'M HOME GETTING A LITTLE PEACE AND QUIET AND THEN—
BUT—
—BAM!
A TELEGRAM FROM THE UNIVERSITY SAYING YOU DITCHED YOUR PROFESSOR HALFWAY BETWEEN LONDON AND AFRICA.
BE GRATEFUL IT WAS ME. IF YOU'RE LUCKY, WE CAN STILL MAKE IT HOME BEFORE YOUR MOTHER FINDS OUT.

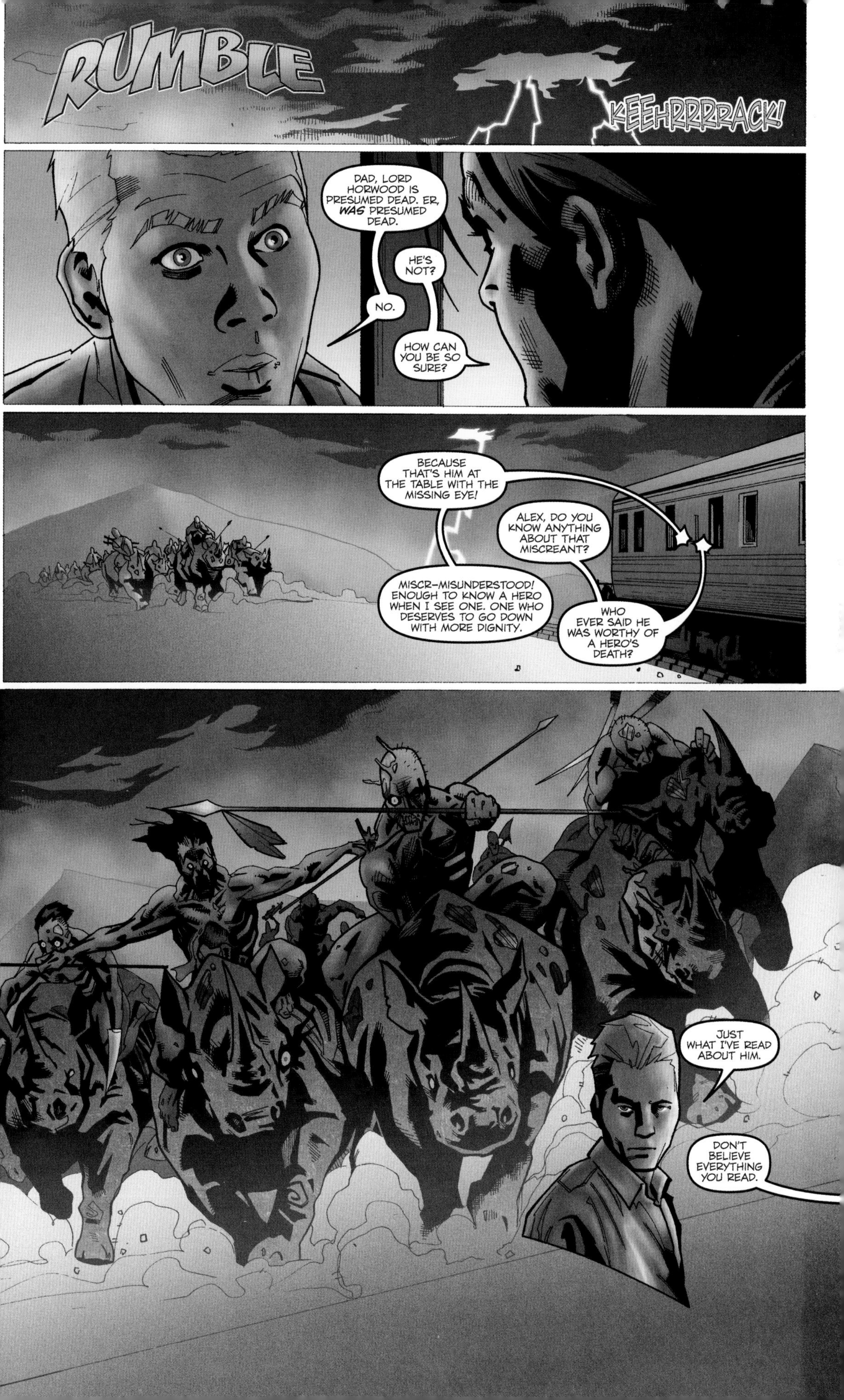
RUMBLE
KEEHRRRRACK!
DAD, LORD HORWOOD IS PRESUMED DEAD. ER, *WAS* PRESUMED DEAD.
HE'S NOT?
NO.
HOW CAN YOU BE SO SURE?
BECAUSE THAT'S HIM AT THE TABLE WITH THE MISSING EYE!
ALEX, DO YOU KNOW ANYTHING ABOUT THAT MISCREANT?
MISCR--MISUNDERSTOOD! ENOUGH TO KNOW A HERO WHEN I SEE ONE. ONE WHO DESERVES TO GO DOWN WITH MORE DIGNITY.
WHO EVER SAID HE WAS WORTHY OF A HERO'S DEATH?
JUST WHAT I'VE READ ABOUT HIM.
DON'T BELIEVE EVERYTHING YOU READ.

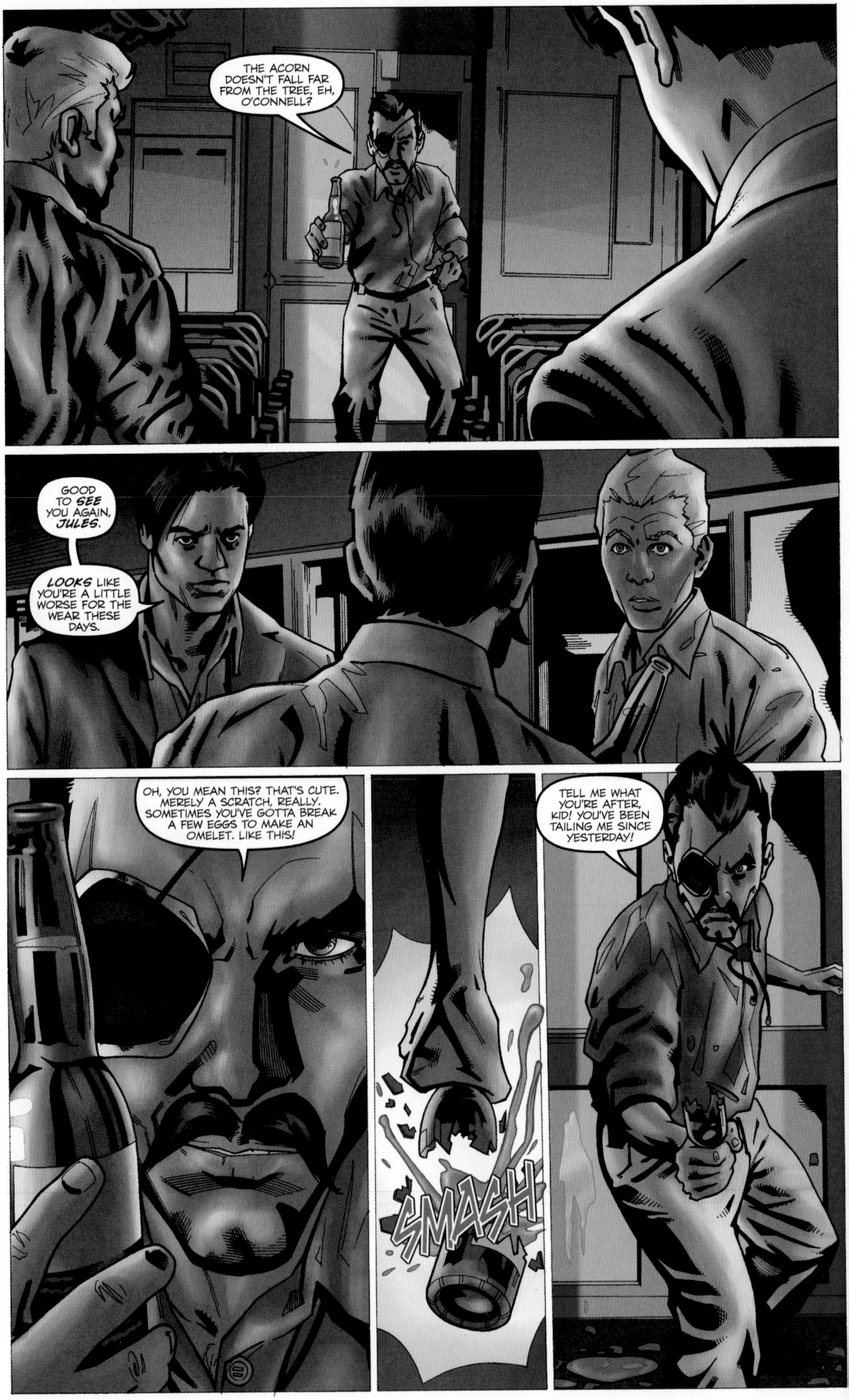
THE ACORN DOESN'T FALL FAR FROM THE TREE, EH, O'CONNELL?
GOOD TO **SEE** YOU AGAIN, **JULES**.
LOOKS LIKE YOU'RE A LITTLE WORSE FOR THE WEAR THESE DAYS.
OH, YOU MEAN THIS? THAT'S CUTE. MERELY A SCRATCH, REALLY. SOMETIMES YOU'VE GOTTA BREAK A FEW EGGS TO MAKE AN OMELET. LIKE THIS!
SMASH
TELL ME WHAT YOU'RE AFTER, KID! YOU'VE BEEN TAILING ME SINCE YESTERDAY!

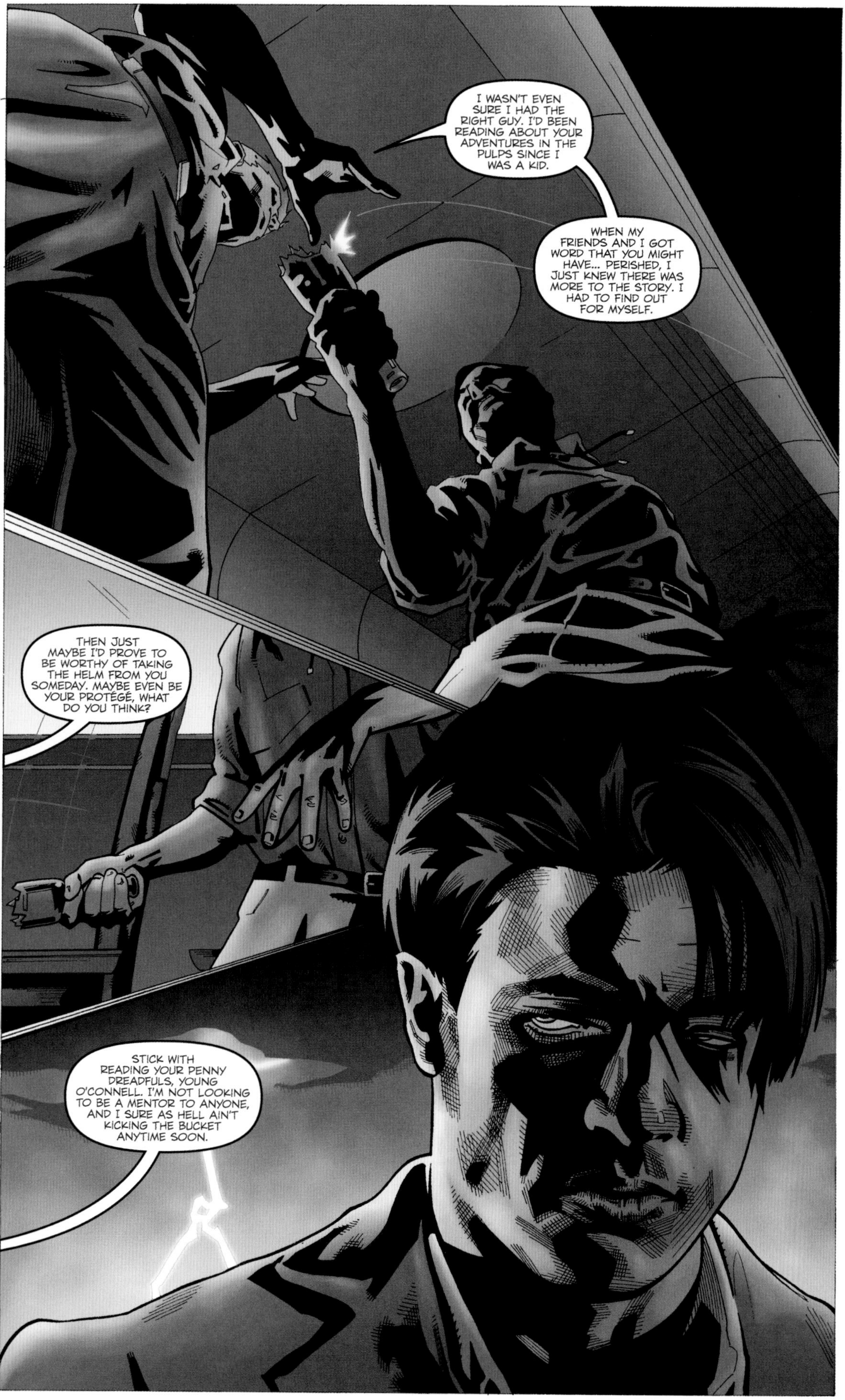
I WASN'T EVEN SURE I HAD THE RIGHT GUY. I'D BEEN READING ABOUT YOUR ADVENTURES IN THE PULPS SINCE I WAS A KID.
WHEN MY FRIENDS AND I GOT WORD THAT YOU MIGHT HAVE... PERISHED, I JUST KNEW THERE WAS MORE TO THE STORY. I HAD TO FIND OUT FOR MYSELF.
THEN JUST MAYBE I'D PROVE TO BE WORTHY OF TAKING THE HELM FROM YOU SOMEDAY. MAYBE EVEN BE YOUR PROTÉGÉ, WHAT DO YOU THINK?
STICK WITH READING YOUR PENNY DREADFULS, YOUNG O'CONNELL. I'M NOT LOOKING TO BE A MENTOR TO ANYONE, AND I SURE AS HELL AIN'T KICKING THE BUCKET ANYTIME SOON.

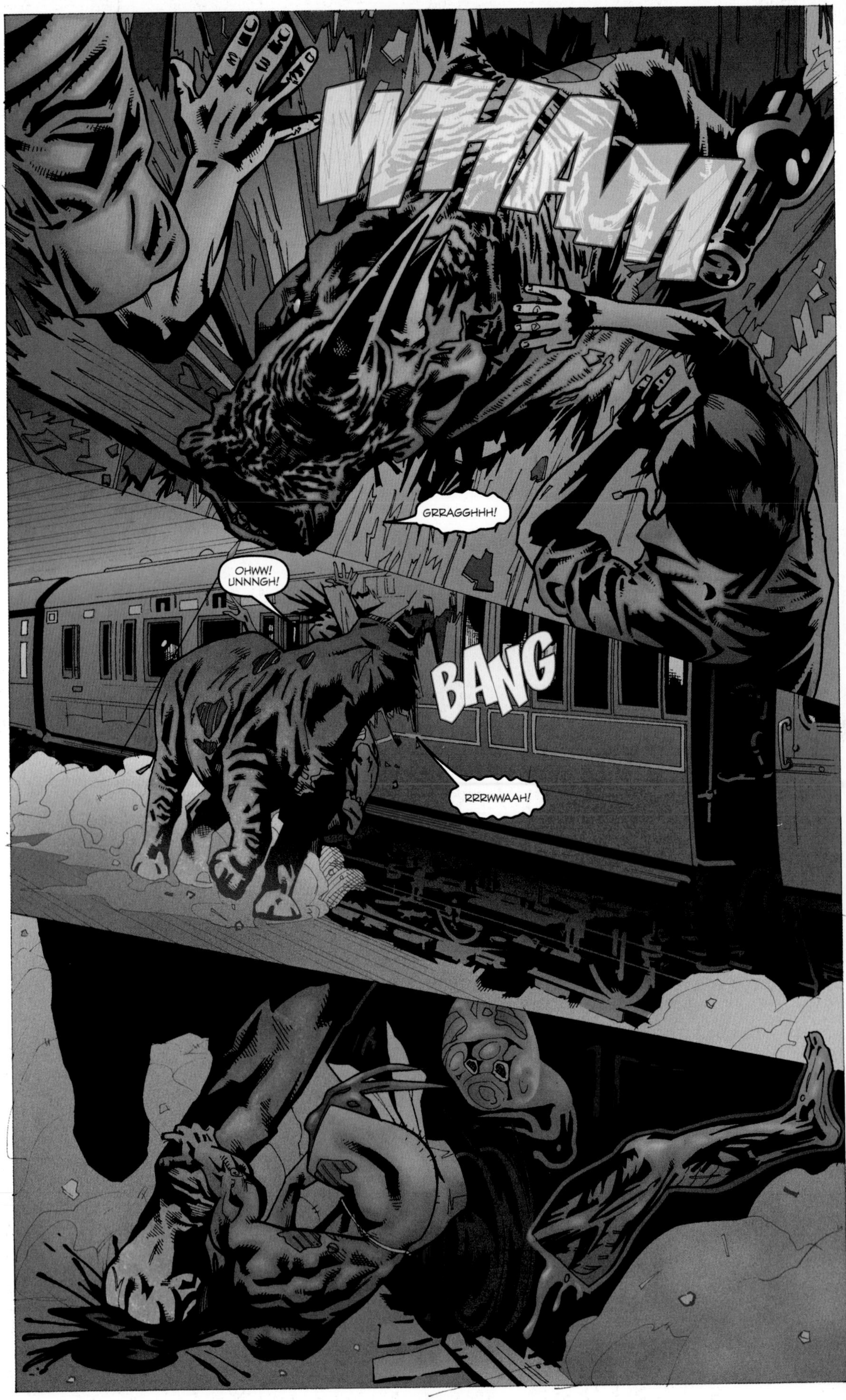
WHAM
GRRAGGHHH!
OHWW! UNNNGH!
BANG
RRRWWAAH!

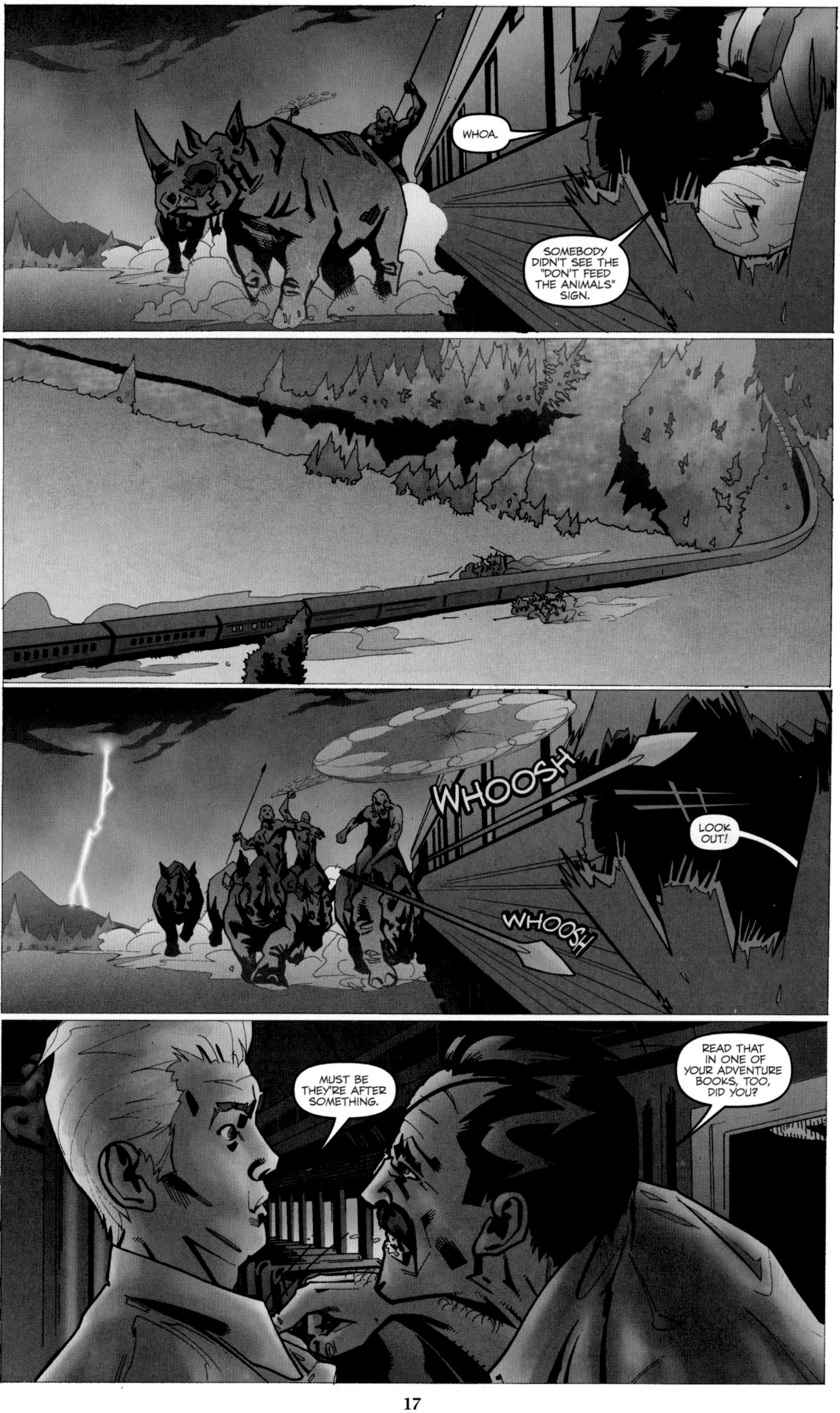
WHOA.
SOMEBODY DIDN'T SEE THE "DON'T FEED THE ANIMALS" SIGN.
WHOOSH
LOOK OUT!
WHOOSH
MUST BE THEY'RE AFTER SOMETHING.
READ THAT IN ONE OF YOUR ADVENTURE BOOKS, TOO, DID YOU?

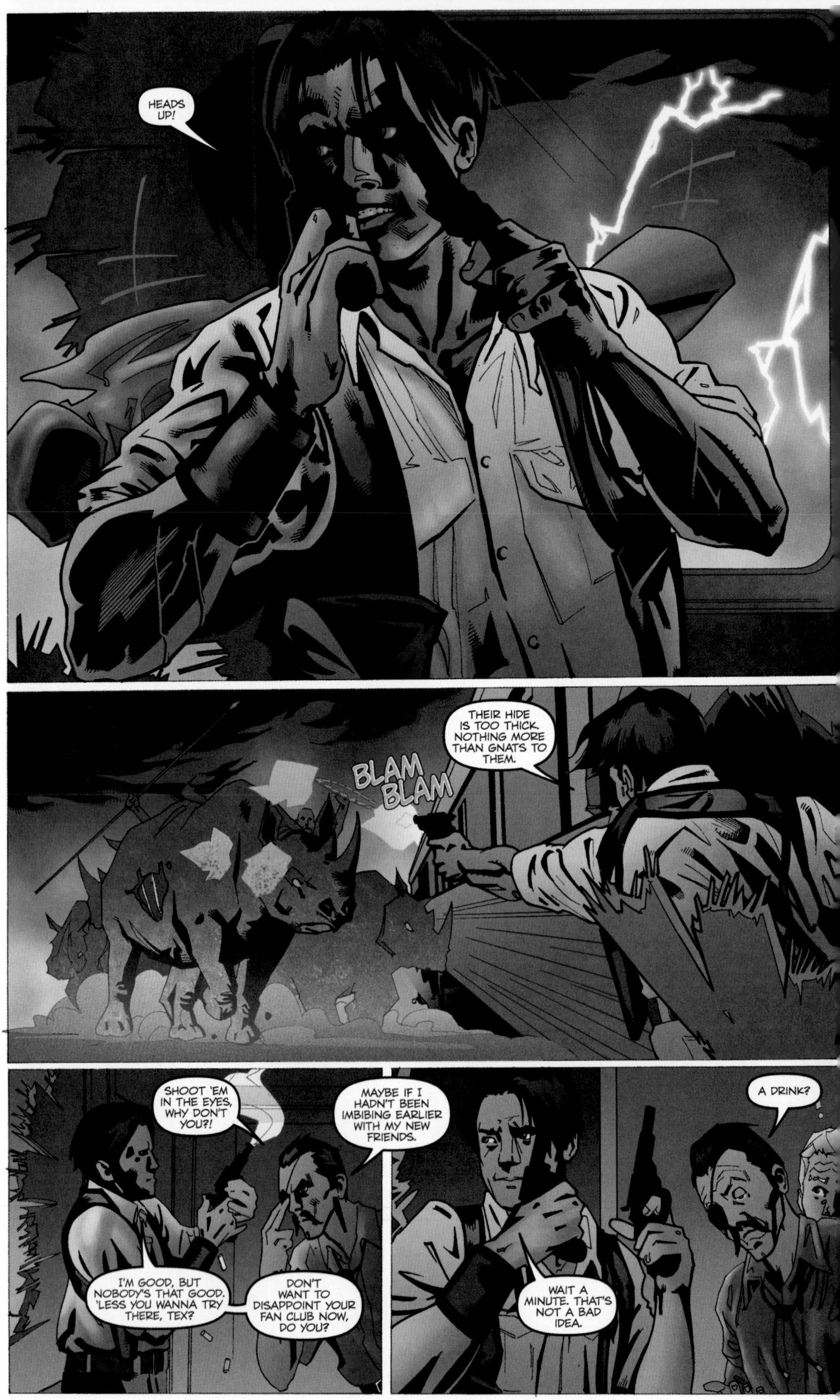

HEADS UP!
THEIR HIDE IS TOO THICK. NOTHING MORE THAN GNATS TO THEM.
BLAM BLAM
SHOOT 'EM IN THE EYES, WHY DON'T YOU?!
MAYBE IF I HADN'T BEEN IMBIBING EARLIER WITH MY NEW FRIENDS.
I'M GOOD, BUT NOBODY'S THAT GOOD. 'LESS YOU WANNA TRY THERE, TEX?
DON'T WANT TO DISAPPOINT YOUR FAN CLUB NOW, DO YOU?
A DRINK?
WAIT A MINUTE. THAT'S NOT A BAD IDEA.

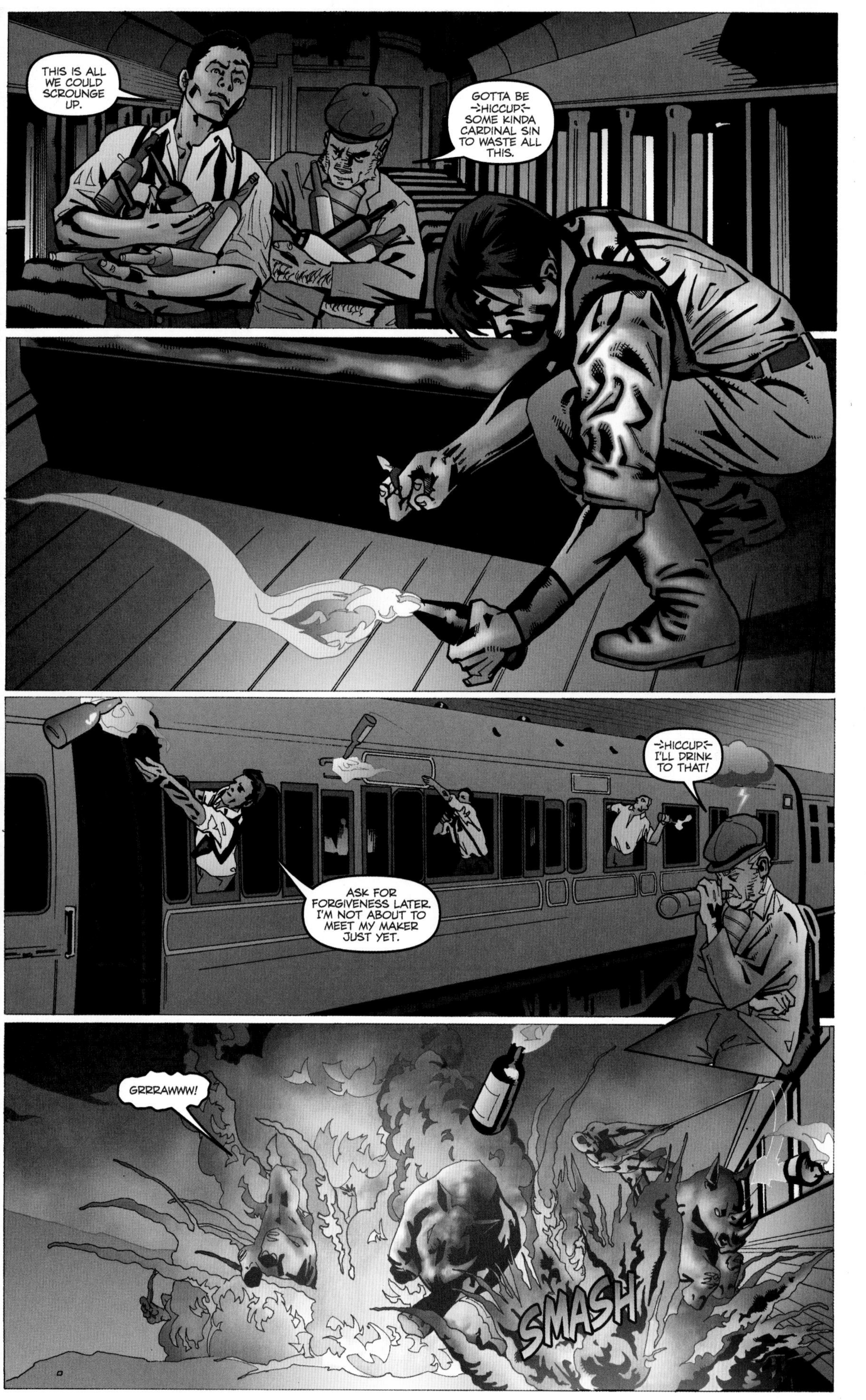
THIS IS ALL WE COULD SCROUNGE UP.
GOTTA BE -HICCUP- SOME KINDA CARDINAL SIN TO WASTE ALL THIS.
-HICCUP- I'LL DRINK TO THAT!
ASK FOR FORGIVENESS LATER. I'M NOT ABOUT TO MEET MY MAKER JUST YET.
GRRRAWWW!
SMASH

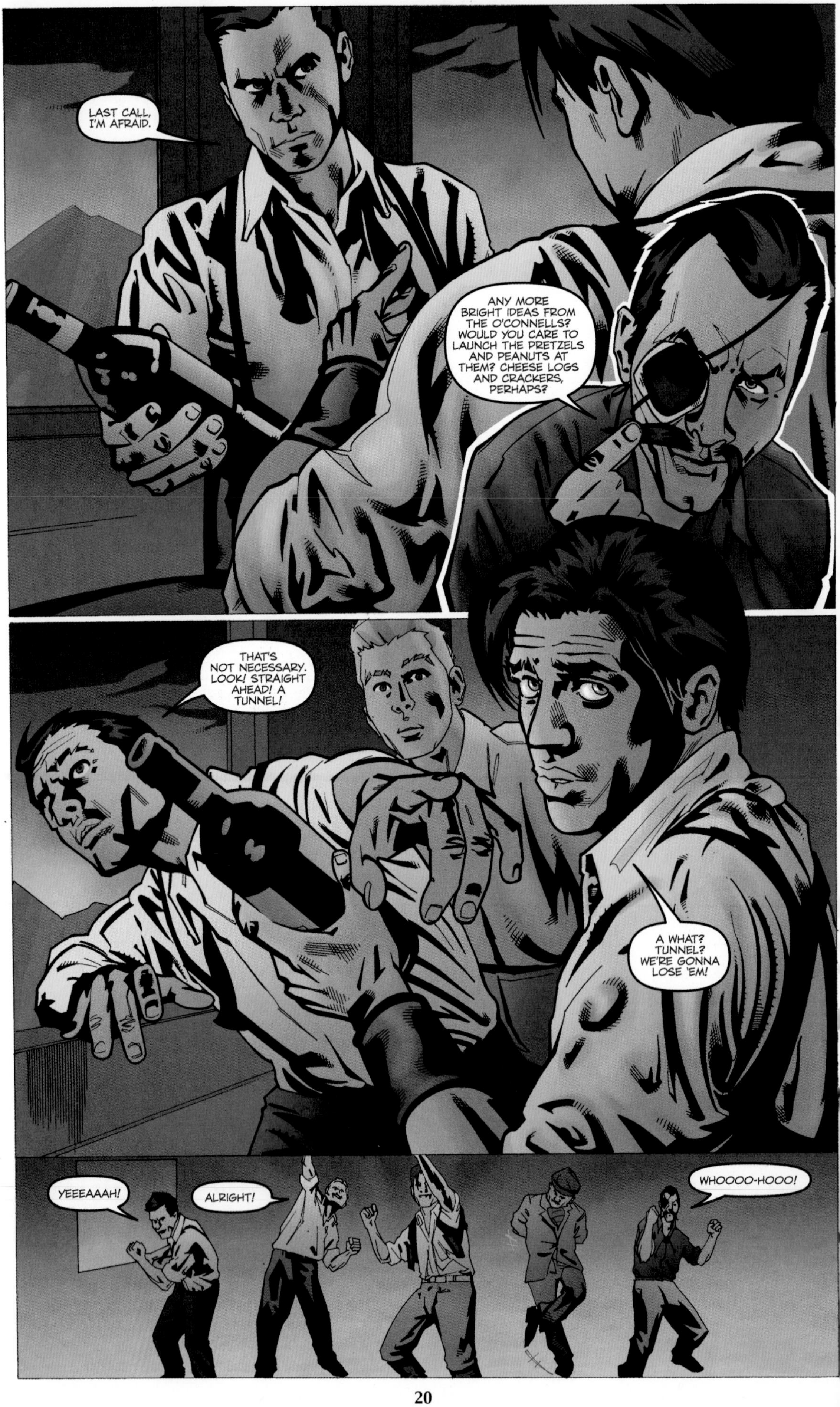
LAST CALL, I'M AFRAID.
ANY MORE BRIGHT IDEAS FROM THE O'CONNELLS? WOULD YOU CARE TO LAUNCH THE PRETZELS AND PEANUTS AT THEM? CHEESE LOGS AND CRACKERS, PERHAPS?
THAT'S NOT NECESSARY. LOOK! STRAIGHT AHEAD! A TUNNEL!
A WHAT? TUNNEL? WE'RE GONNA LOSE 'EM!
YEEEAAAH!
ALRIGHT!
WHOOOO-HOOO!

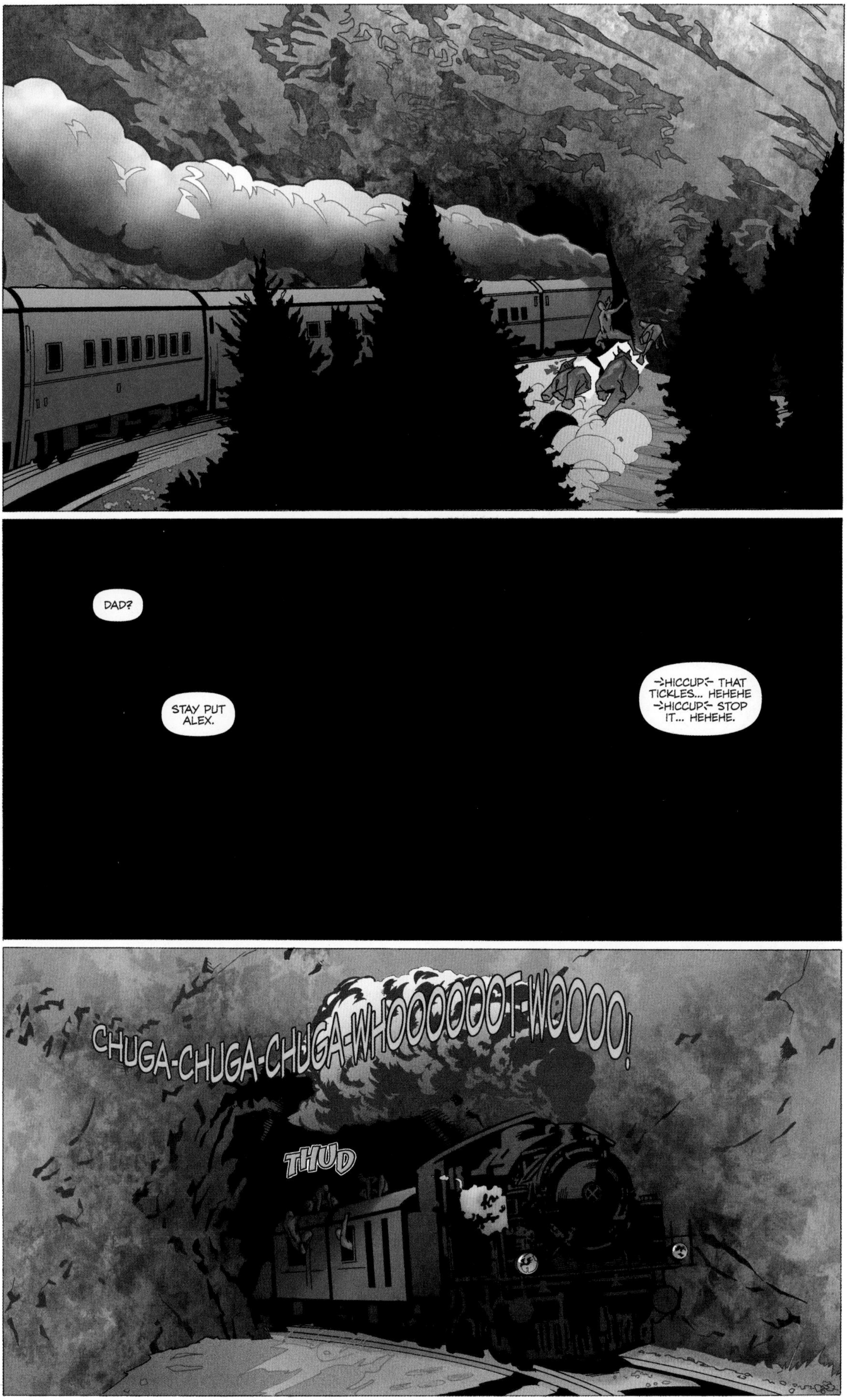
DAD?
STAY PUT ALEX.
->HICCUP<- THAT TICKLES... HEHEHE ->HICCUP<- STOP IT... HEHEHE.
CHUGA-CHUGA-CHUGA-WHOOOOOOT-WOOOO!
THUD

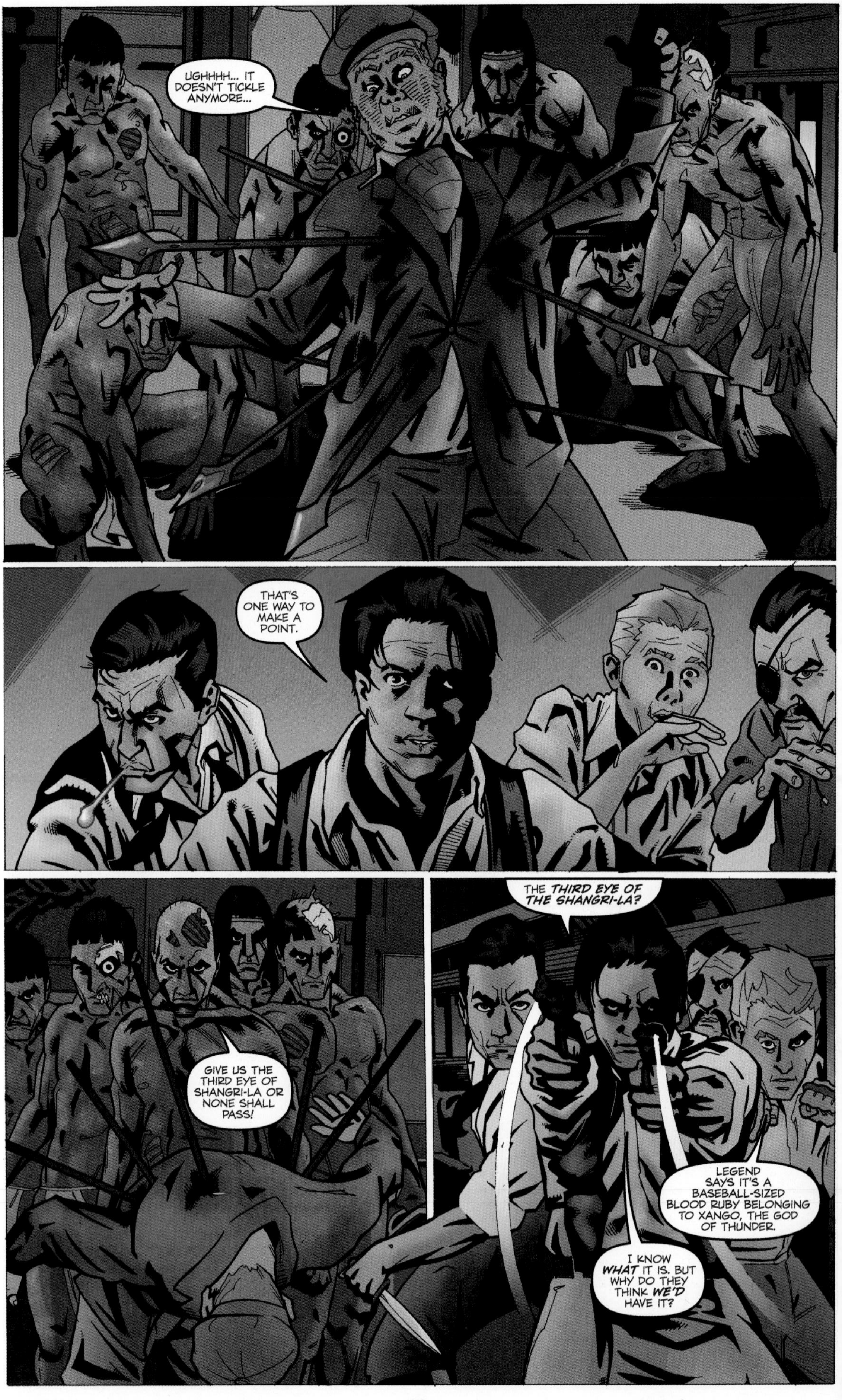
UGHHHH... IT DOESN'T TICKLE ANYMORE...
THAT'S ONE WAY TO MAKE A POINT.
GIVE US THE THIRD EYE OF SHANGRI-LA OR NONE SHALL PASS!
THE THIRD EYE OF THE SHANGRI-LA?
LEGEND SAYS IT'S A BASEBALL-SIZED BLOOD RUBY BELONGING TO XANGO, THE GOD OF THUNDER.
I KNOW WHAT IT IS. BUT WHY DO THEY THINK WE'D HAVE IT?

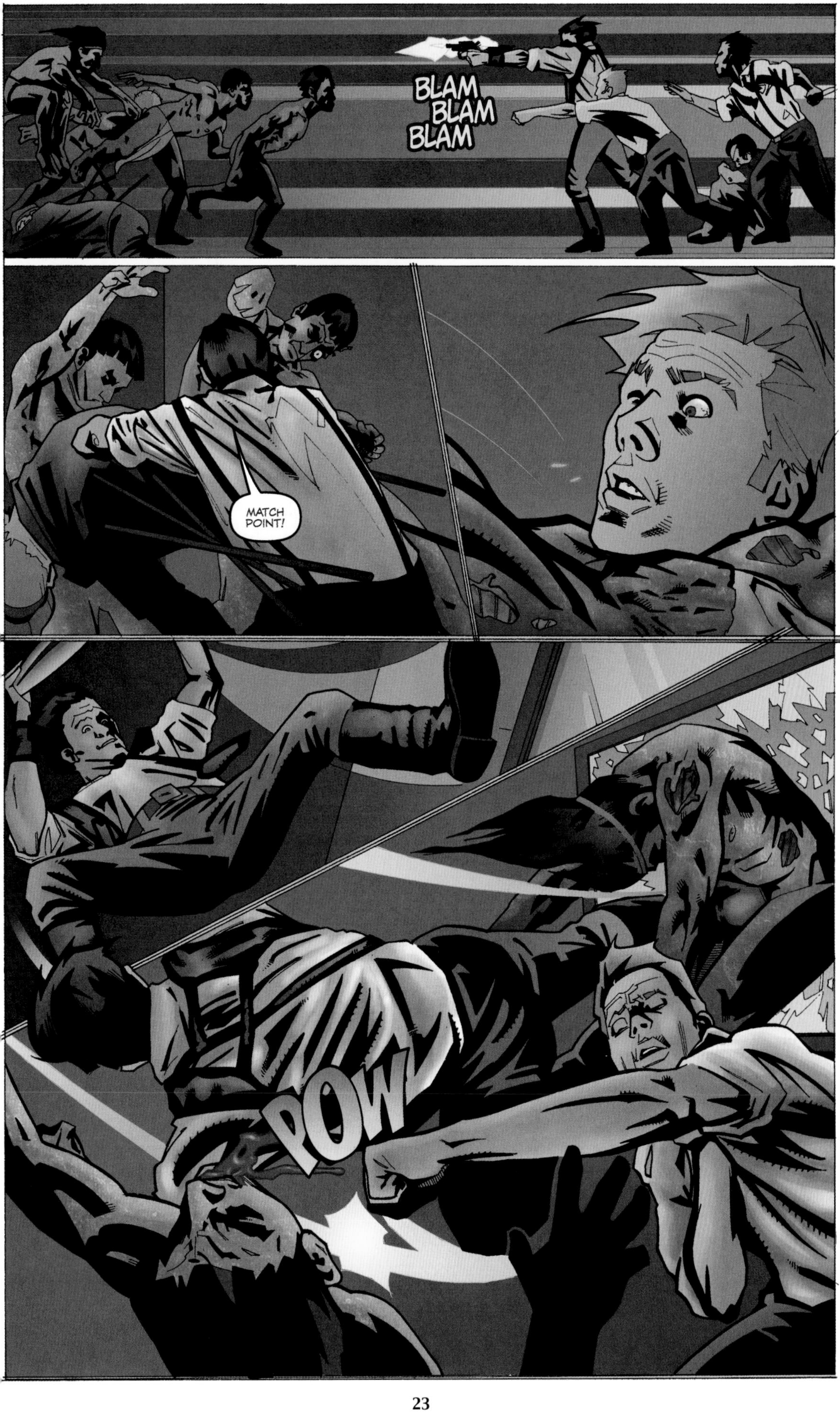
BLAM
BLAM
BLAM
MATCH POINT!
POW

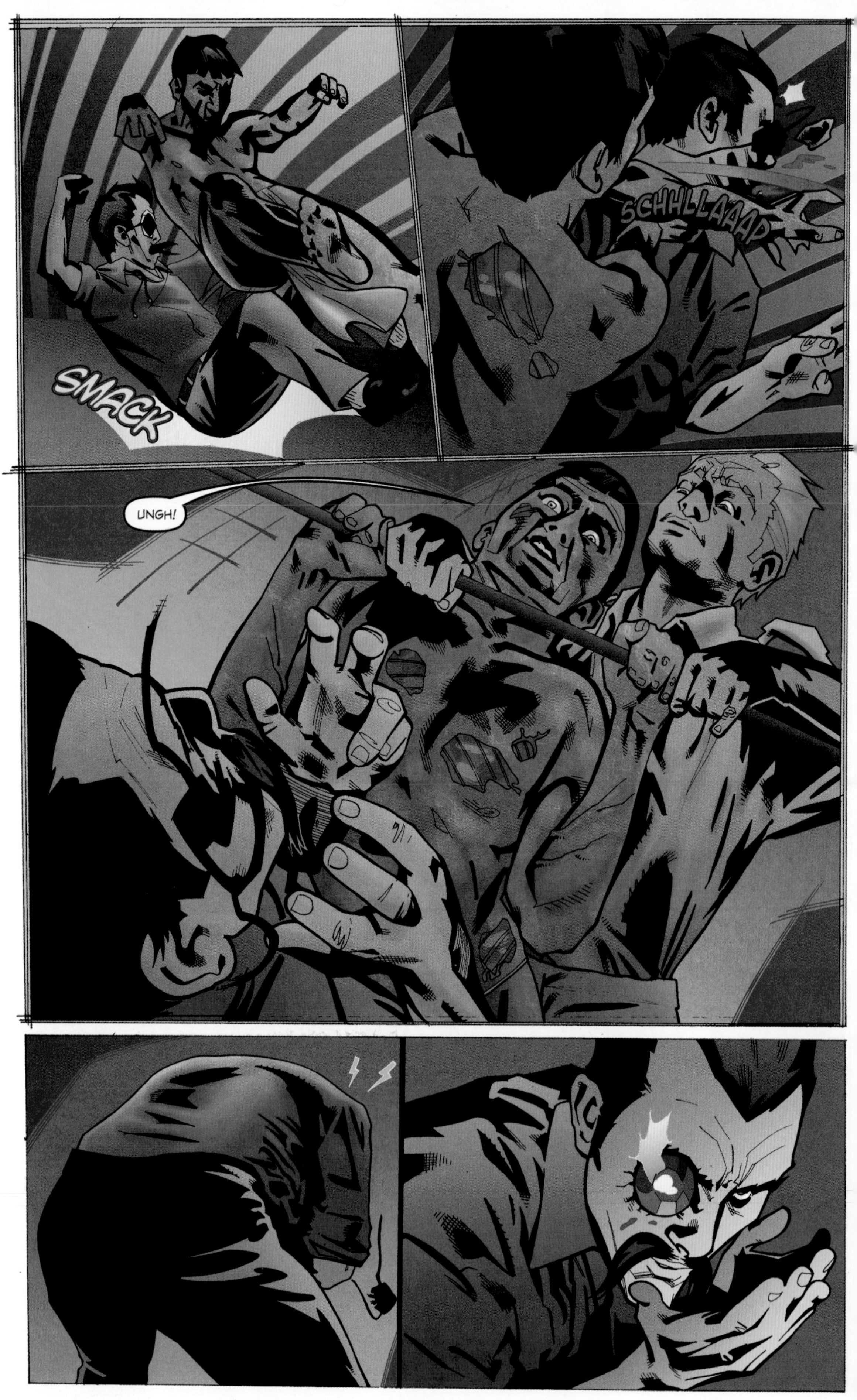

SMACK
SCHHLLAAAP
UNGH!

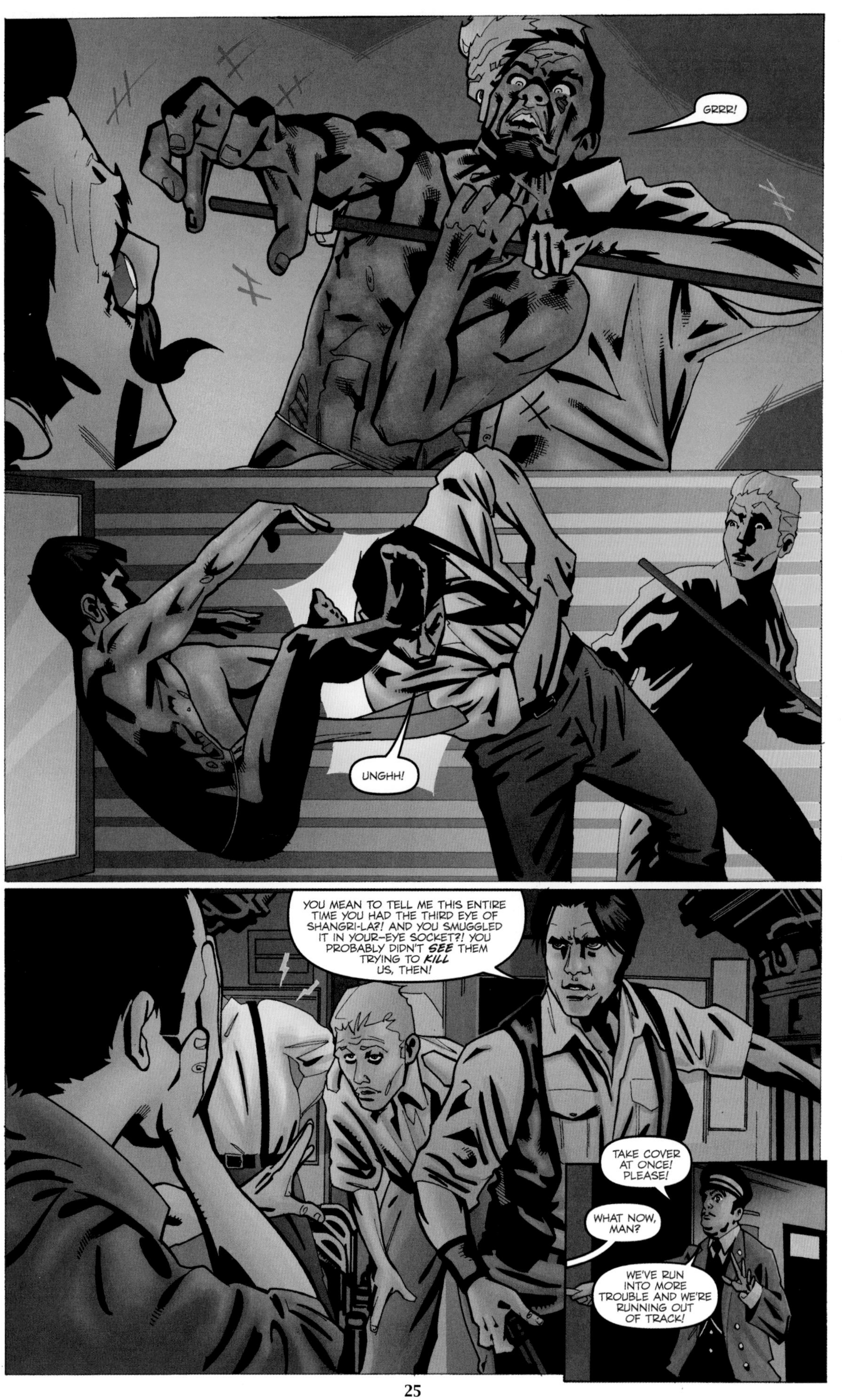
GRRR!
UNGHH!
YOU MEAN TO TELL ME THIS ENTIRE TIME YOU HAD THE THIRD EYE OF SHANGRI-LA?! AND YOU SMUGGLED IT IN YOUR-EYE SOCKET?! YOU PROBABLY DIDN'T SEE THEM TRYING TO KILL US, THEN!
TAKE COVER AT ONCE! PLEASE!
WHAT NOW, MAN?
WE'VE RUN INTO MORE TROUBLE AND WE'RE RUNNING OUT OF TRACK!

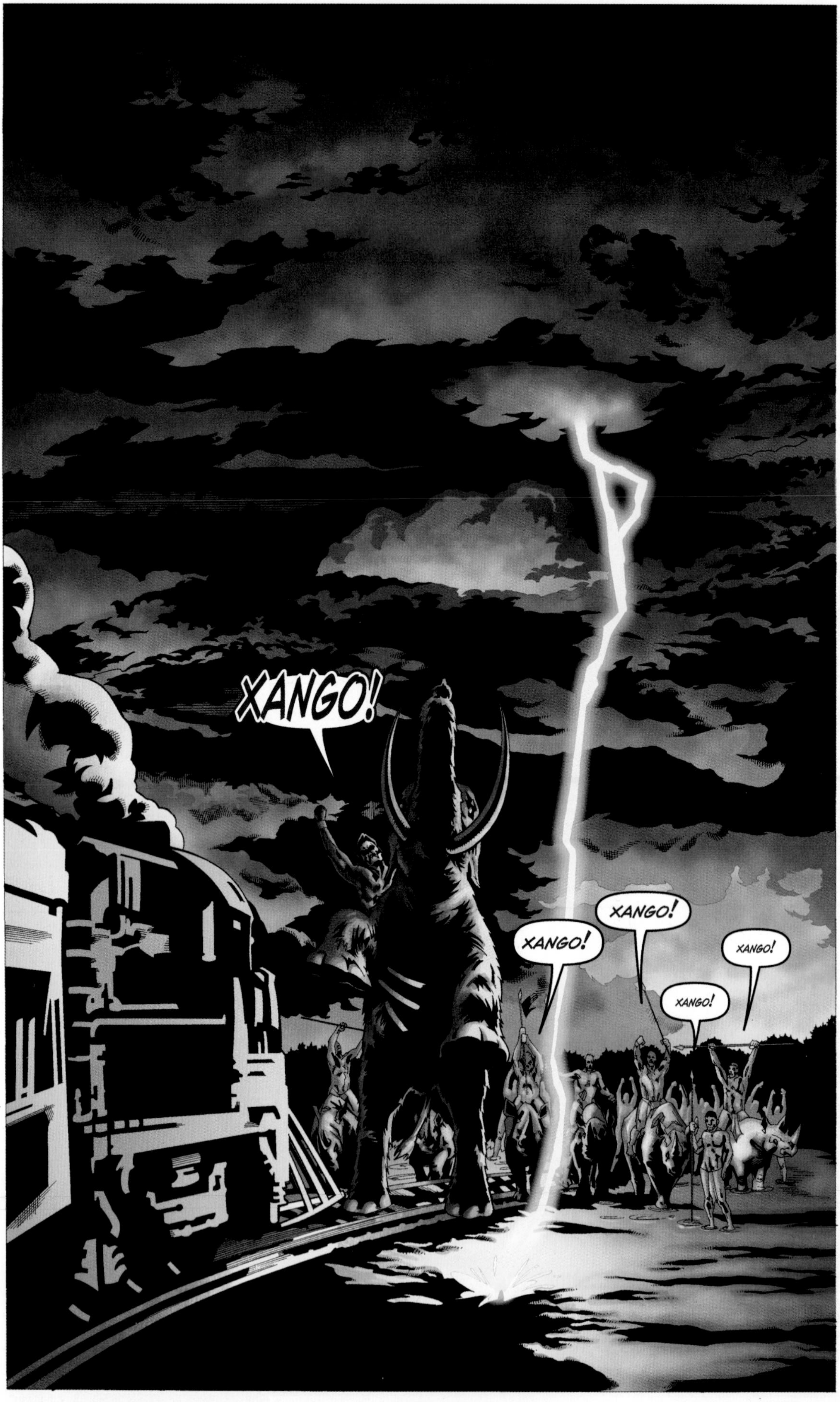
XANGO!
XANGO!
XANGO!
XANGO!
XANGO!

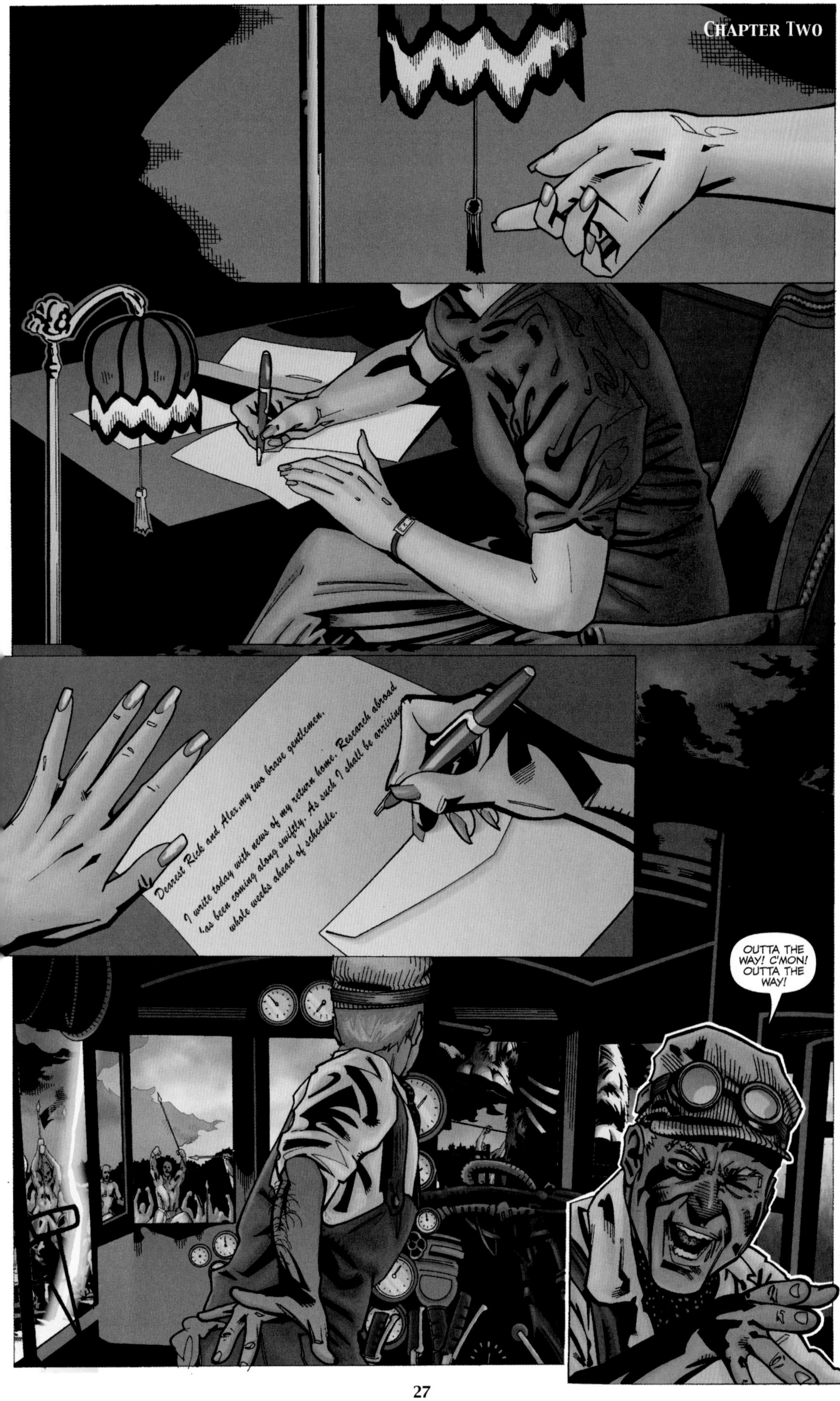
CHAPTER TWO
Dearest Rick and Alex, my two brave gentlemen.
I write today with news of my return home. Research abroad
as been coming along swiftly. As such I shall be arrivin
whole weeks ahead of schedule.
OUTTA THE WAY! C'MON! OUTTA THE WAY!

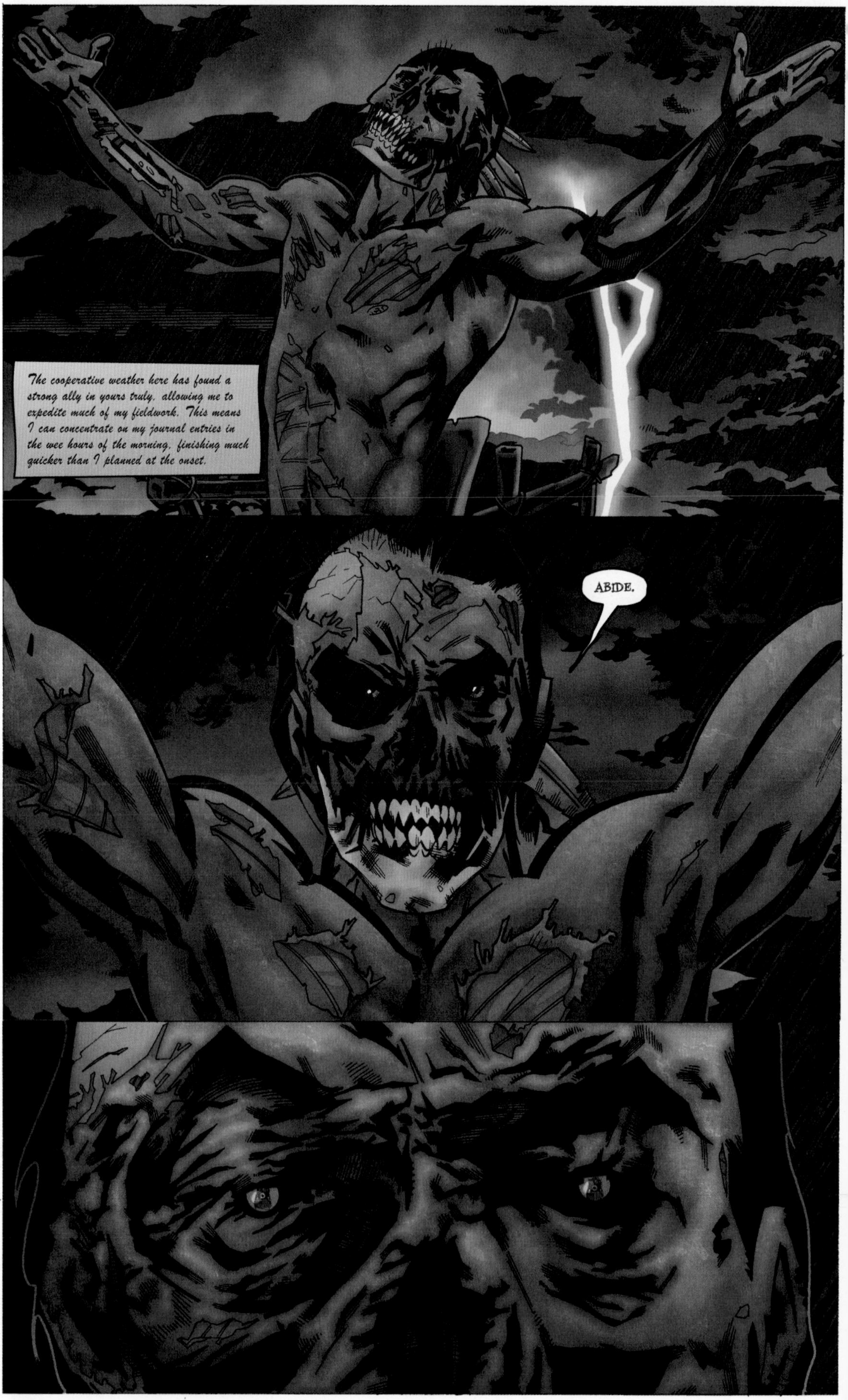
The cooperative weather here has found a strong ally in yours truly, allowing me to expedite much of my fieldwork. This means I can concentrate on my journal entries in the wee hours of the morning, finishing much quicker than I planned at the onset.
ABIDE.

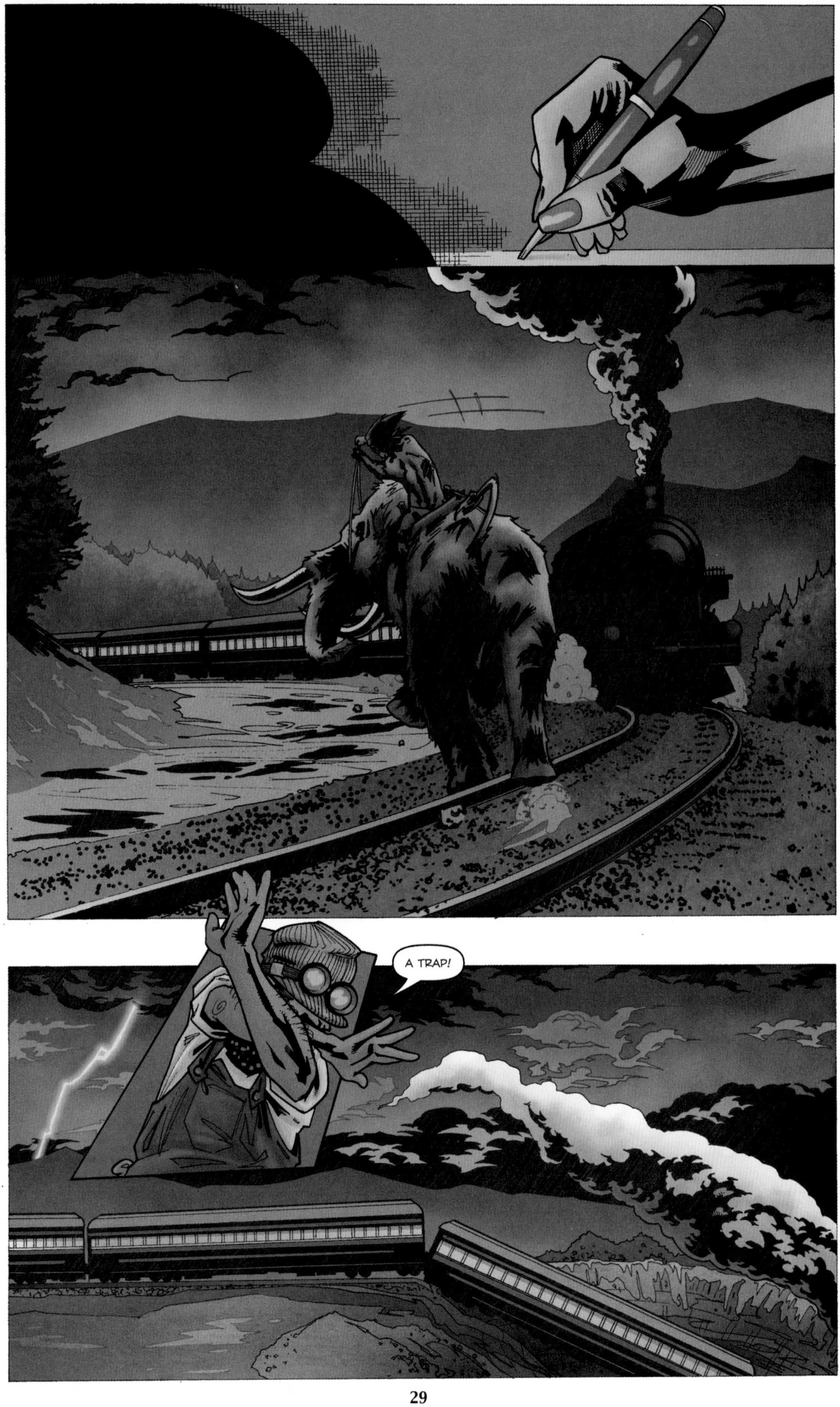
A TRAP!

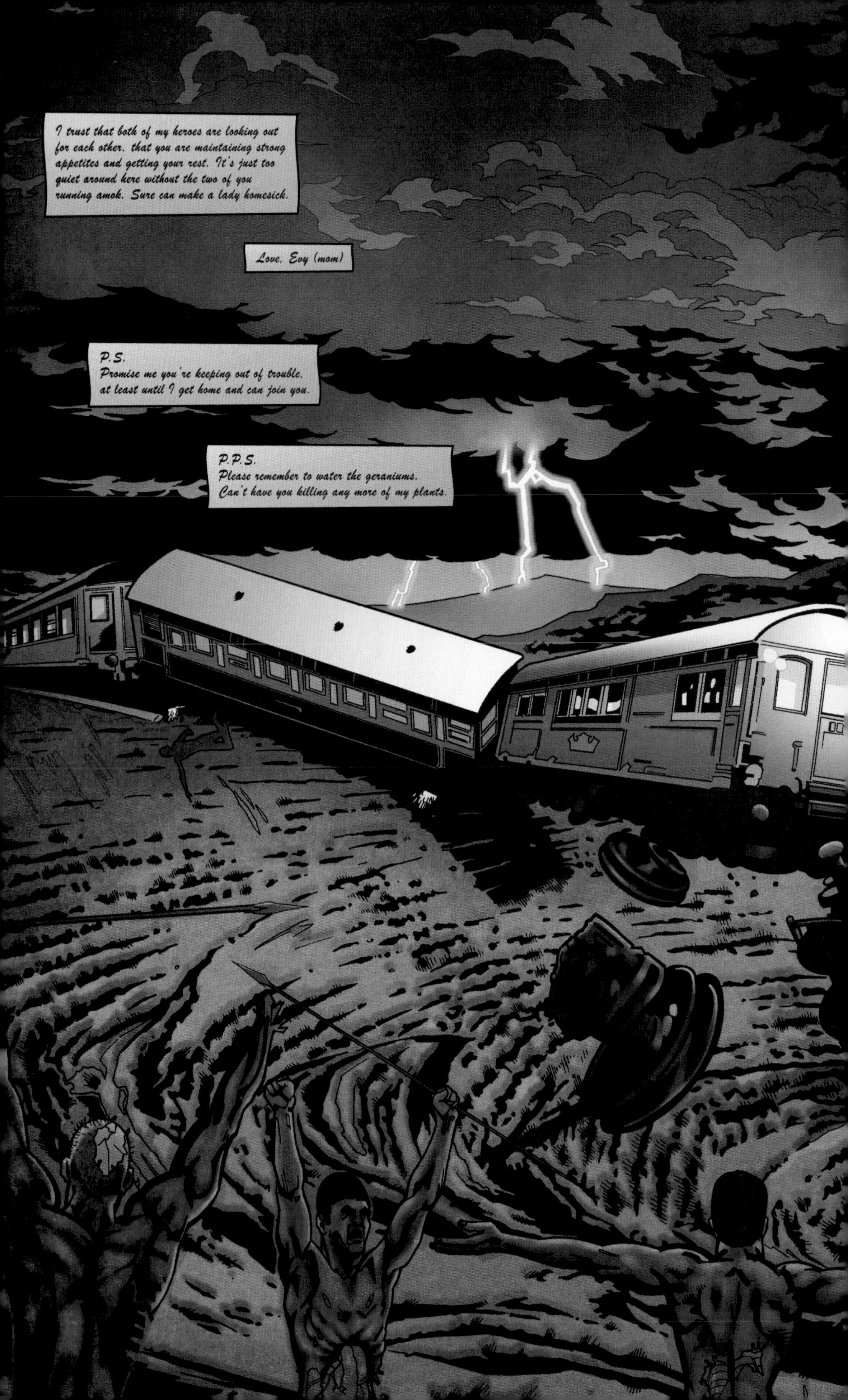
I trust that both of my heroes are looking out for each other, that you are maintaining strong appetites and getting your rest. It's just too quiet around here without the two of you running amok. Sure can make a lady homesick.
Love, Evy (mom)
P.S.
Promise me you're keeping out of trouble, at least until I get home and can join you.
P.P.S.
Please remember to water the geraniums. Can't have you killing any more of my plants.

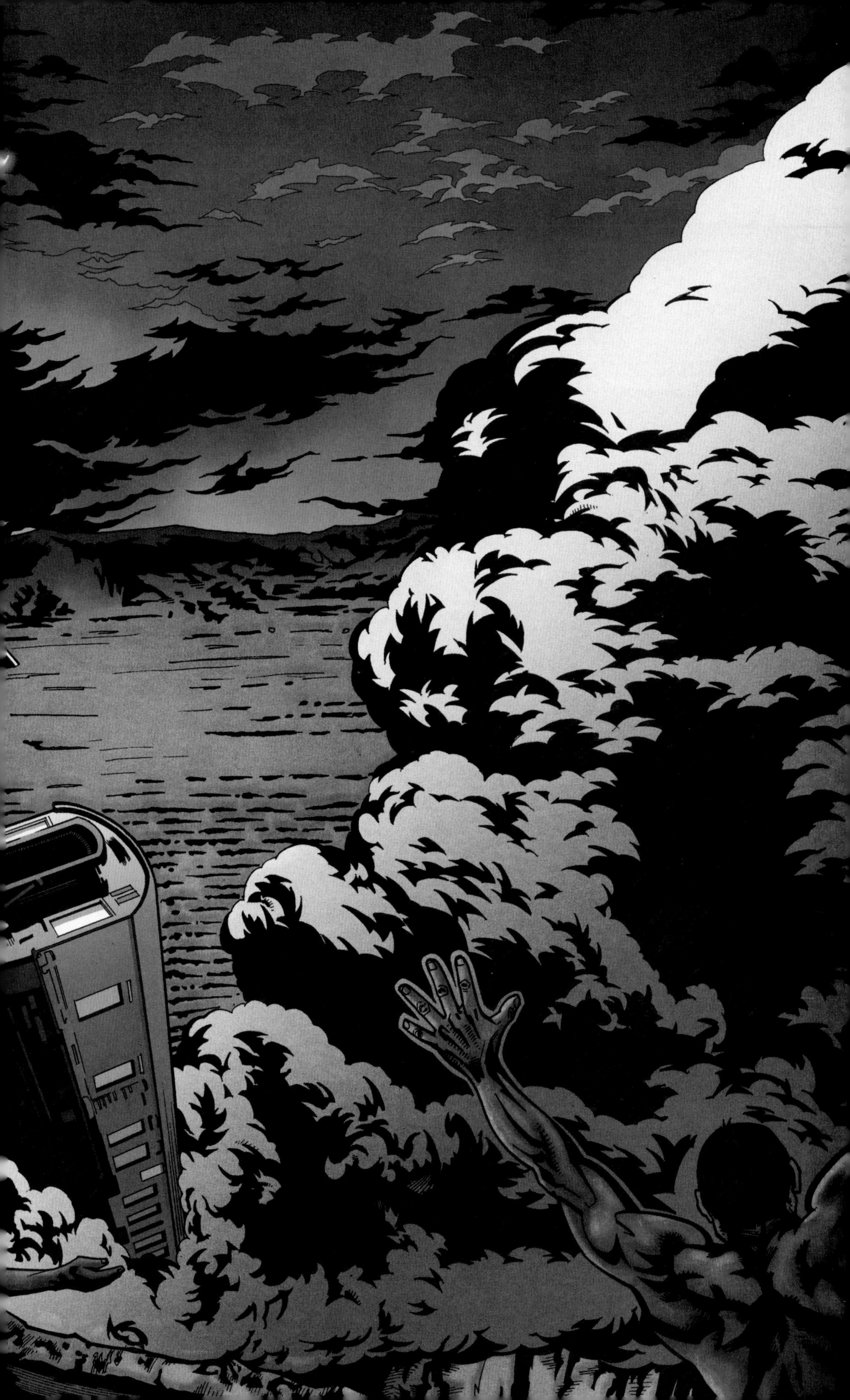

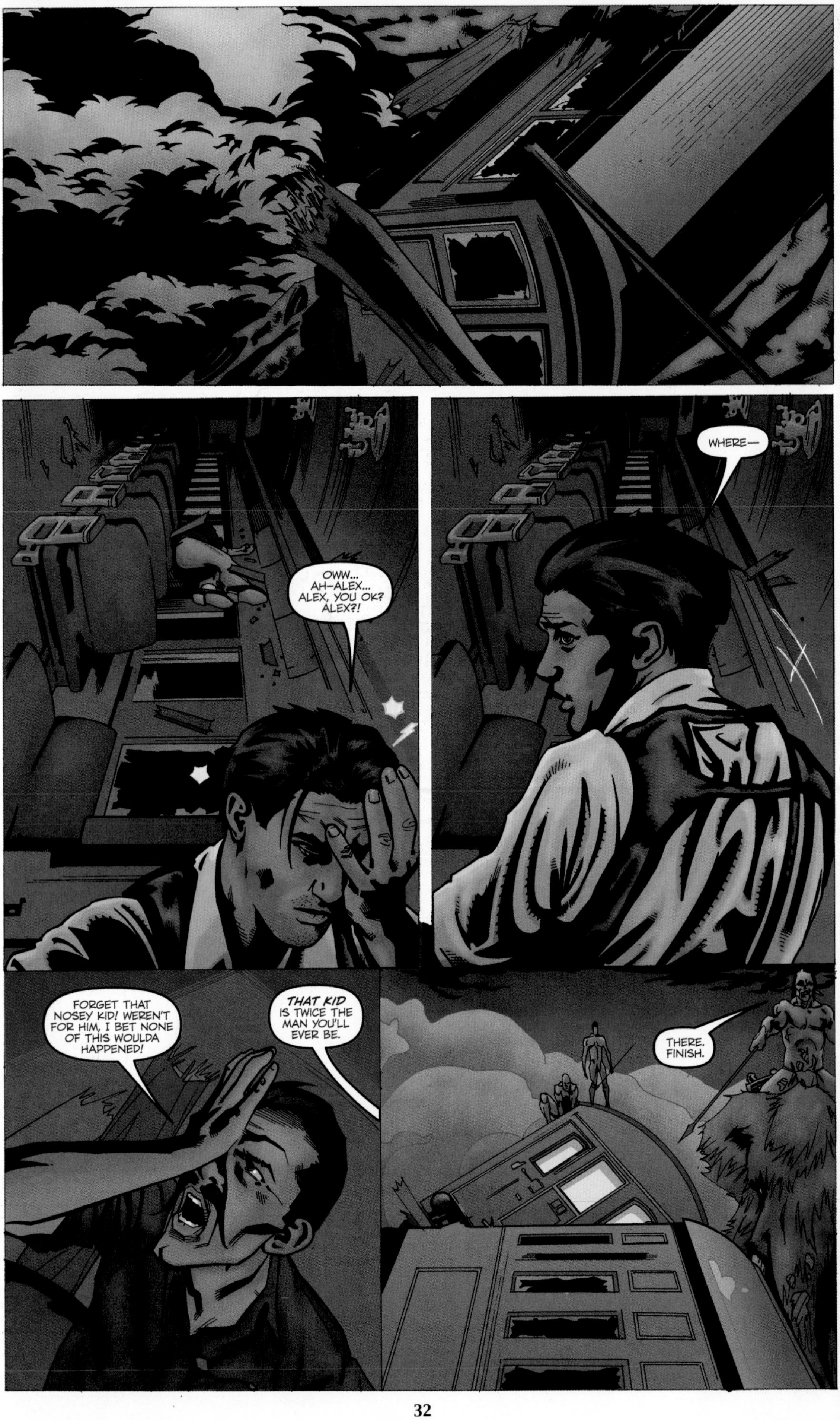
OWW... AH-ALEX... ALEX, YOU OK? ALEX?!
WHERE—
FORGET THAT NOSEY KID! WEREN'T FOR HIM, I BET NONE OF THIS WOULDA HAPPENED!
THAT KID IS TWICE THE MAN YOU'LL EVER BE.
THERE. FINISH.

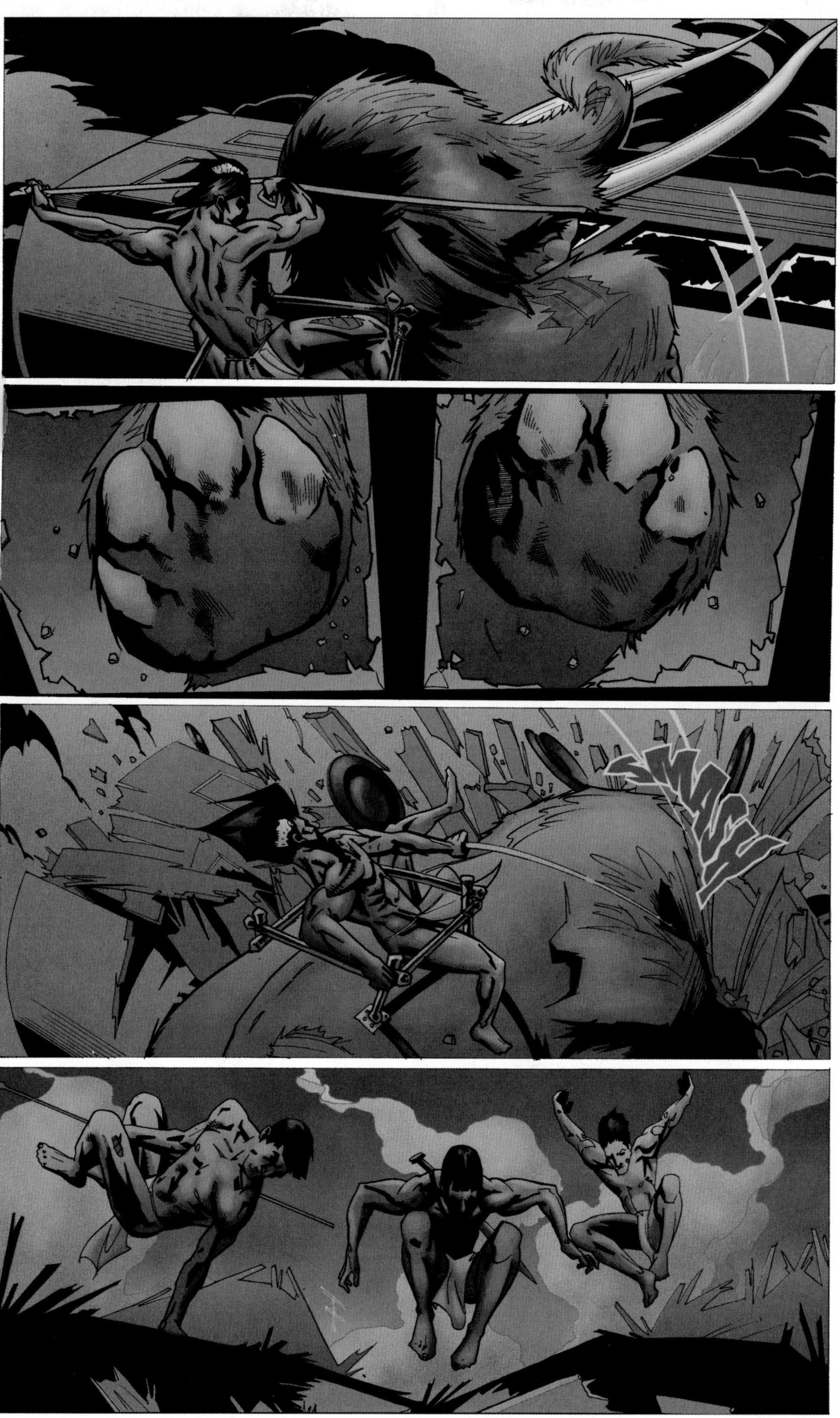
SMACK

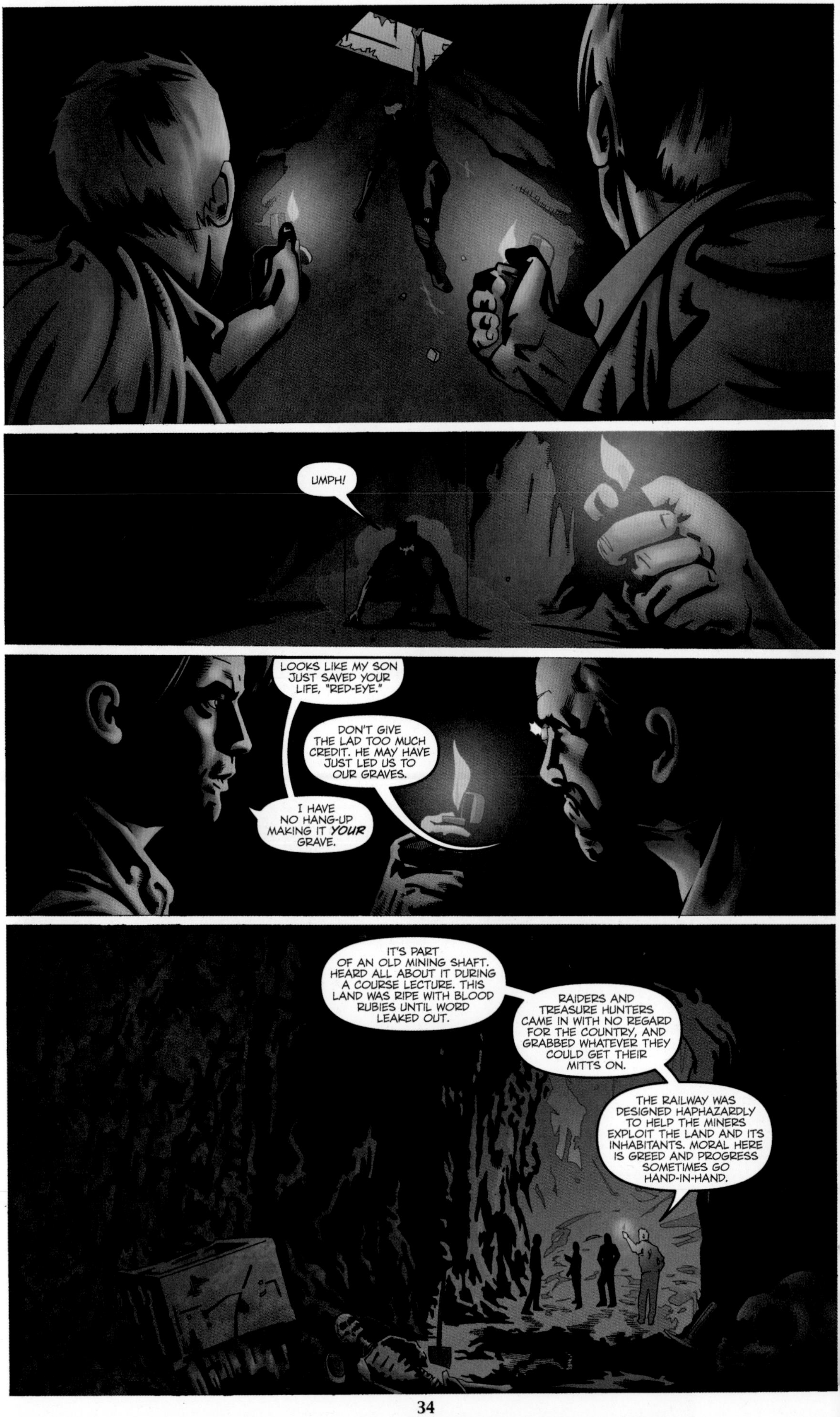
UMPH!
LOOKS LIKE MY SON JUST SAVED YOUR LIFE, "RED-EYE."
DON'T GIVE THE LAD TOO MUCH CREDIT. HE MAY HAVE JUST LED US TO OUR GRAVES.
I HAVE NO HANG-UP MAKING IT *YOUR* GRAVE.
IT'S PART OF AN OLD MINING SHAFT. HEARD ALL ABOUT IT DURING A COURSE LECTURE. THIS LAND WAS RIPE WITH BLOOD RUBIES UNTIL WORD LEAKED OUT.
RAIDERS AND TREASURE HUNTERS CAME IN WITH NO REGARD FOR THE COUNTRY, AND GRABBED WHATEVER THEY COULD GET THEIR MITTS ON.
THE RAILWAY WAS DESIGNED HAPHAZARDLY TO HELP THE MINERS EXPLOIT THE LAND AND ITS INHABITANTS. MORAL HERE IS GREED AND PROGRESS SOMETIMES GO HAND-IN-HAND.

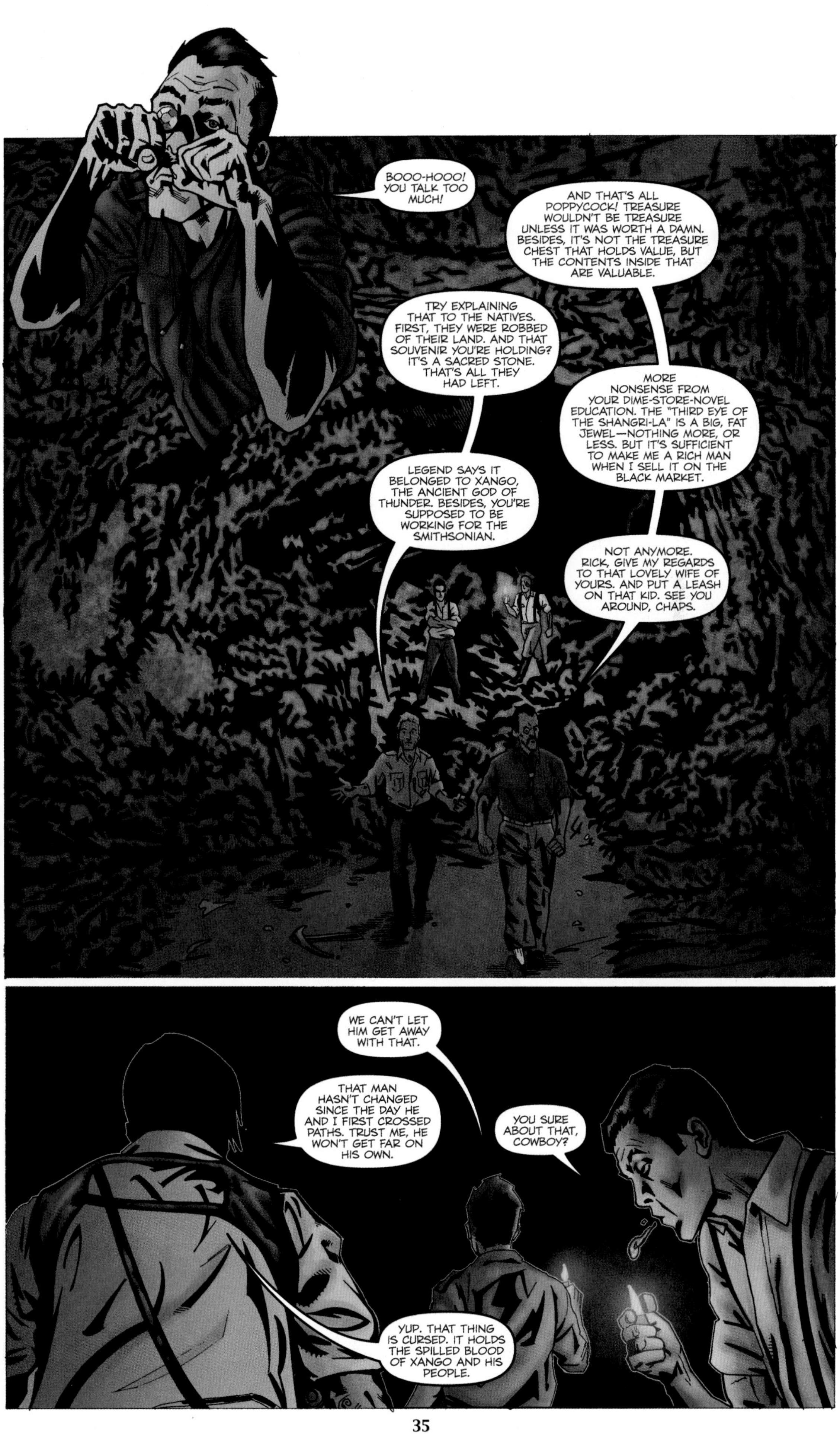
BOOO-HOOO! YOU TALK TOO MUCH!
AND THAT'S ALL POPPYCOCK! TREASURE WOULDN'T BE TREASURE UNLESS IT WAS WORTH A DAMN. BESIDES, IT'S NOT THE TREASURE CHEST THAT HOLDS VALUE, BUT THE CONTENTS INSIDE THAT ARE VALUABLE.
TRY EXPLAINING THAT TO THE NATIVES. FIRST, THEY WERE ROBBED OF THEIR LAND. AND THAT SOUVENIR YOU'RE HOLDING? IT'S A SACRED STONE. THAT'S ALL THEY HAD LEFT.
MORE NONSENSE FROM YOUR DIME-STORE-NOVEL EDUCATION. THE "THIRD EYE OF THE SHANGRI-LA" IS A BIG, FAT JEWEL—NOTHING MORE, OR LESS. BUT IT'S SUFFICIENT TO MAKE ME A RICH MAN WHEN I SELL IT ON THE BLACK MARKET.
LEGEND SAYS IT BELONGED TO XANGO, THE ANCIENT GOD OF THUNDER. BESIDES, YOU'RE SUPPOSED TO BE WORKING FOR THE SMITHSONIAN.
NOT ANYMORE. RICK, GIVE MY REGARDS TO THAT LOVELY WIFE OF YOURS. AND PUT A LEASH ON THAT KID. SEE YOU AROUND, CHAPS.
WE CAN'T LET HIM GET AWAY WITH THAT.
THAT MAN HASN'T CHANGED SINCE THE DAY HE AND I FIRST CROSSED PATHS. TRUST ME, HE WON'T GET FAR ON HIS OWN.
YOU SURE ABOUT THAT, COWBOY?
YUP. THAT THING IS CURSED. IT HOLDS THE SPILLED BLOOD OF XANGO AND HIS PEOPLE.

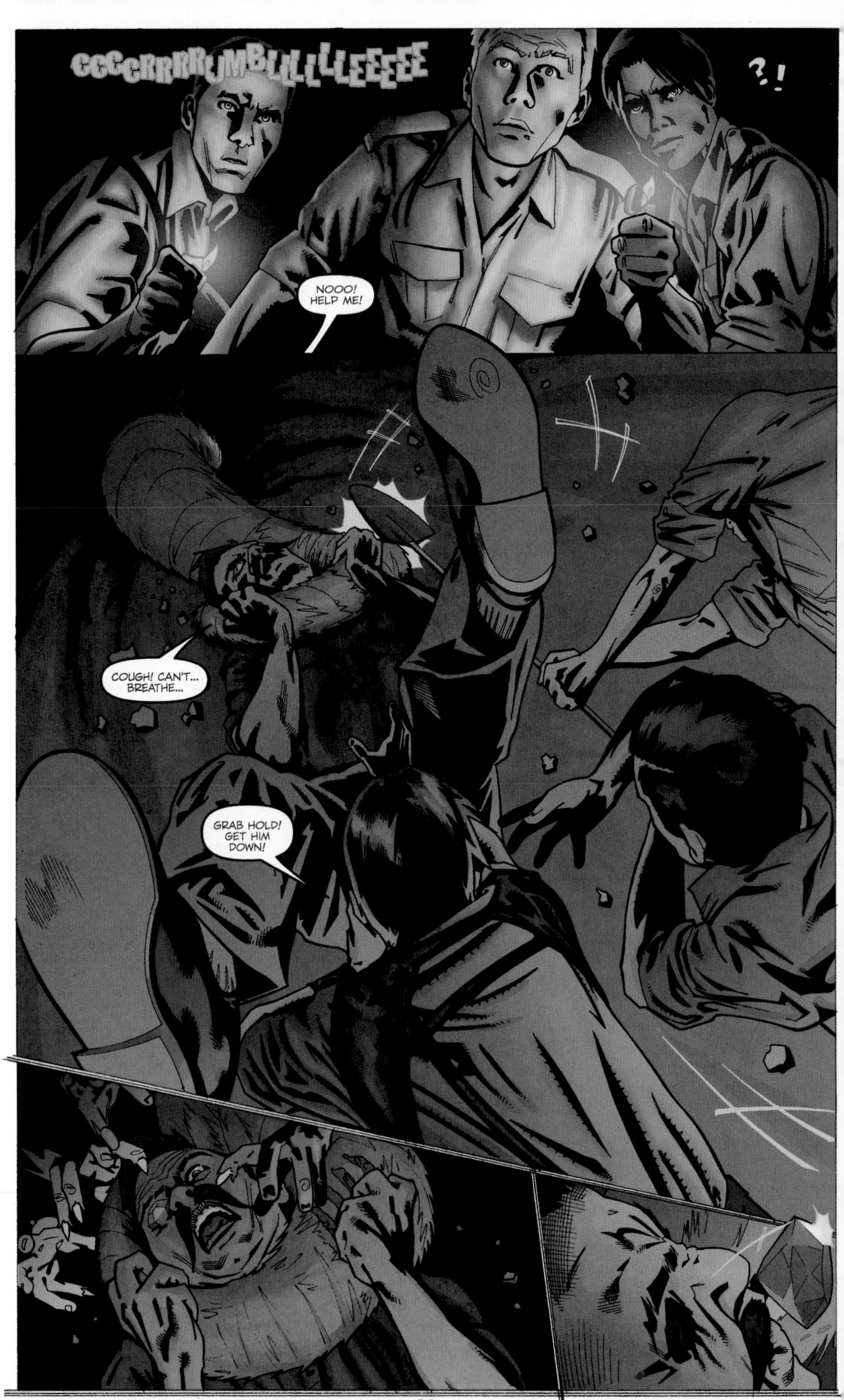
CCCCRRRRUMBLLLLLEEEEEE
?!
NOOO! HELP ME!
COUGH! CAN'T... BREATHE...
GRAB HOLD! GET HIM DOWN!

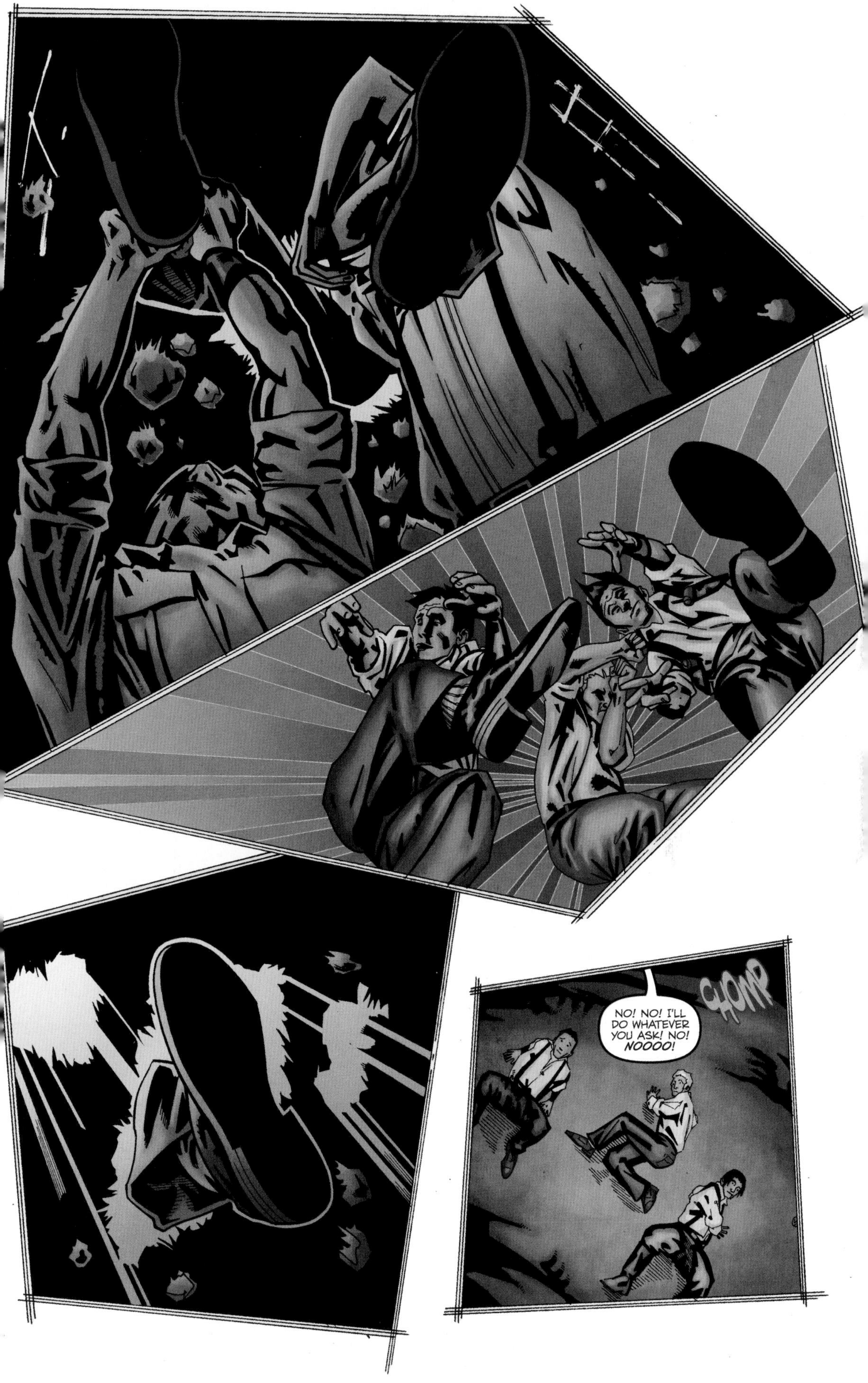
NO! NO! I'LL DO WHATEVER YOU ASK! NO! NOOOO!
CHOMP

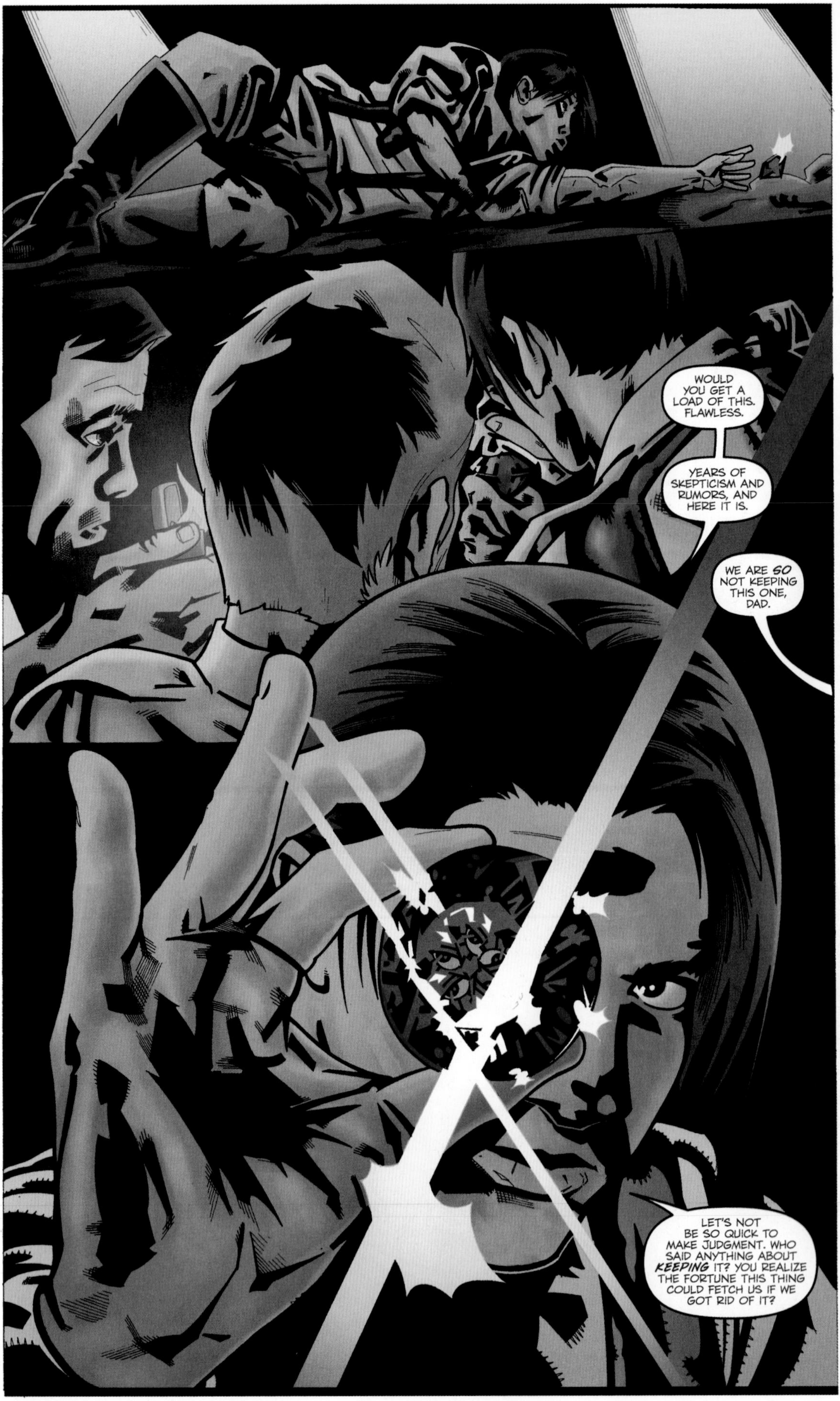
WOULD YOU GET A LOAD OF THIS. FLAWLESS.
YEARS OF SKEPTICISM AND RUMORS, AND HERE IT IS.
WE ARE *SO* NOT KEEPING THIS ONE, DAD.
LET'S NOT BE SO QUICK TO MAKE JUDGMENT. WHO SAID ANYTHING ABOUT *KEEPING* IT? YOU REALIZE THE FORTUNE THIS THING COULD FETCH US IF WE GOT RID OF IT?

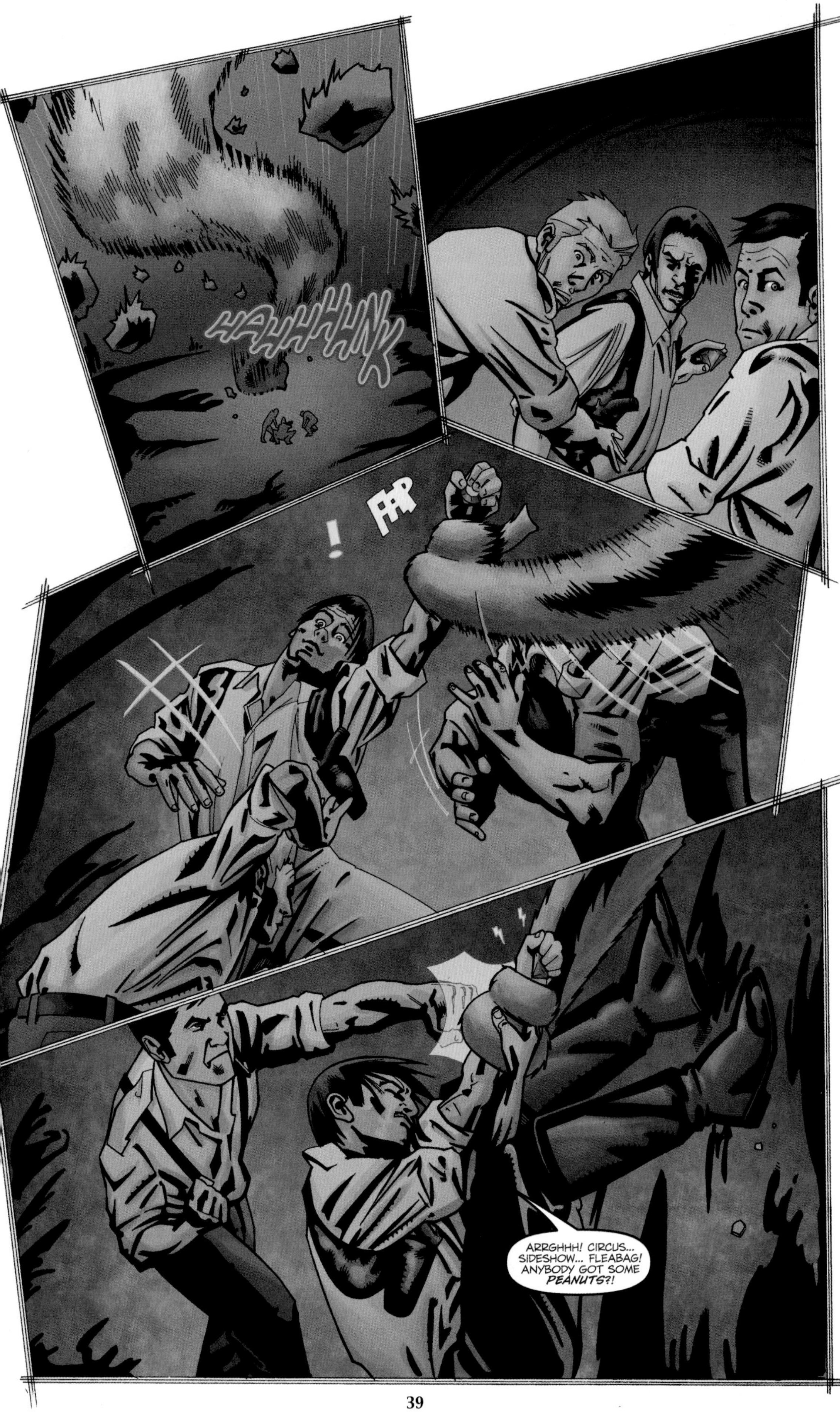
HAWHHUNK
!
FFFP
ARRGHHH! CIRCUS... SIDESHOW... FLEABAG! ANYBODY GOT SOME *PEANUTS*?!

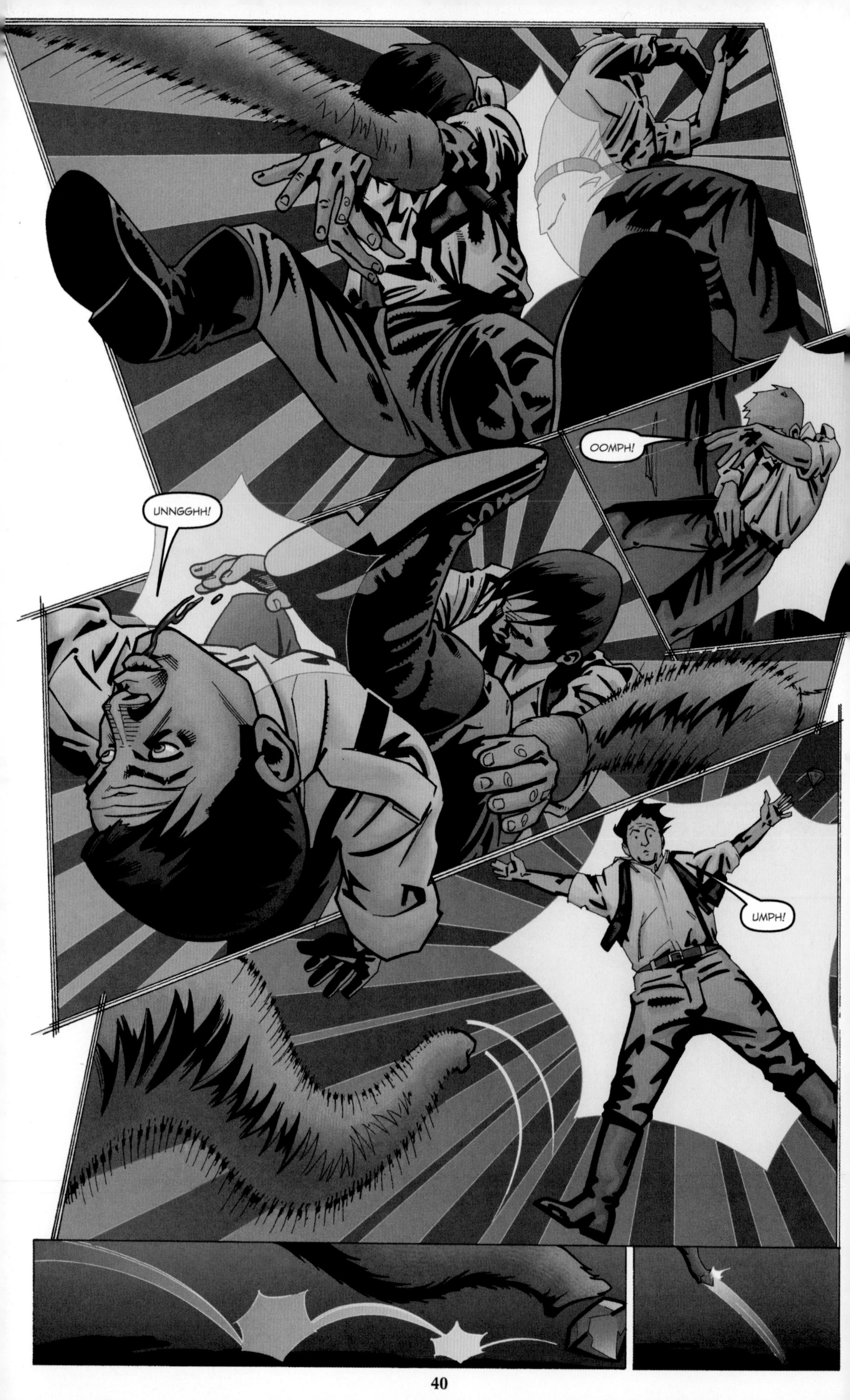

OOMPH!
UNNGGHH!
UMPH!

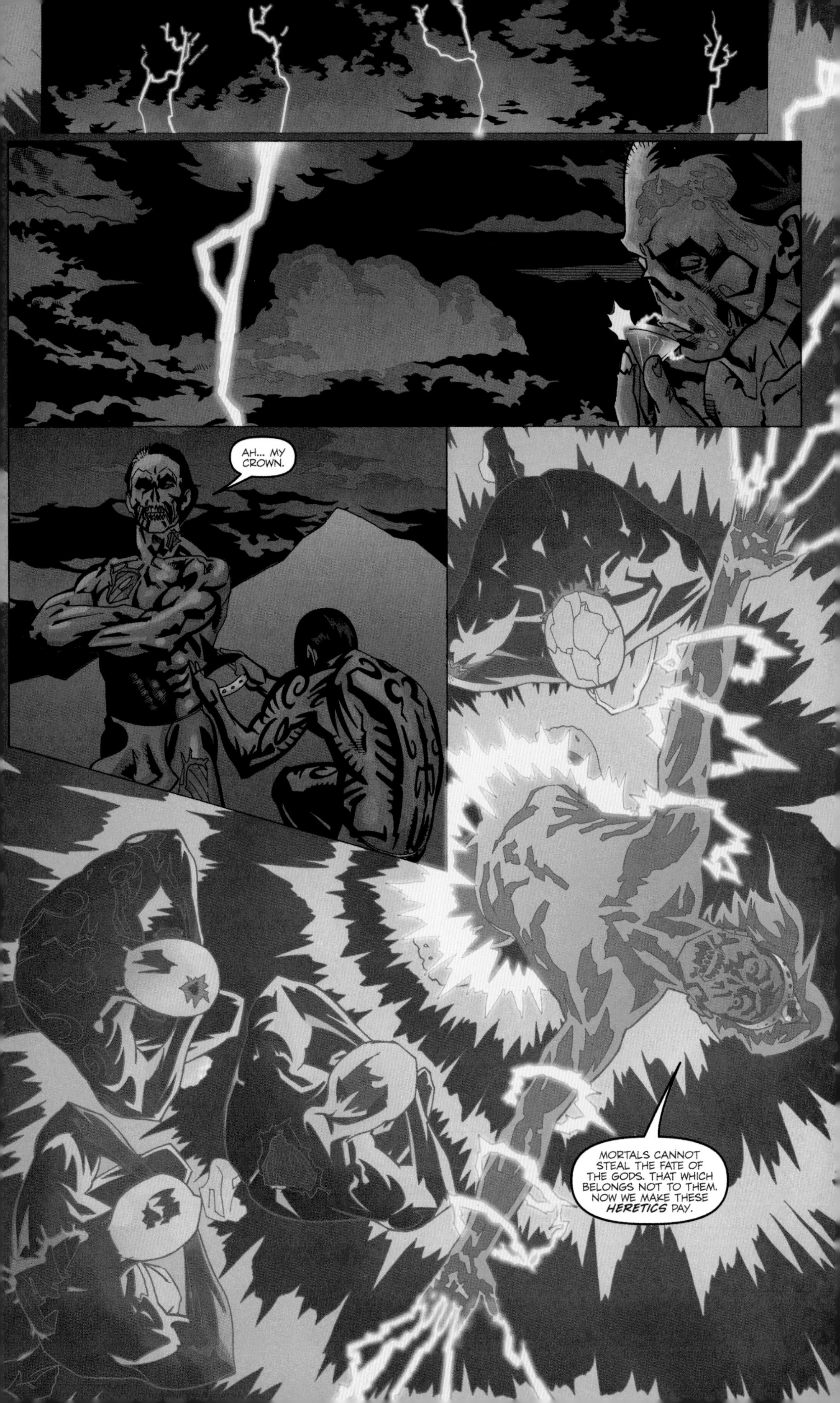
AH... MY CROWN.
MORTALS CANNOT STEAL THE FATE OF THE GODS. THAT WHICH BELONGS NOT TO THEM. NOW WE MAKE THESE *HERETICS* PAY.

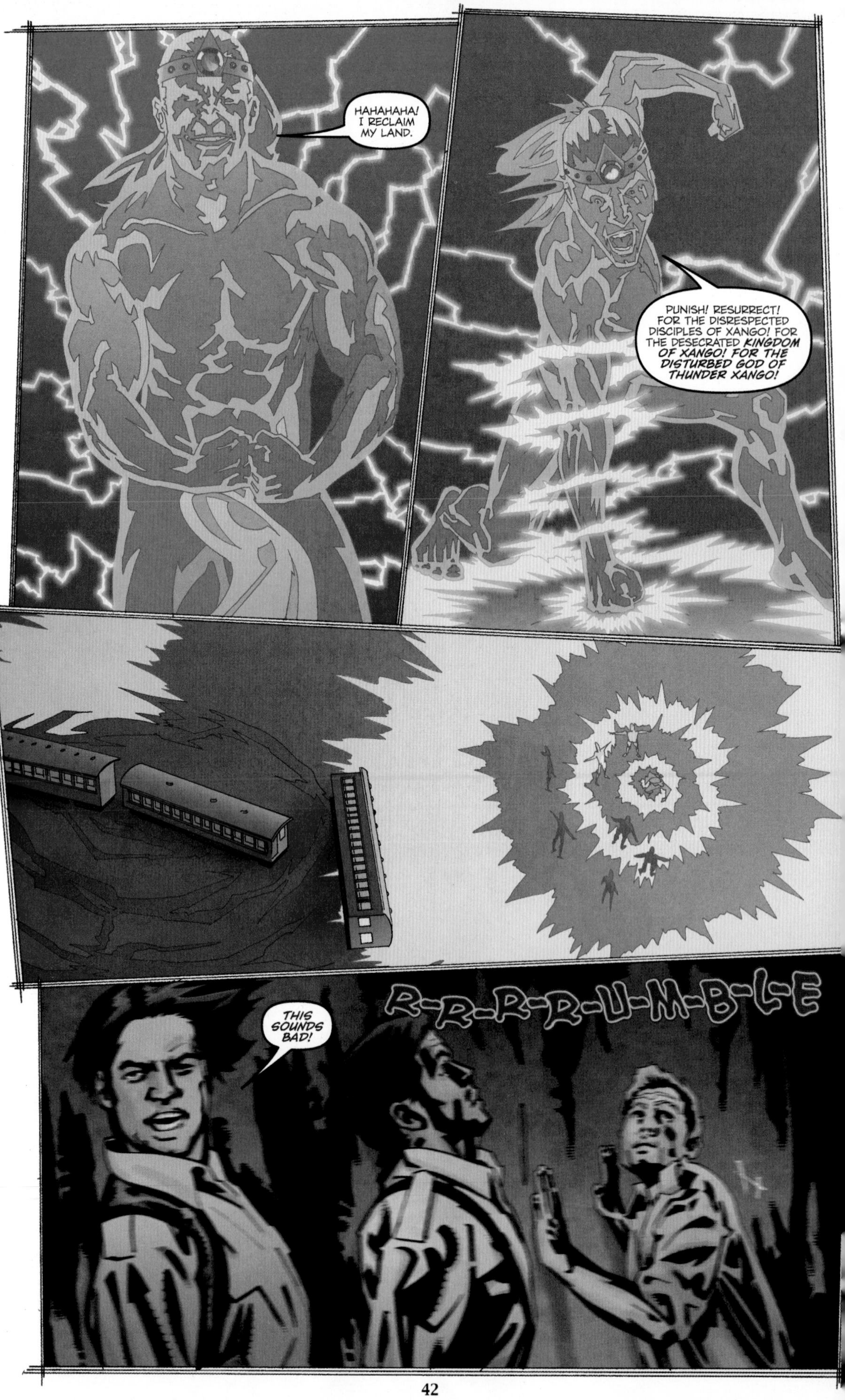
HAHAHAHA! I RECLAIM MY LAND.
PUNISH! RESURRECT! FOR THE DISRESPECTED DISCIPLES OF XANGO! FOR THE DESECRATED KINGDOM OF XANGO! FOR THE DISTURBED GOD OF THUNDER XANGO!
R-R-R-R-U-M-B-L-E
THIS SOUNDS BAD!

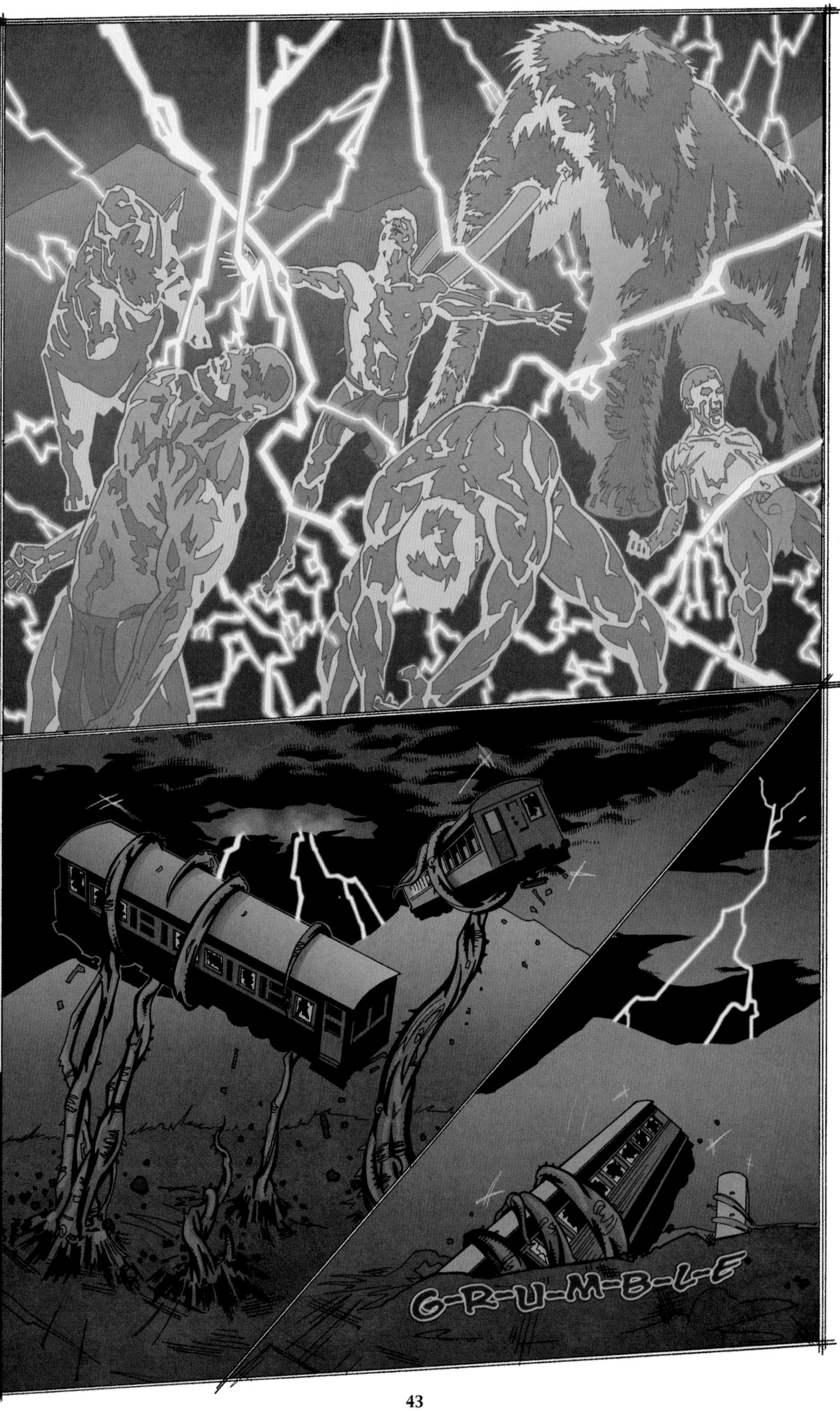
G-R-U-M-B-L-E

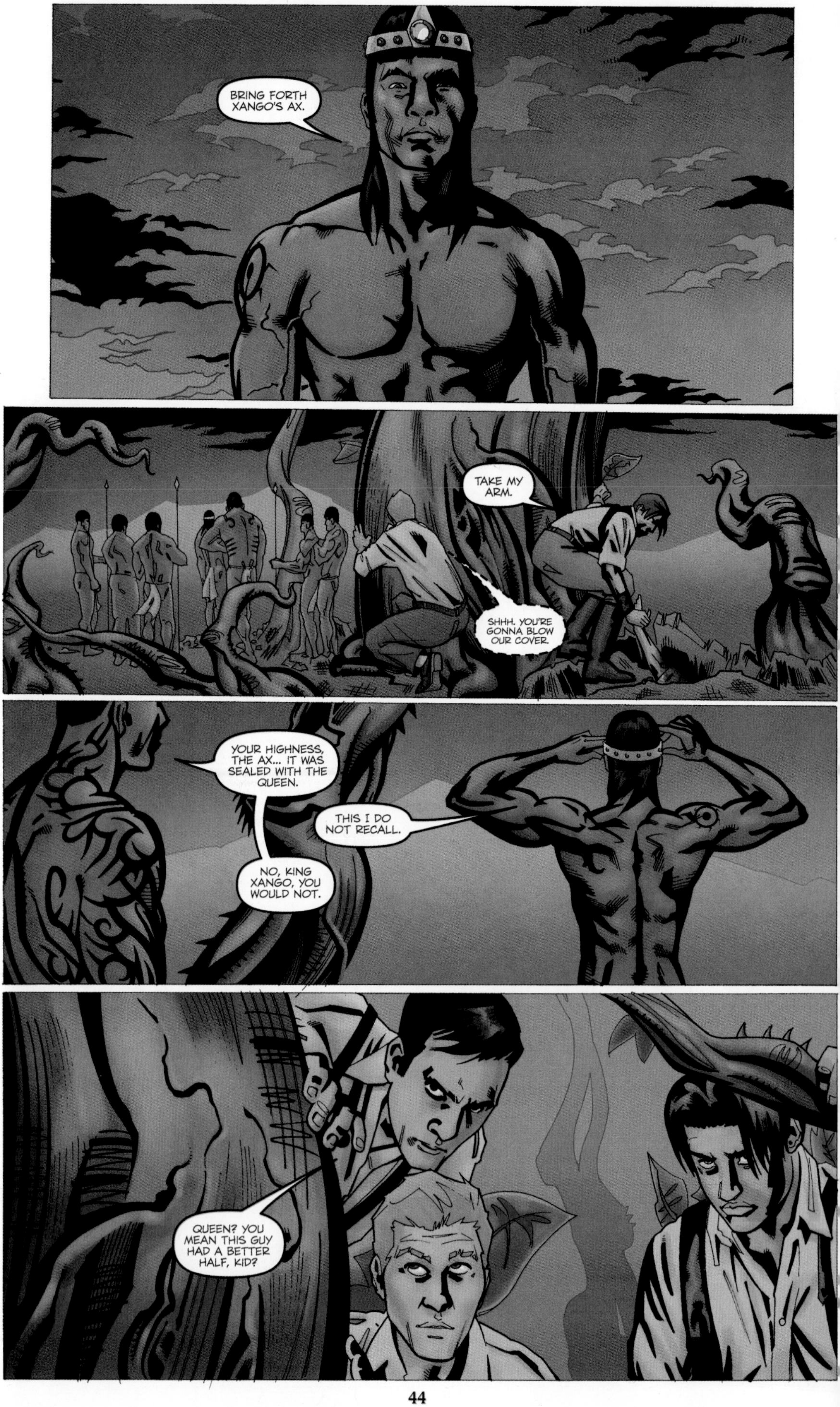
BRING FORTH XANGO'S AX.
TAKE MY ARM.
SHHH. YOU'RE GONNA BLOW OUR COVER.
YOUR HIGHNESS, THE AX... IT WAS SEALED WITH THE QUEEN.
THIS I DO NOT RECALL.
NO, KING XANGO, YOU WOULD NOT.
QUEEN? YOU MEAN THIS GUY HAD A BETTER HALF, KID?

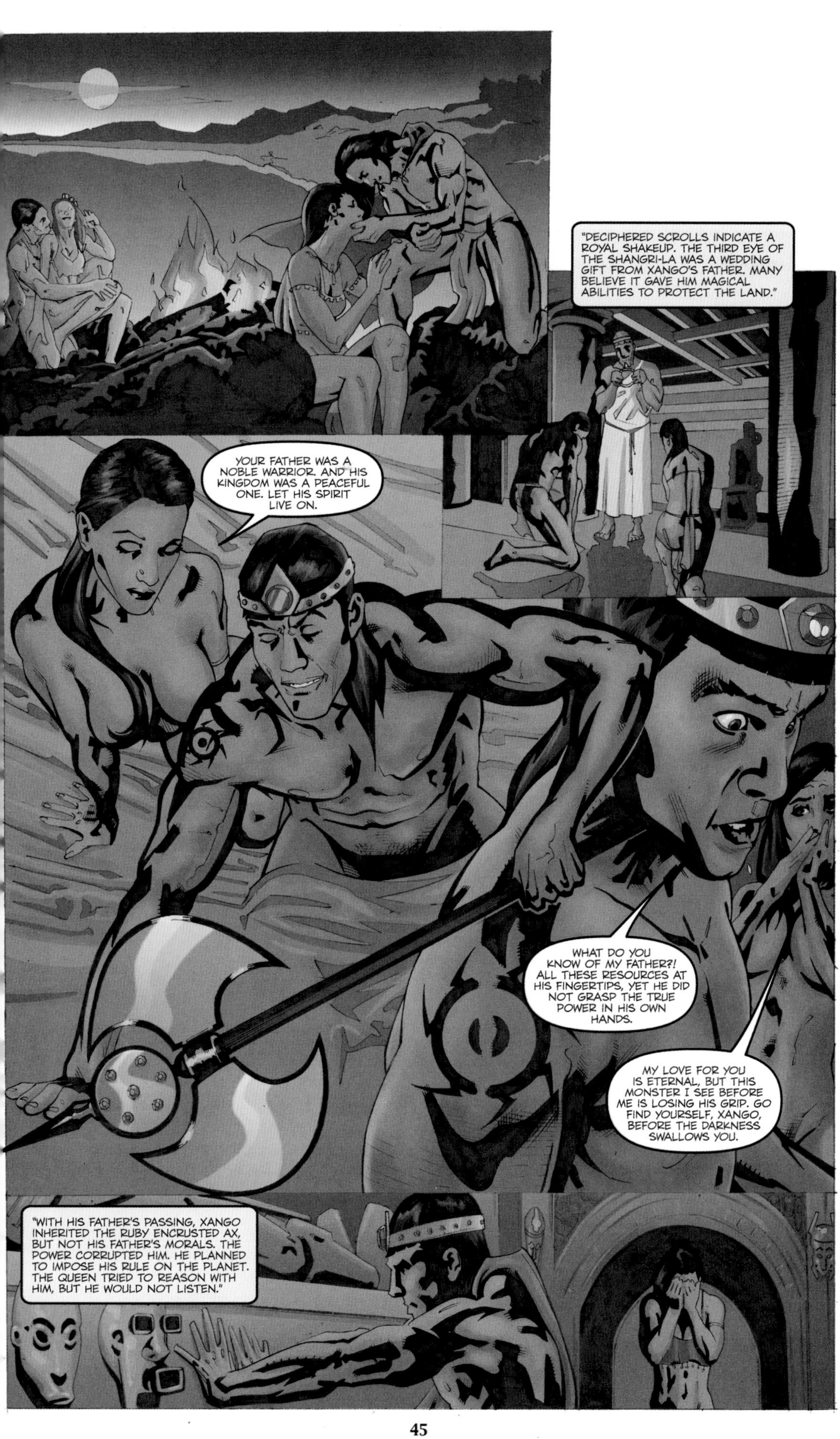
"DECIPHERED SCROLLS INDICATE A ROYAL SHAKEUP. THE THIRD EYE OF THE SHANGRI-LA WAS A WEDDING GIFT FROM XANGO'S FATHER. MANY BELIEVE IT GAVE HIM MAGICAL ABILITIES TO PROTECT THE LAND."
YOUR FATHER WAS A NOBLE WARRIOR. AND HIS KINGDOM WAS A PEACEFUL ONE. LET HIS SPIRIT LIVE ON.
WHAT DO YOU KNOW OF MY FATHER?! ALL THESE RESOURCES AT HIS FINGERTIPS, YET HE DID NOT GRASP THE TRUE POWER IN HIS OWN HANDS.
MY LOVE FOR YOU IS ETERNAL, BUT THIS MONSTER I SEE BEFORE ME IS LOSING HIS GRIP. GO FIND YOURSELF, XANGO, BEFORE THE DARKNESS SWALLOWS YOU.
"WITH HIS FATHER'S PASSING, XANGO INHERITED THE RUBY ENCRUSTED AX, BUT NOT HIS FATHER'S MORALS. THE POWER CORRUPTED HIM. HE PLANNED TO IMPOSE HIS RULE ON THE PLANET. THE QUEEN TRIED TO REASON WITH HIM, BUT HE WOULD NOT LISTEN."

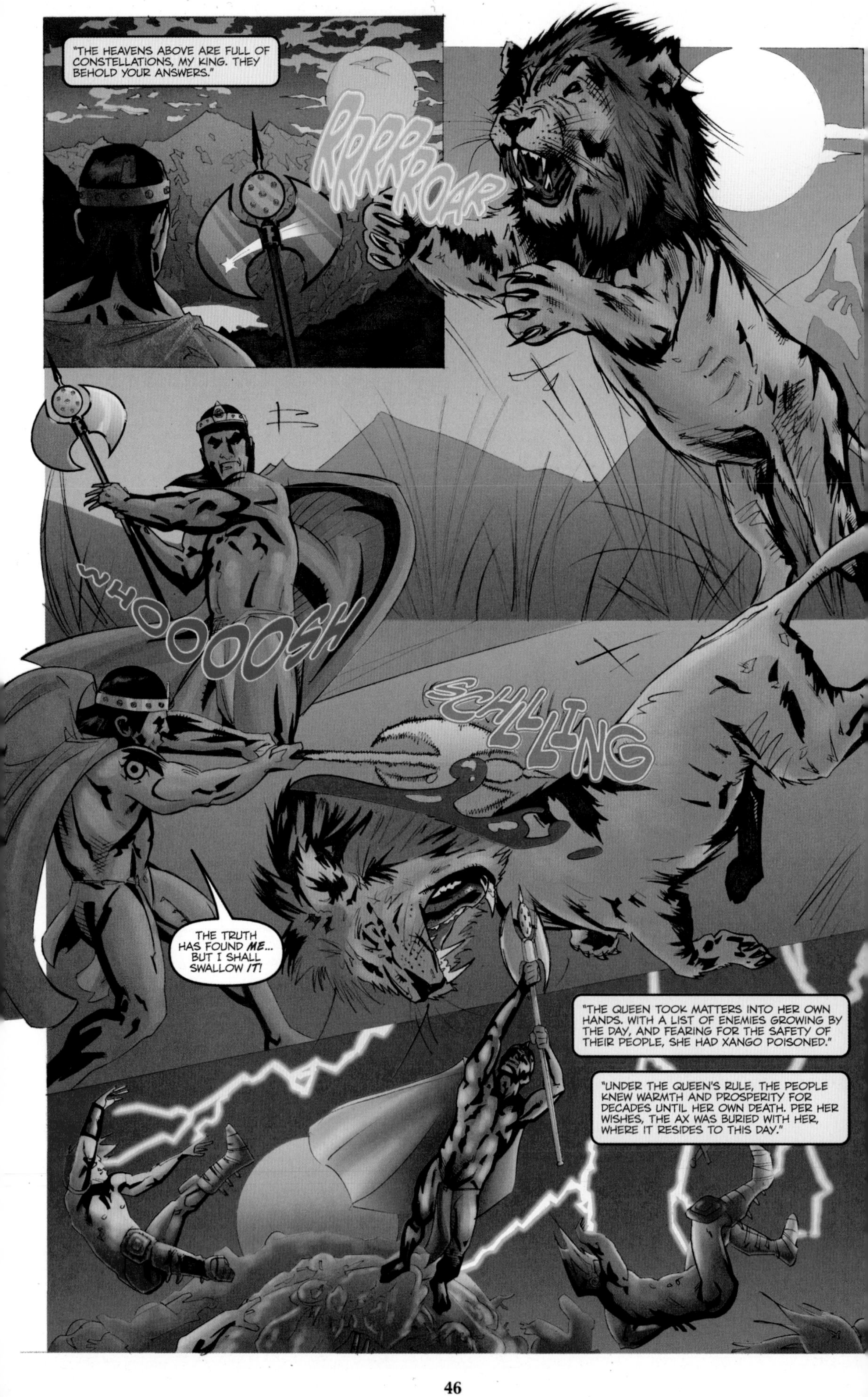
"THE HEAVENS ABOVE ARE FULL OF CONSTELLATIONS, MY KING. THEY BEHOLD YOUR ANSWERS."
RRRRROAR
WHOOOOOSH
SCHLLING
THE TRUTH HAS FOUND *ME*... BUT I SHALL SWALLOW *IT*!
"THE QUEEN TOOK MATTERS INTO HER OWN HANDS. WITH A LIST OF ENEMIES GROWING BY THE DAY, AND FEARING FOR THE SAFETY OF THEIR PEOPLE, SHE HAD XANGO POISONED."
"UNDER THE QUEEN'S RULE, THE PEOPLE KNEW WARMTH AND PROSPERITY FOR DECADES UNTIL HER OWN DEATH. PER HER WISHES, THE AX WAS BURIED WITH HER, WHERE IT RESIDES TO THIS DAY."

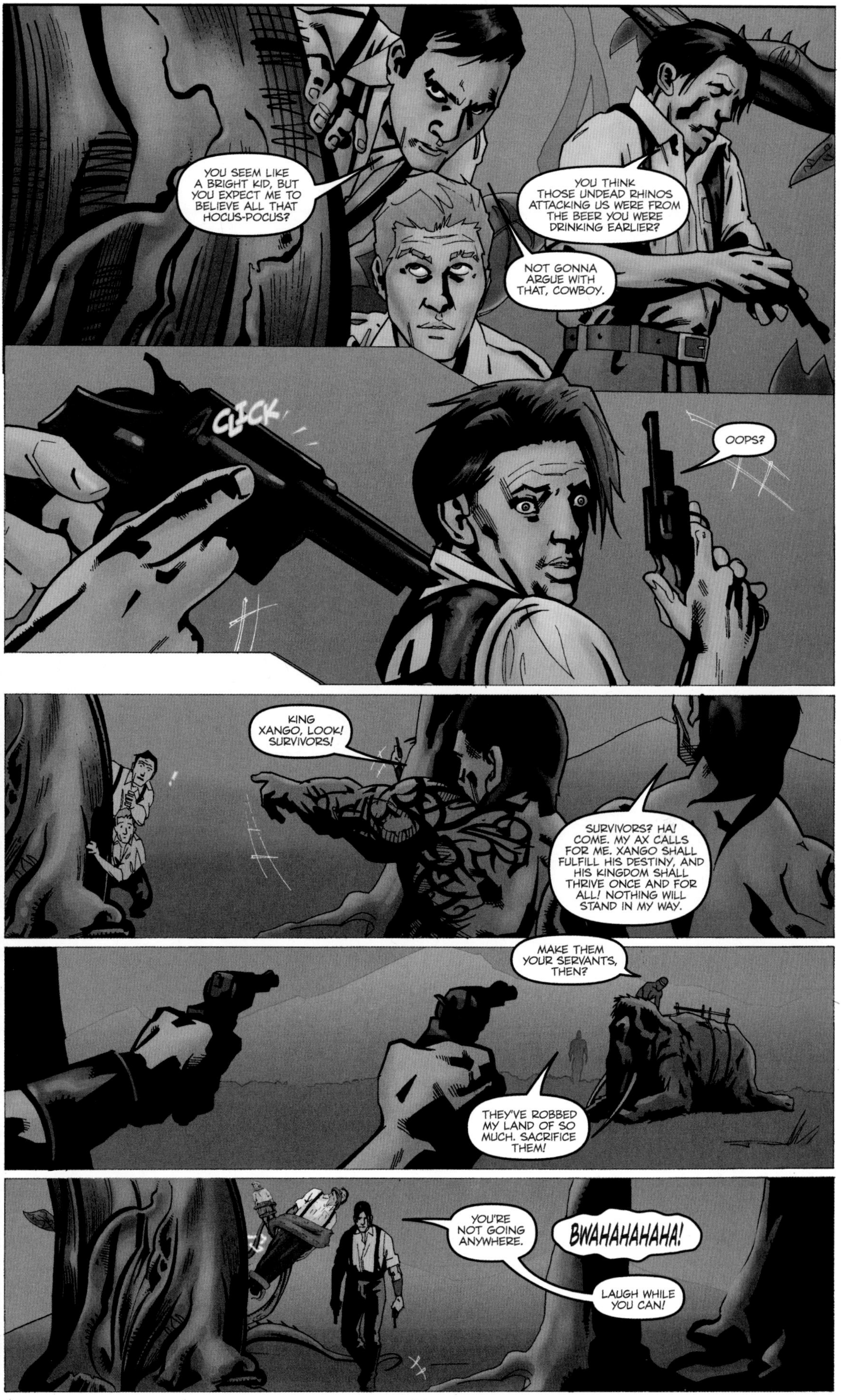
YOU SEEM LIKE A BRIGHT KID, BUT YOU EXPECT ME TO BELIEVE ALL THAT HOCUS-POCUS?
YOU THINK THOSE UNDEAD RHINOS ATTACKING US WERE FROM THE BEER YOU WERE DRINKING EARLIER?
NOT GONNA ARGUE WITH THAT, COWBOY.
CLICK
OOPS?
KING XANGO, LOOK! SURVIVORS!
SURVIVORS? HA! COME. MY AX CALLS FOR ME. XANGO SHALL FULFILL HIS DESTINY, AND HIS KINGDOM SHALL THRIVE ONCE AND FOR ALL! NOTHING WILL STAND IN MY WAY.
MAKE THEM YOUR SERVANTS, THEN?
THEY'VE ROBBED MY LAND OF SO MUCH. SACRIFICE THEM!
YOU'RE NOT GOING ANYWHERE.
BWAHAHAHAHA!
LAUGH WHILE YOU CAN!

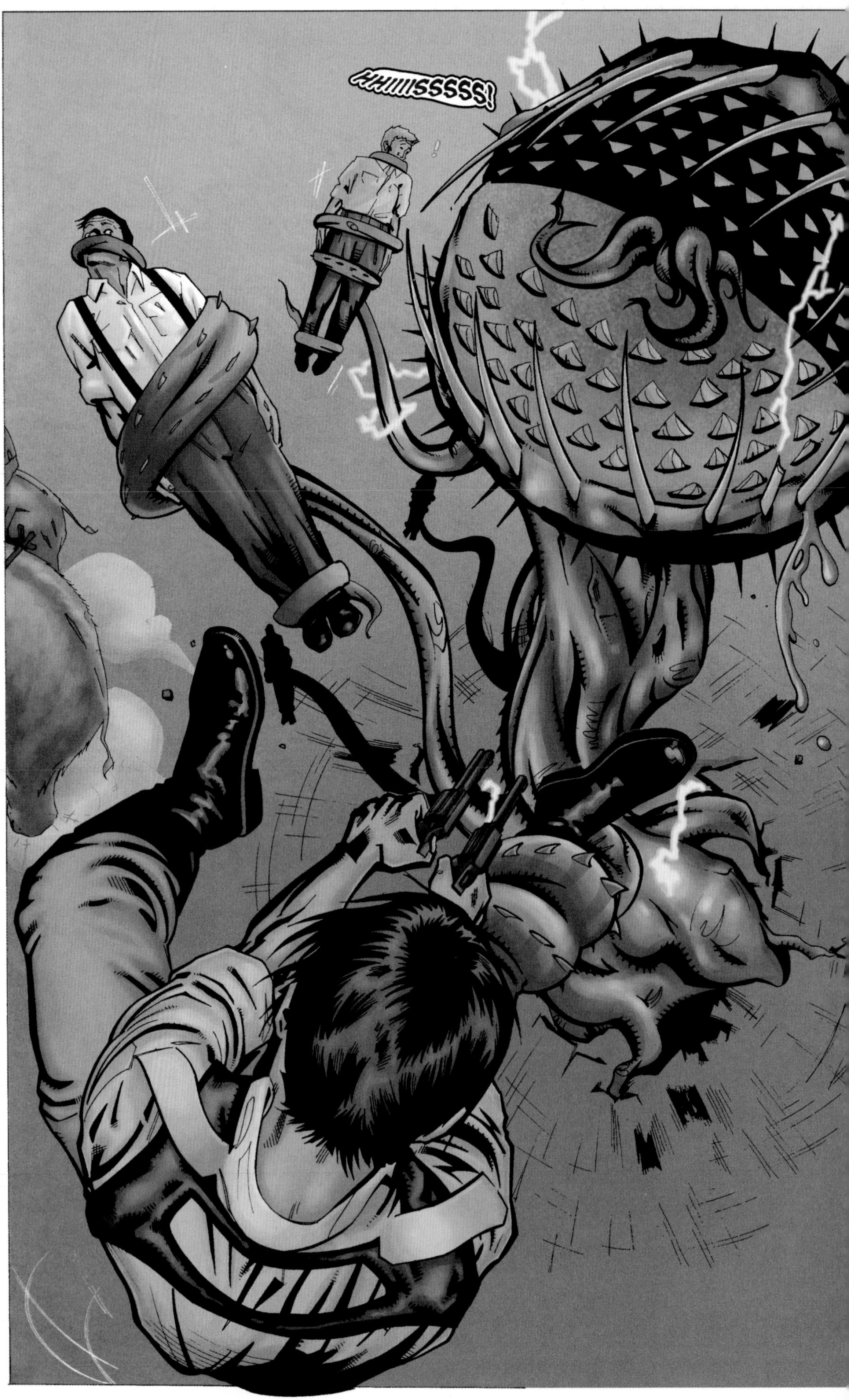
HHIIIISSSSS!
!

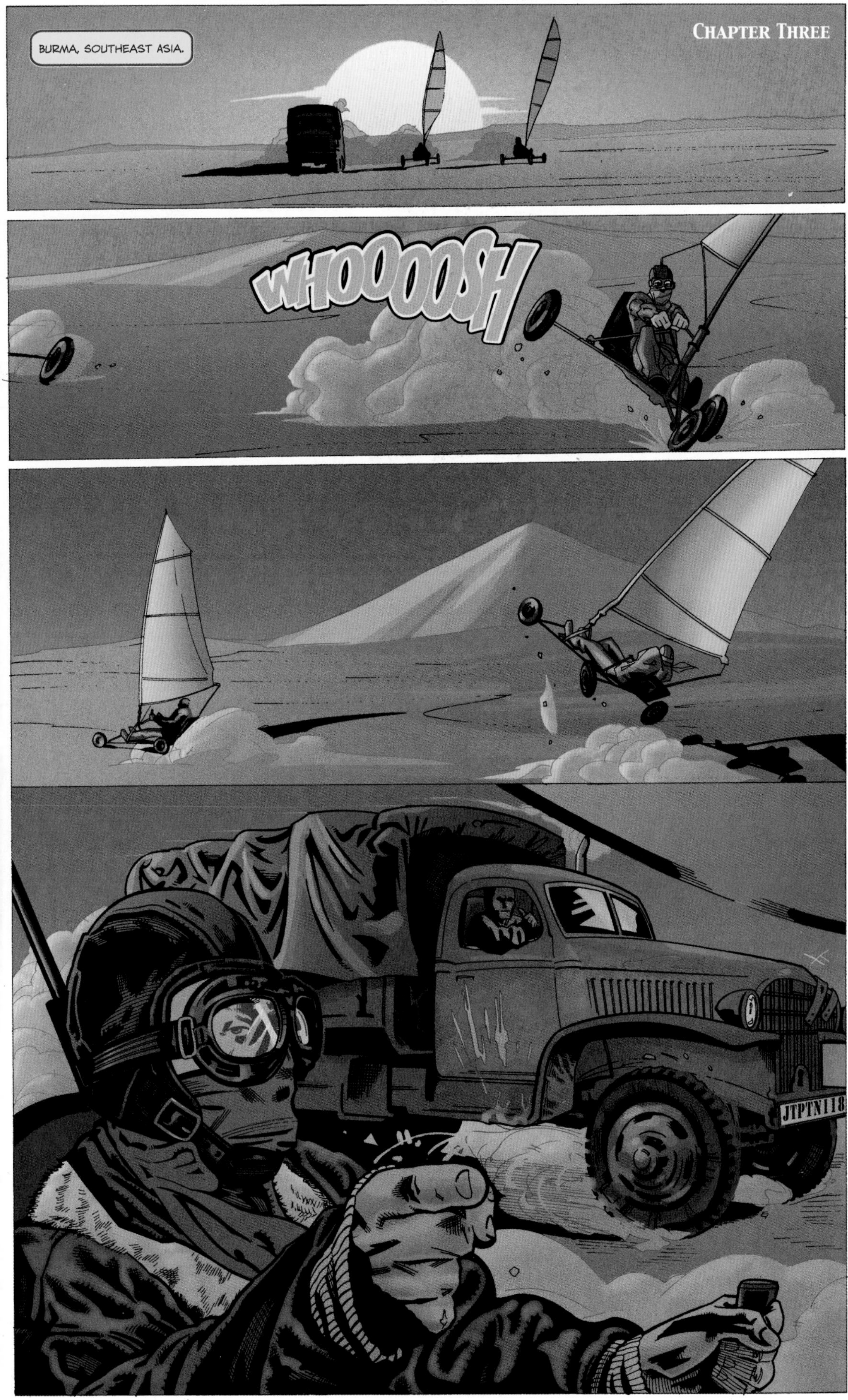
BURMA, SOUTHEAST ASIA.
WHOOOOSH
JTPTN118

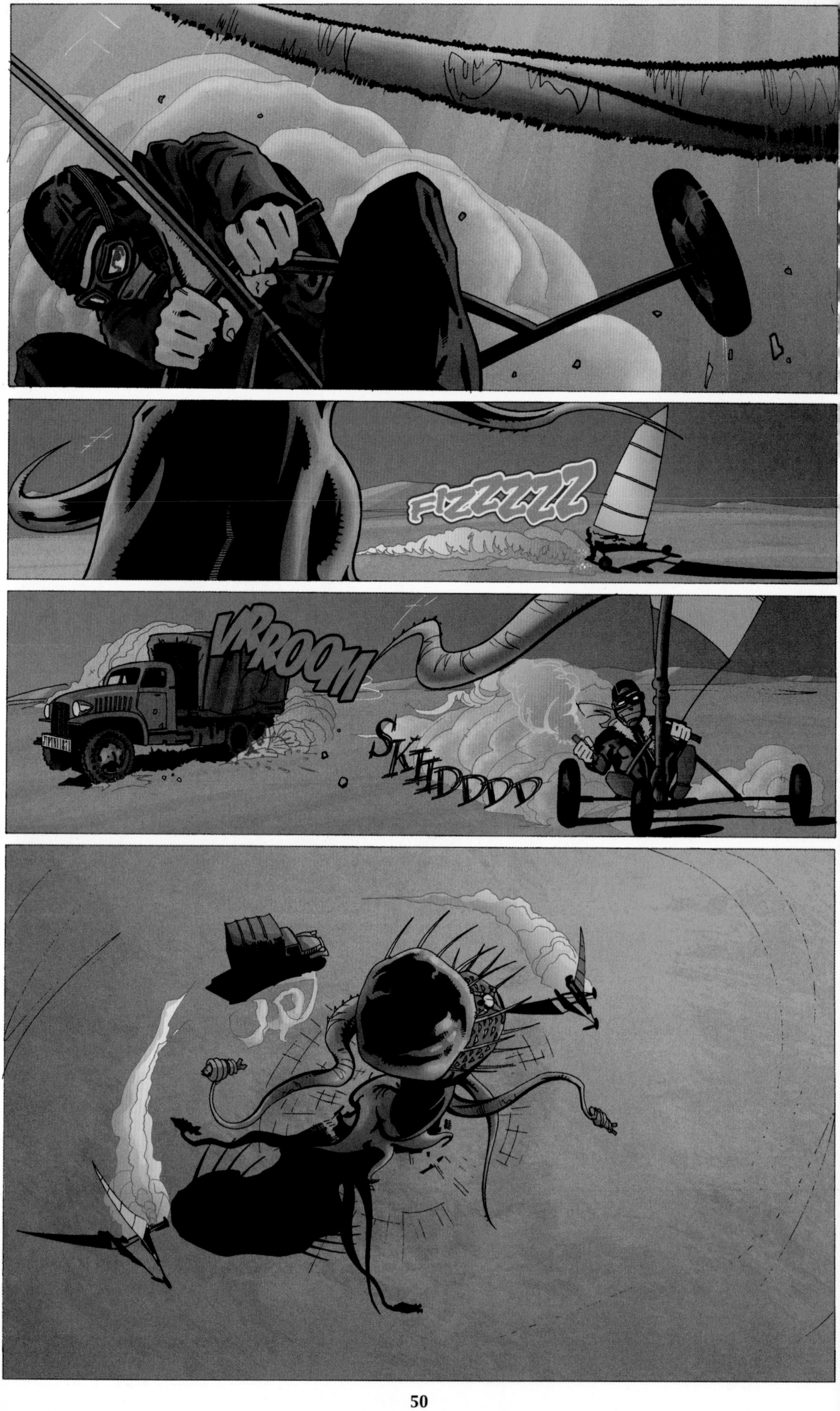
FIZZZZZ
VRROOM
SKEEDDDDD

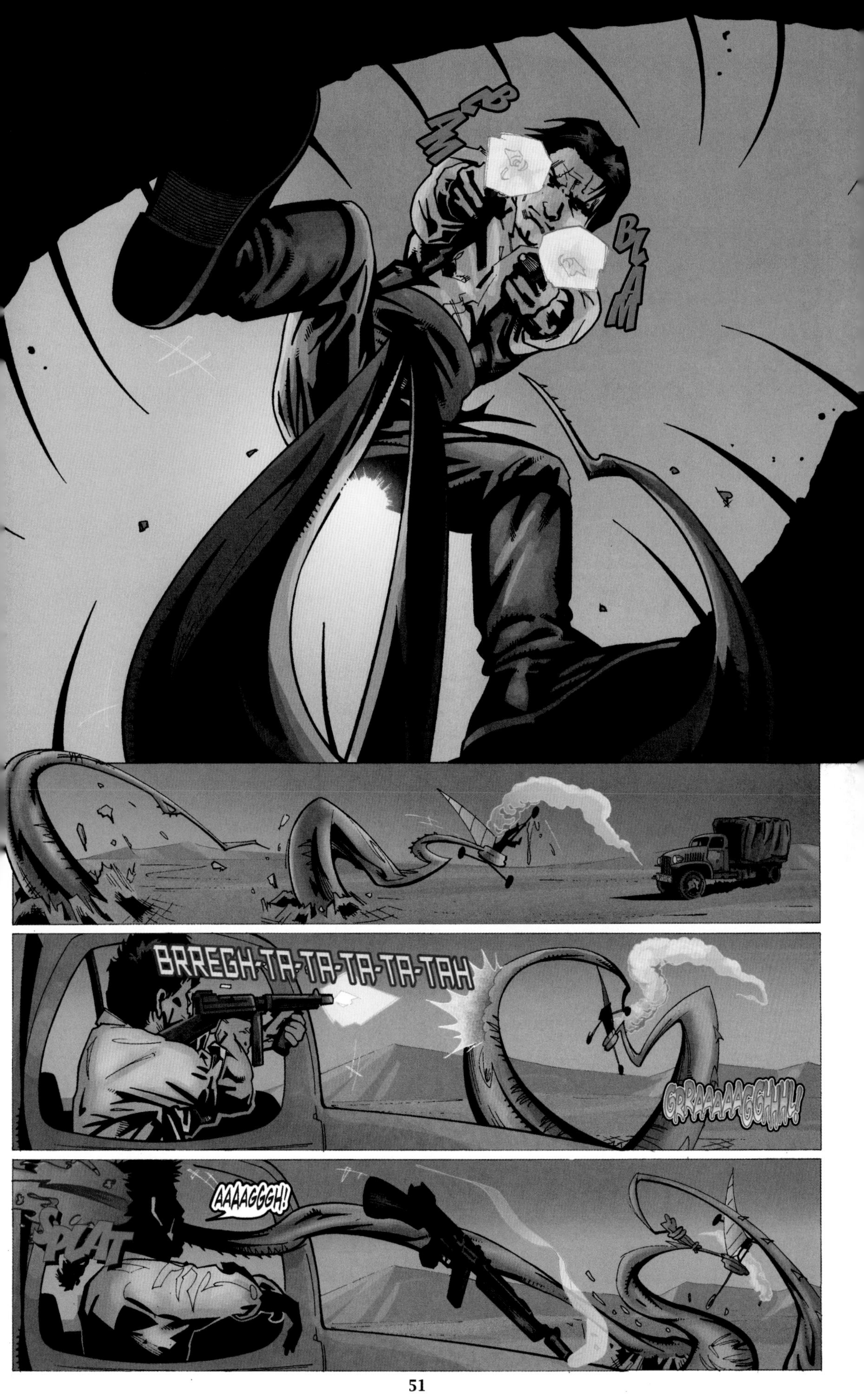
BLAM
BLAM
BRREGH-TA-TA-TA-TA-TAH
GRRAAAAAGGHHHL!
SPLAT
AAAAGGGH!

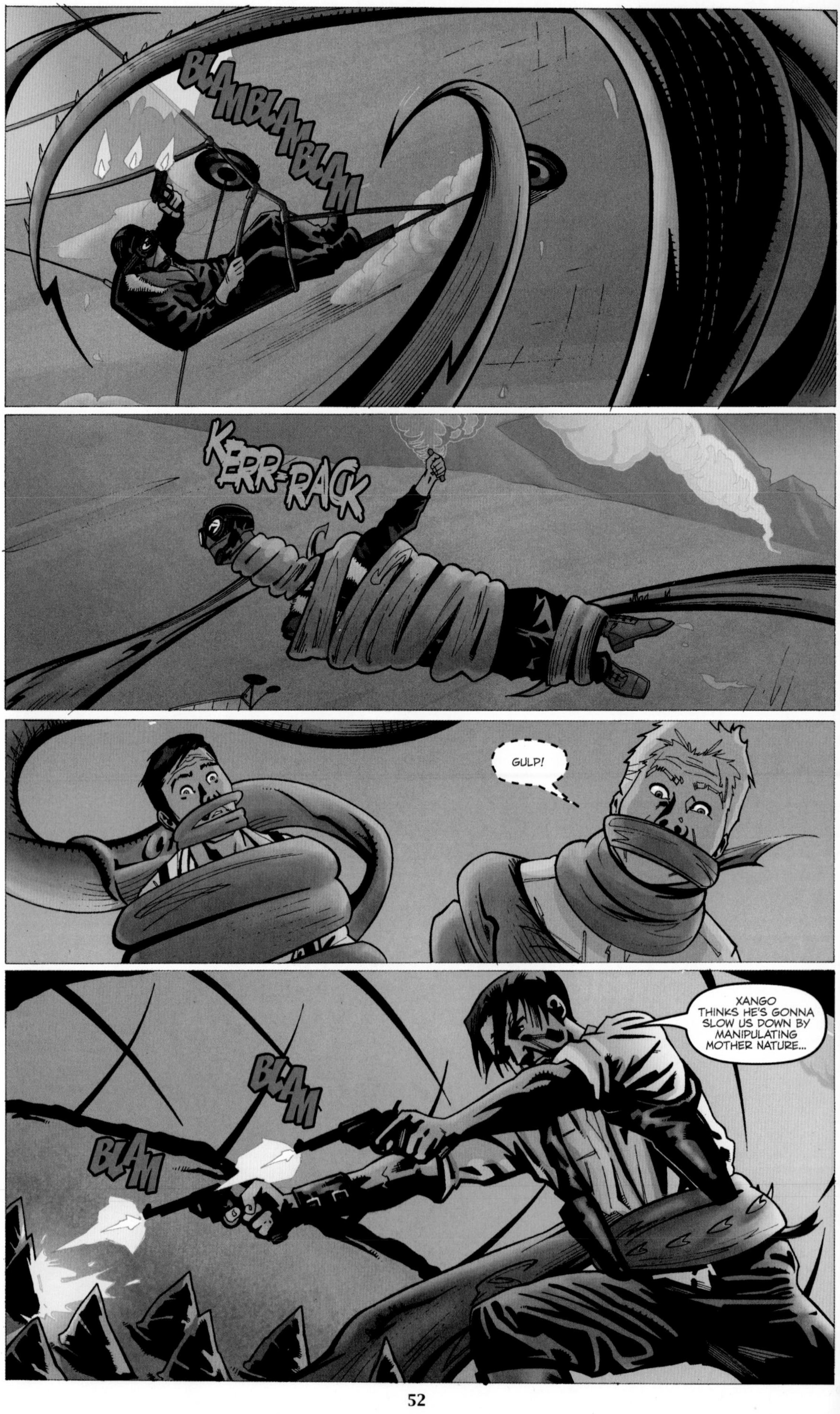
BLAMBLAMBLAM
KERR-RACK
GULP!
BLAM
BLAM
XANGO THINKS HE'S GONNA SLOW US DOWN BY MANIPULATING MOTHER NATURE...

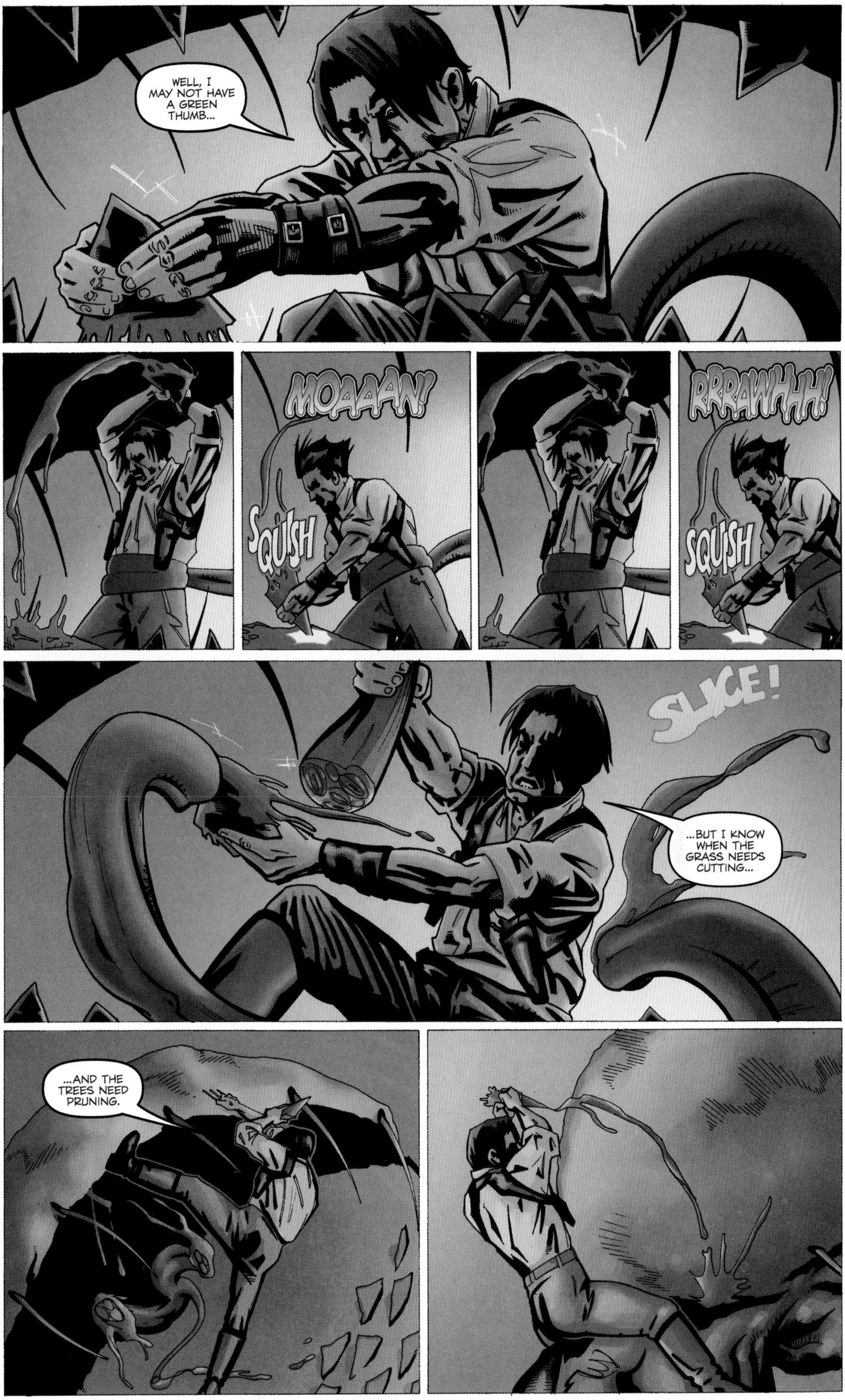
WELL, I MAY NOT HAVE A GREEN THUMB...
MOAAAN!
SQUISH
RRRAWHHH!
SQUISH
SLICE!
...BUT I KNOW WHEN THE GRASS NEEDS CUTTING...
...AND THE TREES NEED PRUNING.

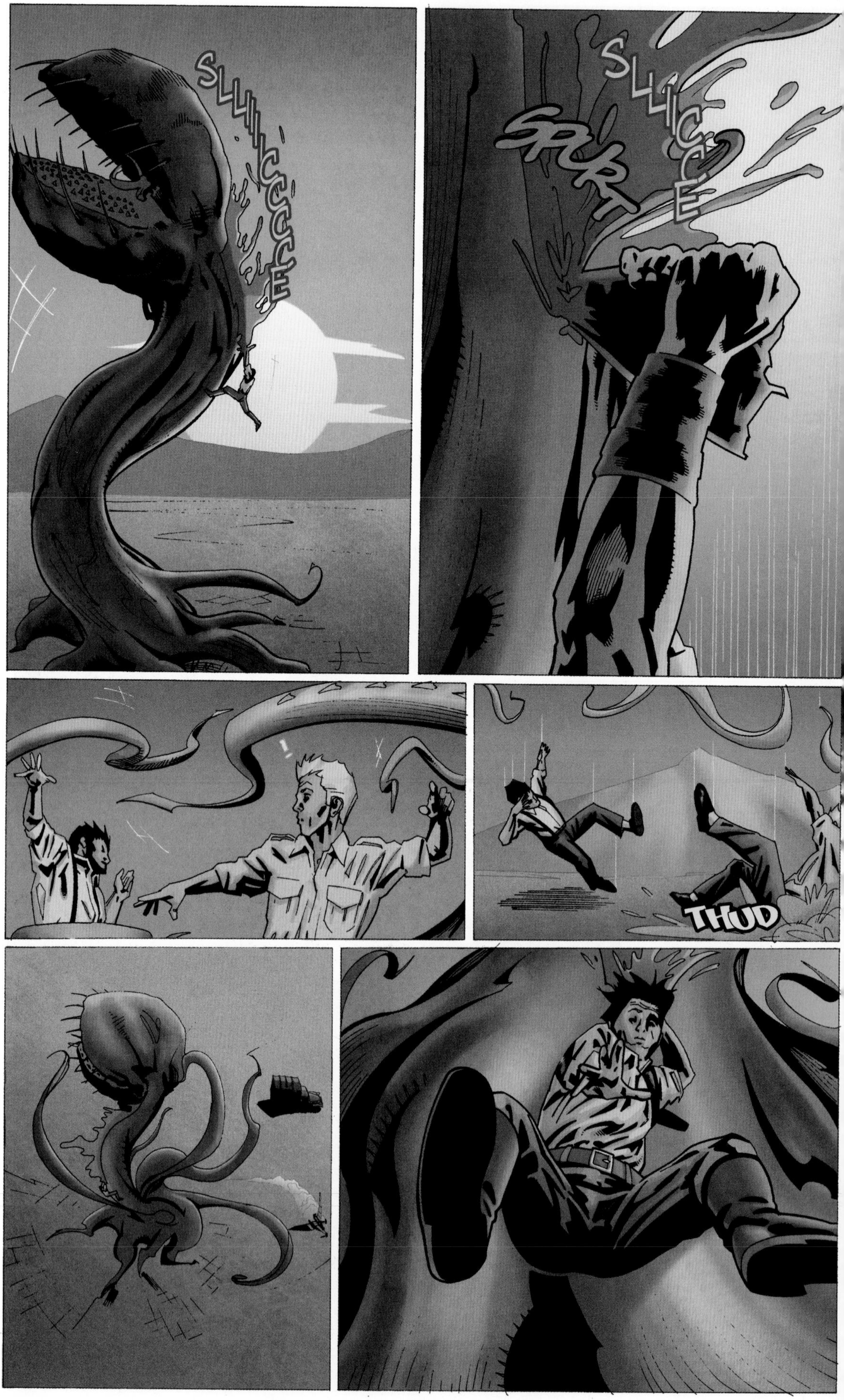
SLIIICCCCE
SLIICCE
SPURT
THUD

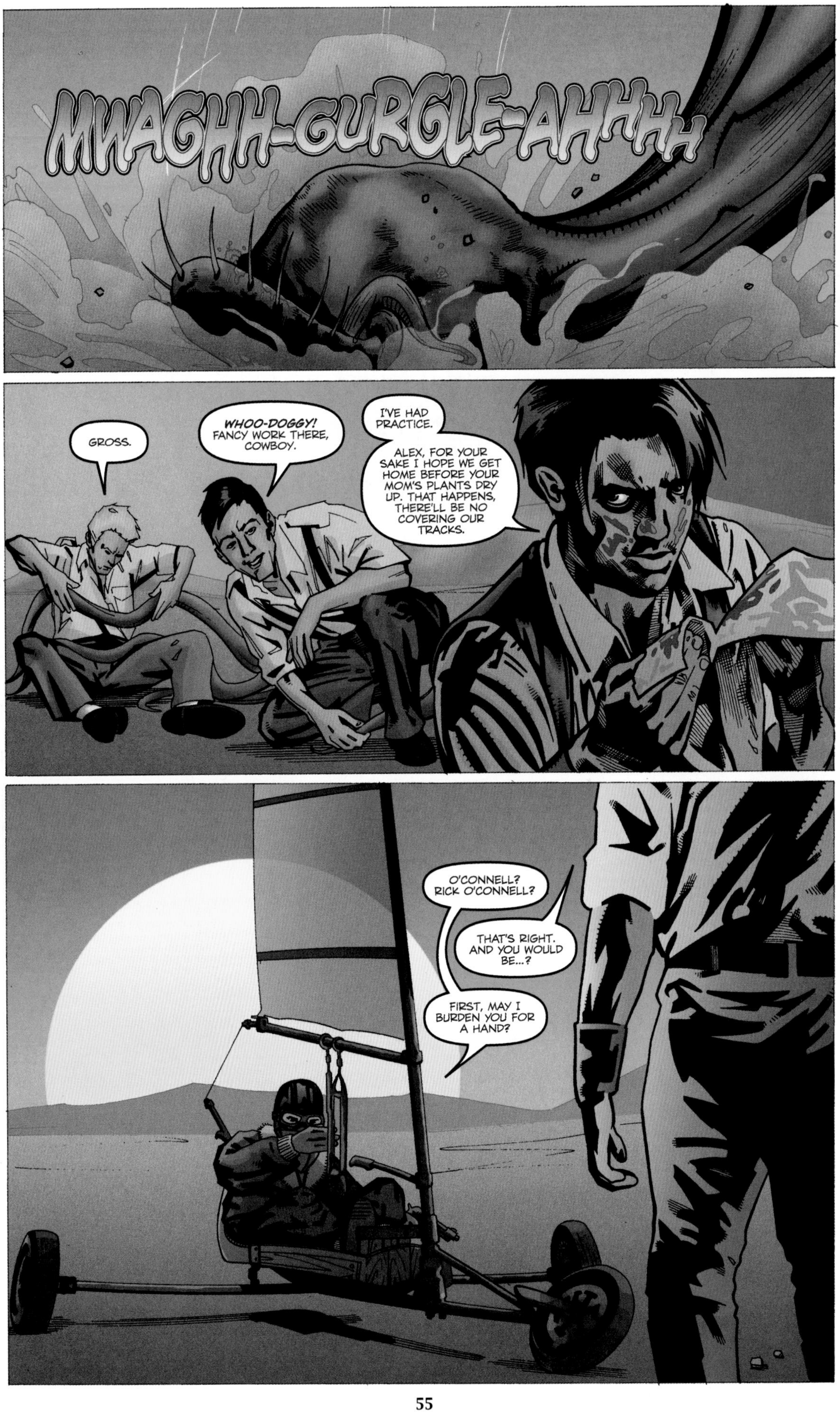
MWAGHH-GURGLE-AHHHH
GROSS.
WHOO-DOGGY! FANCY WORK THERE, COWBOY.
I'VE HAD PRACTICE.
ALEX, FOR YOUR SAKE I HOPE WE GET HOME BEFORE YOUR MOM'S PLANTS DRY UP. THAT HAPPENS, THERE'LL BE NO COVERING OUR TRACKS.
O'CONNELL? RICK O'CONNELL?
THAT'S RIGHT. AND YOU WOULD BE...?
FIRST, MAY I BURDEN YOU FOR A HAND?

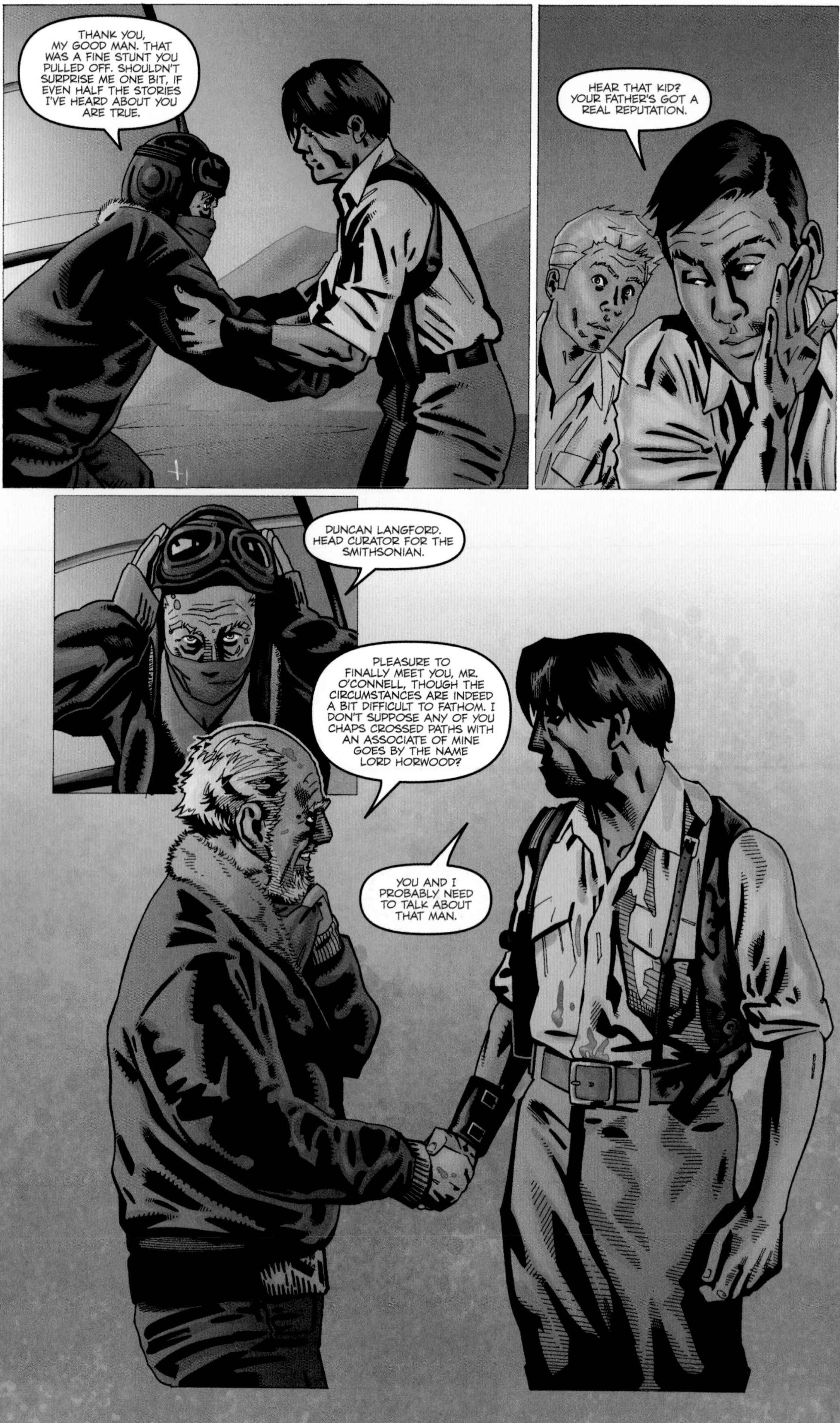

THANK YOU, MY GOOD MAN. THAT WAS A FINE STUNT YOU PULLED OFF. SHOULDN'T SURPRISE ME ONE BIT, IF EVEN HALF THE STORIES I'VE HEARD ABOUT YOU ARE TRUE.
HEAR THAT KID? YOUR FATHER'S GOT A REAL REPUTATION.
DUNCAN LANGFORD. HEAD CURATOR FOR THE SMITHSONIAN.
PLEASURE TO FINALLY MEET YOU, MR. O'CONNELL, THOUGH THE CIRCUMSTANCES ARE INDEED A BIT DIFFICULT TO FATHOM. I DON'T SUPPOSE ANY OF YOU CHAPS CROSSED PATHS WITH AN ASSOCIATE OF MINE GOES BY THE NAME LORD HORWOOD?
YOU AND I PROBABLY NEED TO TALK ABOUT THAT MAN.

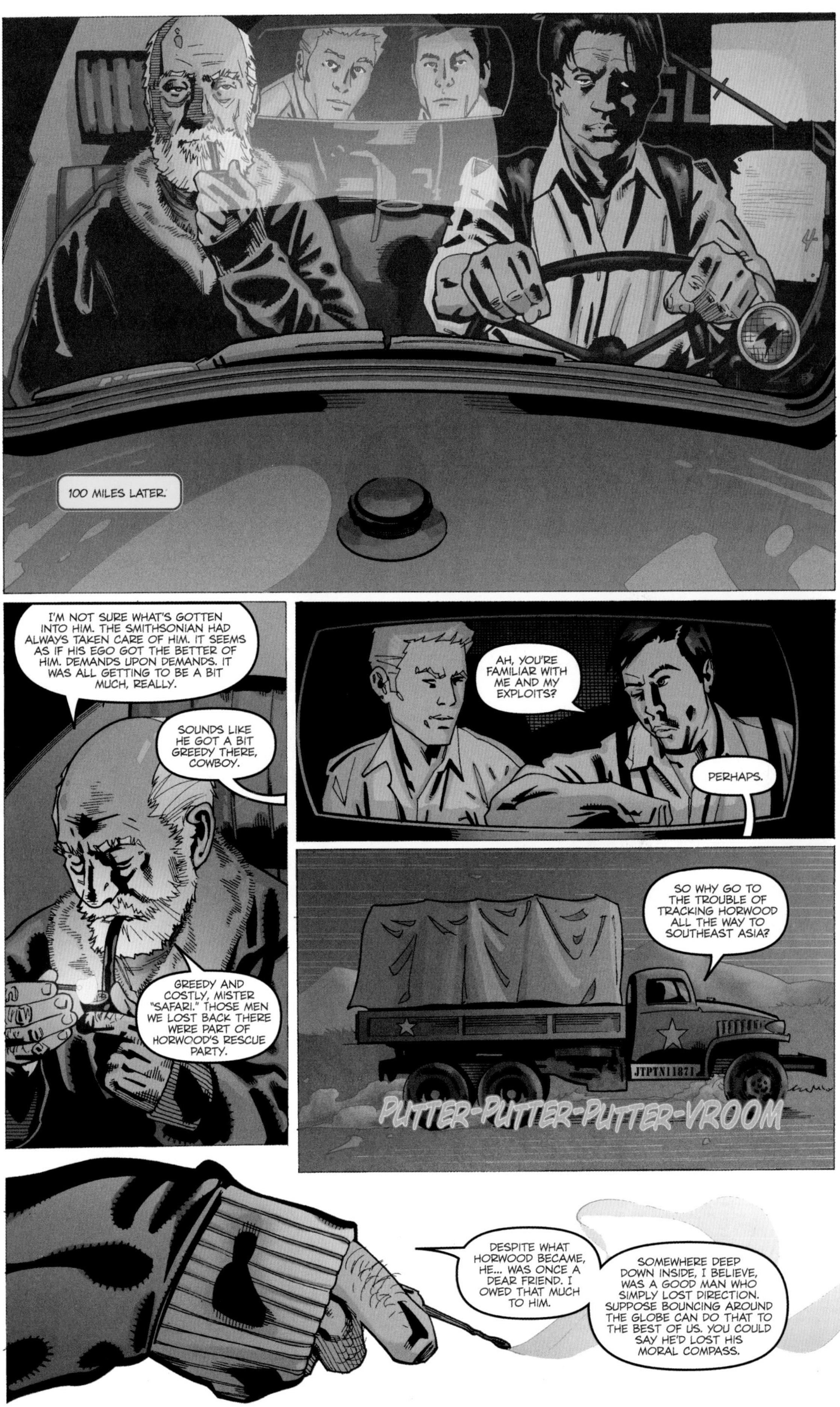
100 MILES LATER.
I'M NOT SURE WHAT'S GOTTEN INTO HIM. THE SMITHSONIAN HAD ALWAYS TAKEN CARE OF HIM. IT SEEMS AS IF HIS EGO GOT THE BETTER OF HIM. DEMANDS UPON DEMANDS. IT WAS ALL GETTING TO BE A BIT MUCH, REALLY.
SOUNDS LIKE HE GOT A BIT GREEDY THERE, COWBOY.
GREEDY AND COSTLY, MISTER "SAFARI." THOSE MEN WE LOST BACK THERE WERE PART OF HORWOOD'S RESCUE PARTY.
AH, YOU'RE FAMILIAR WITH ME AND MY EXPLOITS?
PERHAPS.
SO WHY GO TO THE TROUBLE OF TRACKING HORWOOD ALL THE WAY TO SOUTHEAST ASIA?
JTPTN11871
PUTTER-PUTTER-PUTTER-VROOM
DESPITE WHAT HORWOOD BECAME, HE... WAS ONCE A DEAR FRIEND. I OWED THAT MUCH TO HIM.
SOMEWHERE DEEP DOWN INSIDE, I BELIEVE, WAS A GOOD MAN WHO SIMPLY LOST DIRECTION. SUPPOSE BOUNCING AROUND THE GLOBE CAN DO THAT TO THE BEST OF US. YOU COULD SAY HE'D LOST HIS MORAL COMPASS.

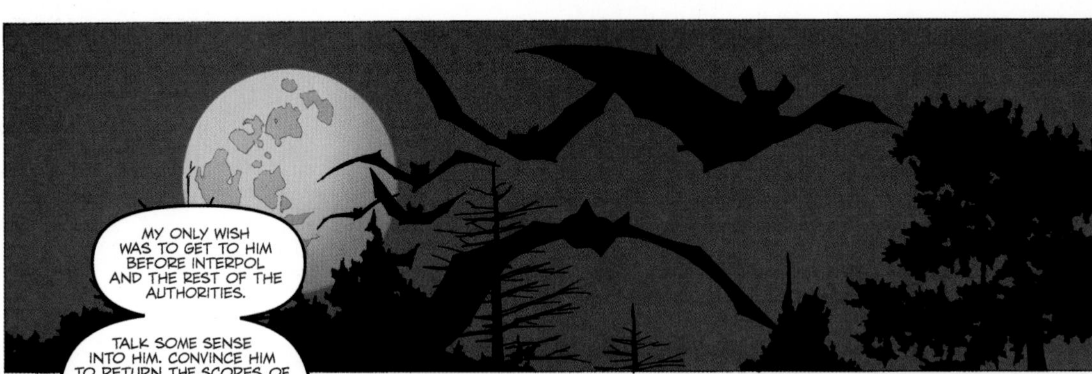
MY ONLY WISH WAS TO GET TO HIM BEFORE INTERPOL AND THE REST OF THE AUTHORITIES.
TALK SOME SENSE INTO HIM. CONVINCE HIM TO RETURN THE SCORES OF ARTIFACTS THAT WENT MISSING FROM THE MUSEUM, ALONG WITH THE MORE RECENT DISCOVERIES HE WAS PITCHING ON THE BLACK MARKET.

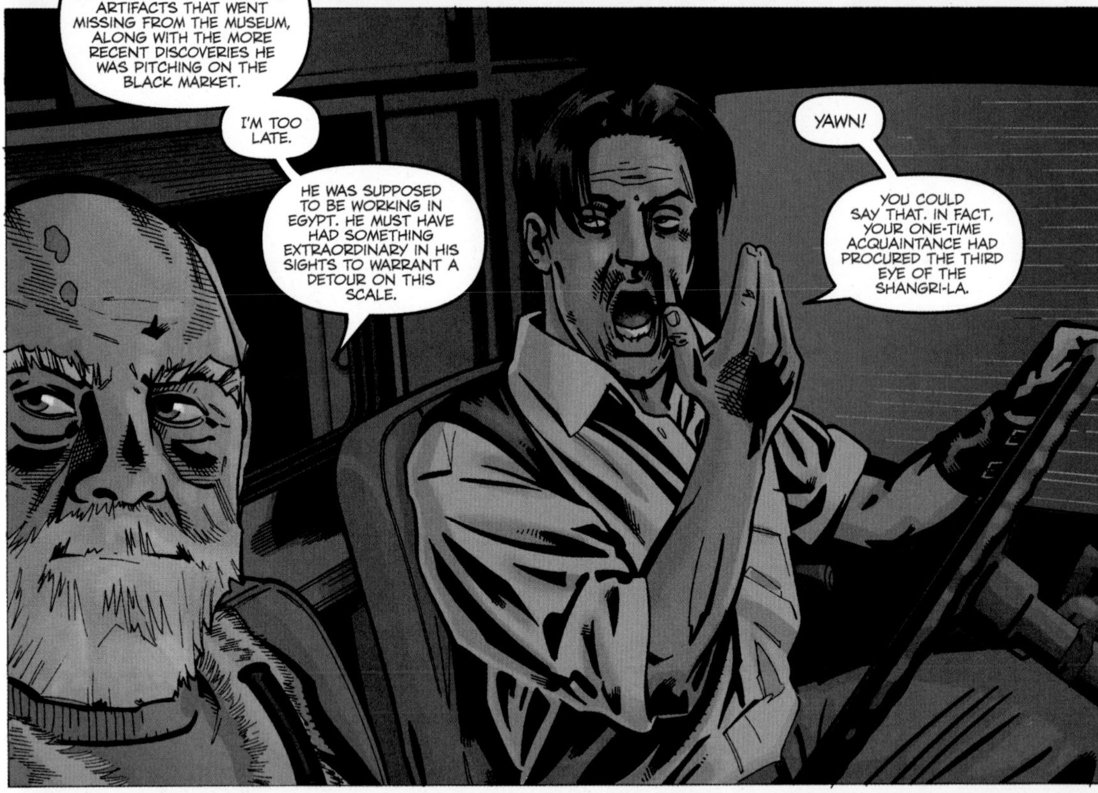
I'M TOO LATE.
HE WAS SUPPOSED TO BE WORKING IN EGYPT. HE MUST HAVE HAD SOMETHING EXTRAORDINARY IN HIS SIGHTS TO WARRANT A DETOUR ON THIS SCALE.
YAWN!
YOU COULD SAY THAT. IN FACT, YOUR ONE-TIME ACQUAINTANCE HAD PROCURED THE THIRD EYE OF THE SHANGRI-LA.

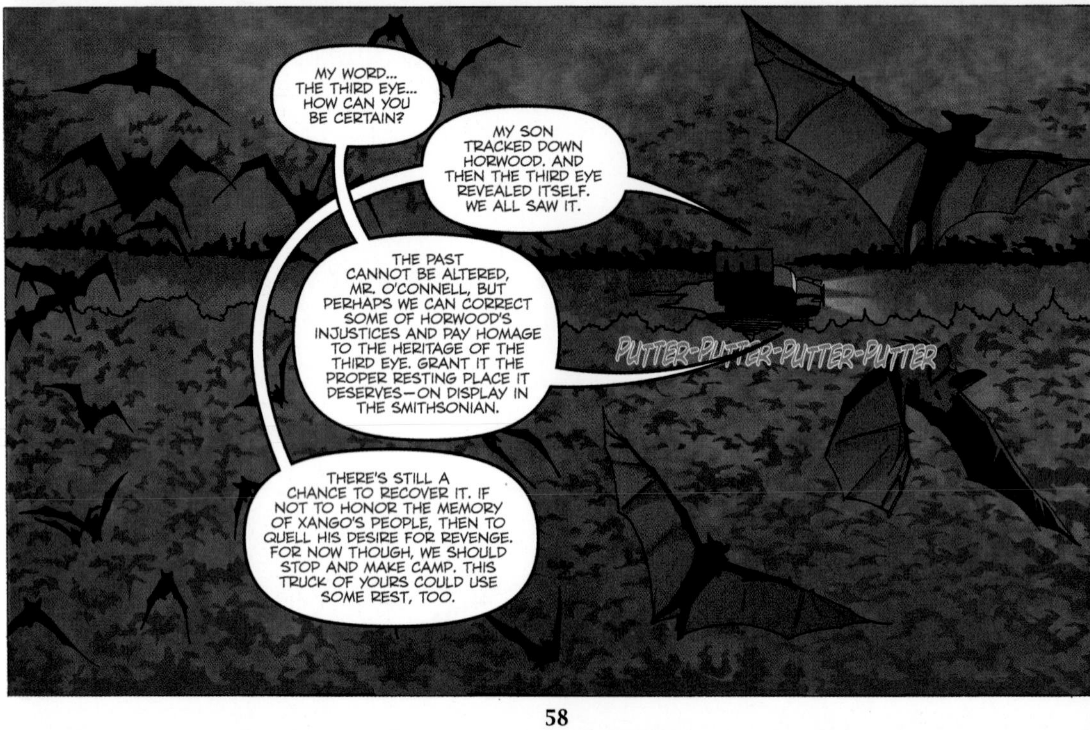
MY WORD... THE THIRD EYE... HOW CAN YOU BE CERTAIN?
MY SON TRACKED DOWN HORWOOD. AND THEN THE THIRD EYE REVEALED ITSELF. WE ALL SAW IT.
THE PAST CANNOT BE ALTERED, MR. O'CONNELL, BUT PERHAPS WE CAN CORRECT SOME OF HORWOOD'S INJUSTICES AND PAY HOMAGE TO THE HERITAGE OF THE THIRD EYE. GRANT IT THE PROPER RESTING PLACE IT DESERVES—ON DISPLAY IN THE SMITHSONIAN.
PUTTER-PUTTER-PUTTER-PUTTER
THERE'S STILL A CHANCE TO RECOVER IT. IF NOT TO HONOR THE MEMORY OF XANGO'S PEOPLE, THEN TO QUELL HIS DESIRE FOR REVENGE. FOR NOW THOUGH, WE SHOULD STOP AND MAKE CAMP. THIS TRUCK OF YOURS COULD USE SOME REST, TOO.

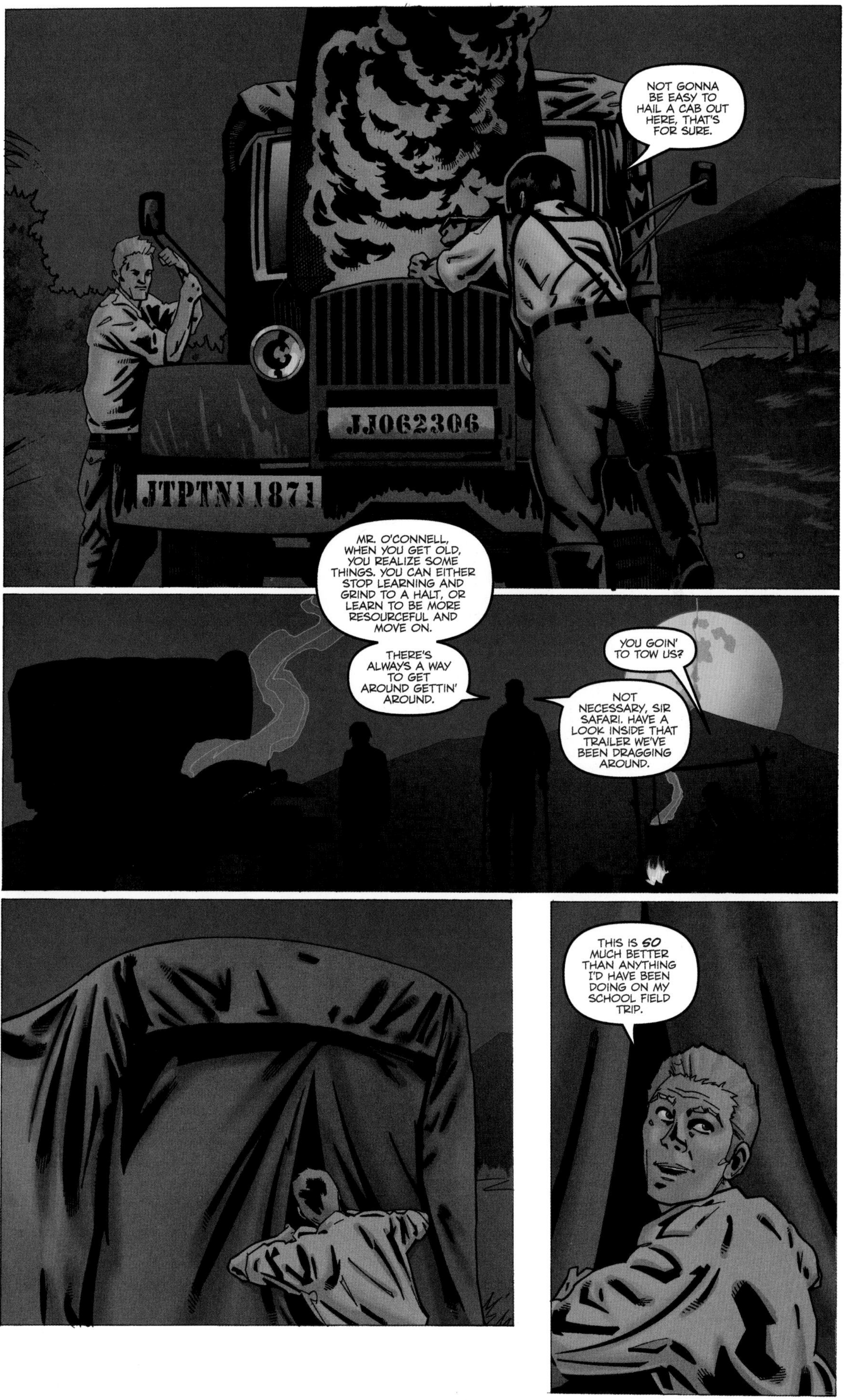
NOT GONNA BE EASY TO HAIL A CAB OUT HERE, THAT'S FOR SURE.
JJ062306
JTPTN1 1871
MR. O'CONNELL, WHEN YOU GET OLD, YOU REALIZE SOME THINGS. YOU CAN EITHER STOP LEARNING AND GRIND TO A HALT, OR LEARN TO BE MORE RESOURCEFUL AND MOVE ON.
THERE'S ALWAYS A WAY TO GET AROUND GETTIN' AROUND.
YOU GOIN' TO TOW US?
NOT NECESSARY, SIR SAFARI. HAVE A LOOK INSIDE THAT TRAILER WE'VE BEEN DRAGGING AROUND.
THIS IS SO MUCH BETTER THAN ANYTHING I'D HAVE BEEN DOING ON MY SCHOOL FIELD TRIP.

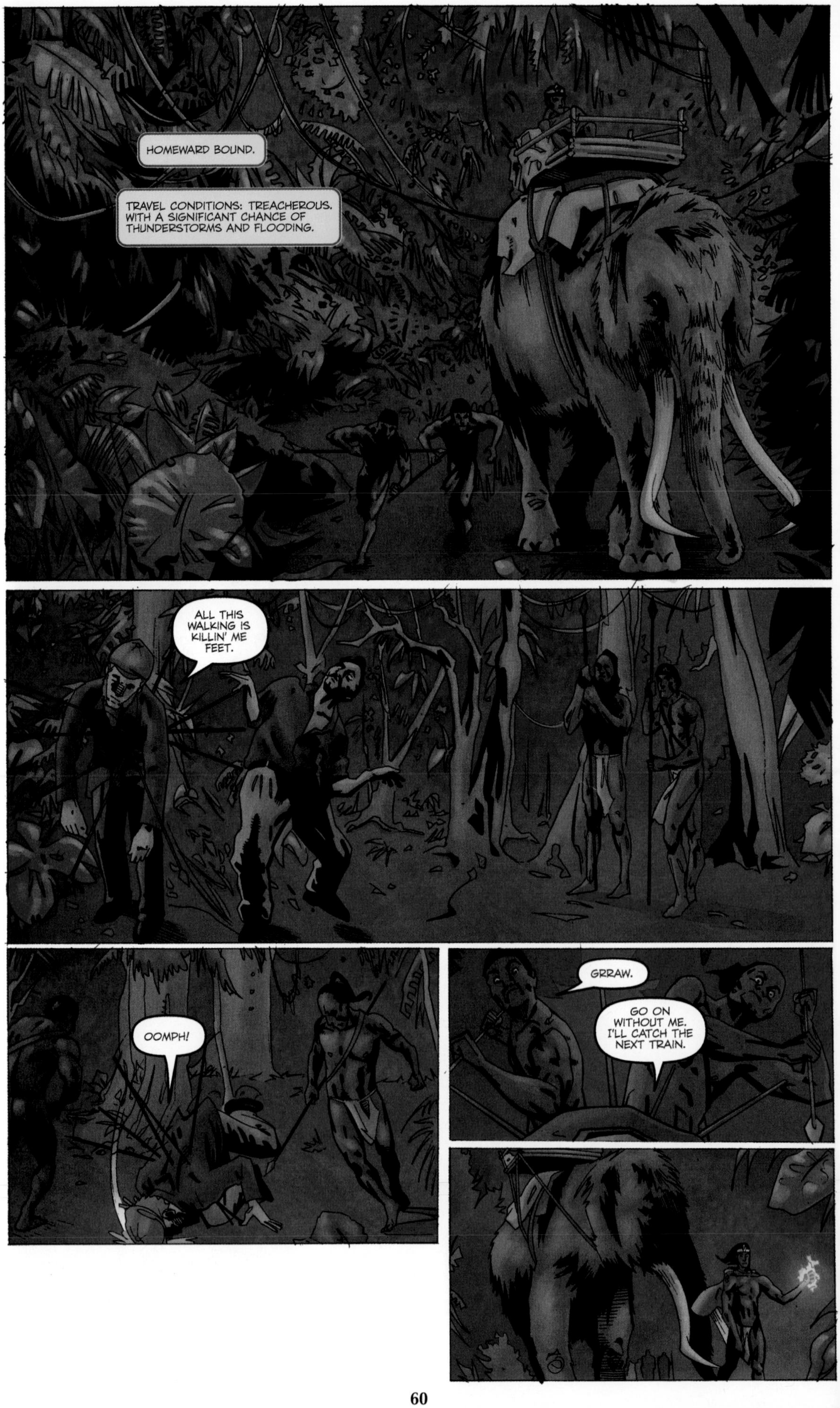
HOMEWARD BOUND.
TRAVEL CONDITIONS: TREACHEROUS. WITH A SIGNIFICANT CHANCE OF THUNDERSTORMS AND FLOODING.
ALL THIS WALKING IS KILLIN' ME FEET.
OOMPH!
GRRAW.
GO ON WITHOUT ME. I'LL CATCH THE NEXT TRAIN.

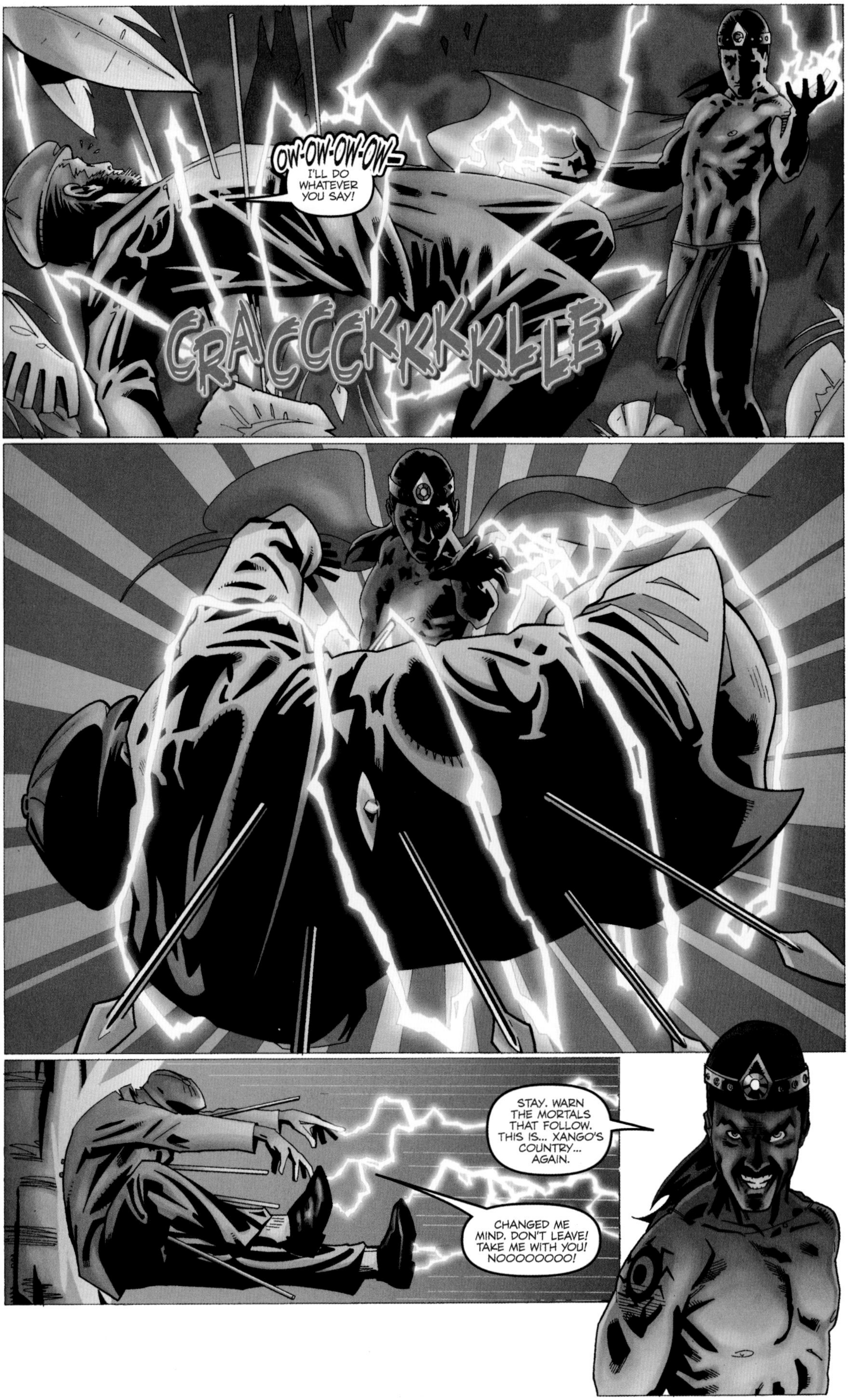
OW-OW-OW-OW-
I'LL DO WHATEVER YOU SAY!
CRACCCCKKKKLLE
STAY. WARN THE MORTALS THAT FOLLOW. THIS IS... XANGO'S COUNTRY... AGAIN.
CHANGED ME MIND. DON'T LEAVE! TAKE ME WITH YOU! NOOOOOOOO!

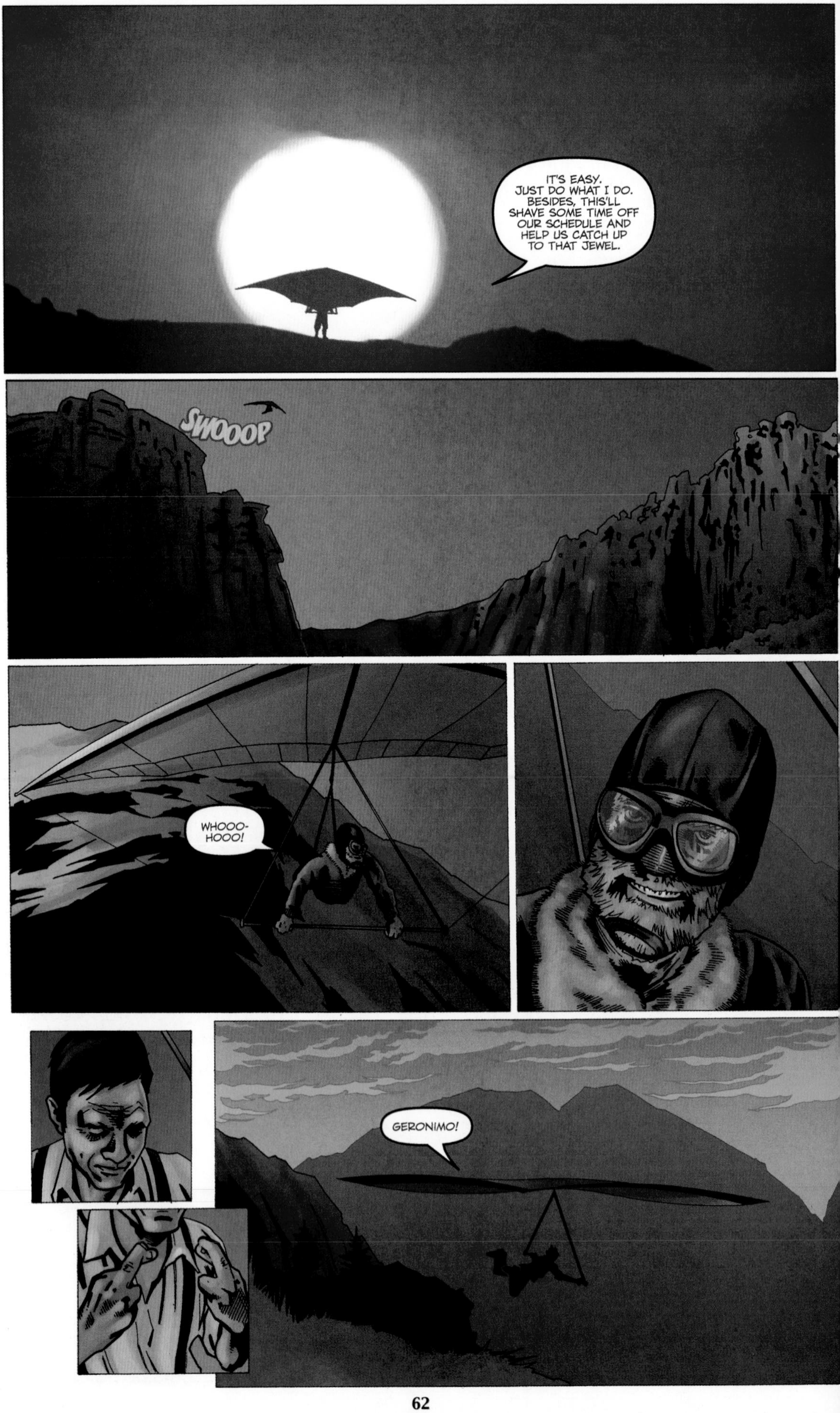
IT'S EASY. JUST DO WHAT I DO. BESIDES, THIS'LL SHAVE SOME TIME OFF OUR SCHEDULE AND HELP US CATCH UP TO THAT JEWEL.
SWOOOP
WHOOO-HOOO!
GERONIMO!

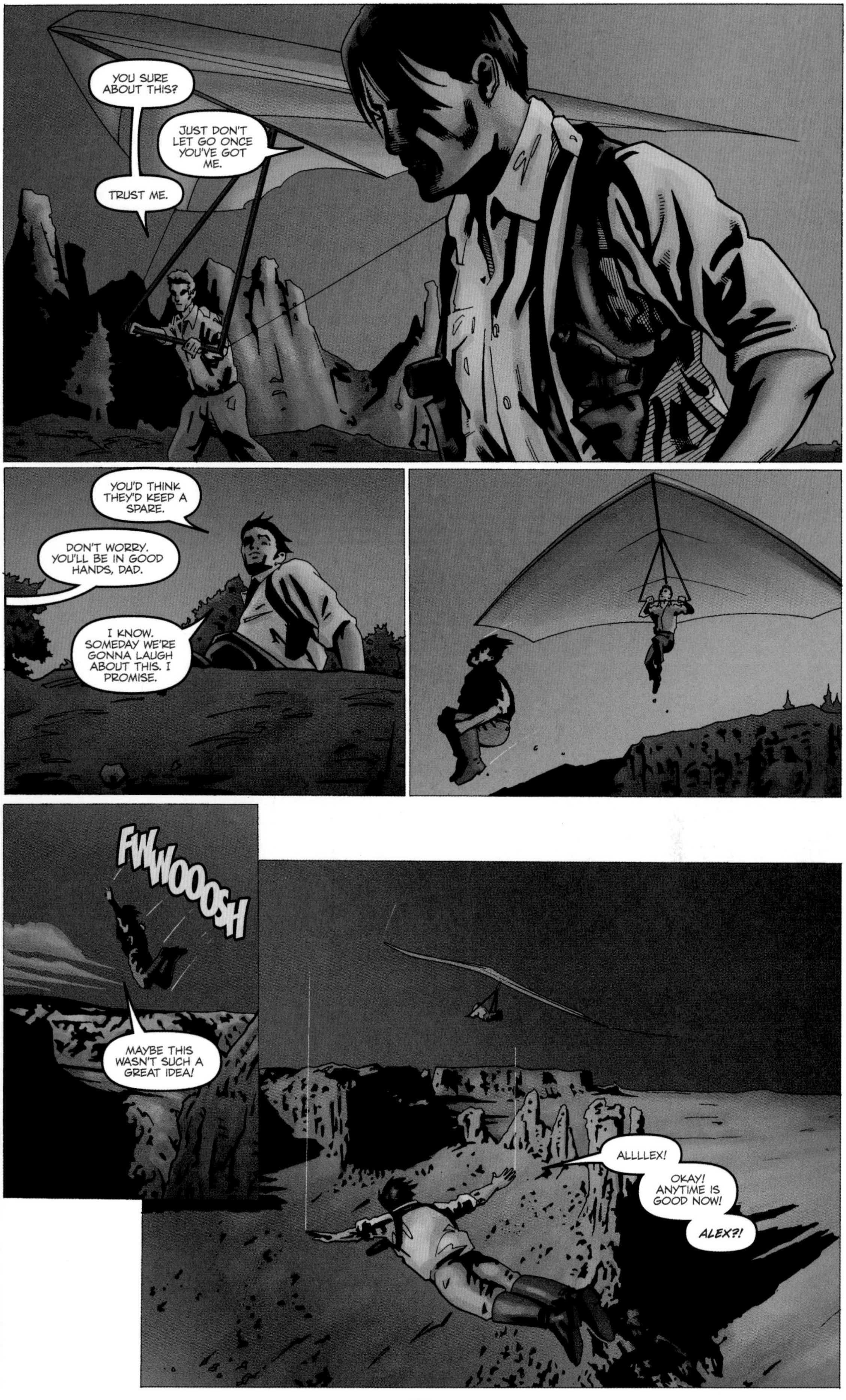
YOU SURE ABOUT THIS?
JUST DON'T LET GO ONCE YOU'VE GOT ME.
TRUST ME.
YOU'D THINK THEY'D KEEP A SPARE.
DON'T WORRY. YOU'LL BE IN GOOD HANDS, DAD.
I KNOW. SOMEDAY WE'RE GONNA LAUGH ABOUT THIS. I PROMISE.
FWWOOOSH
MAYBE THIS WASN'T SUCH A GREAT IDEA!
ALLLLEX!
OKAY! ANYTIME IS GOOD NOW!
ALEX?!

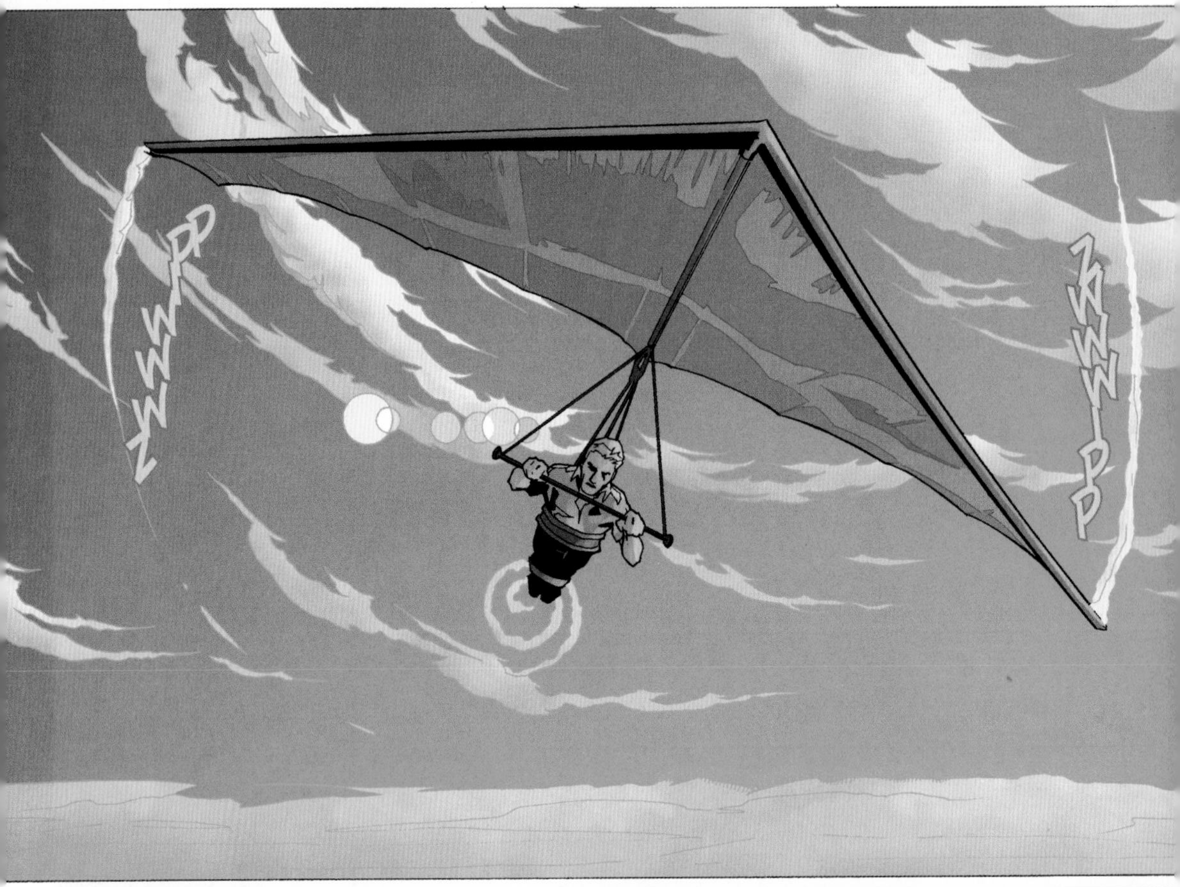
ZWWWWPP
ZWWWIPP

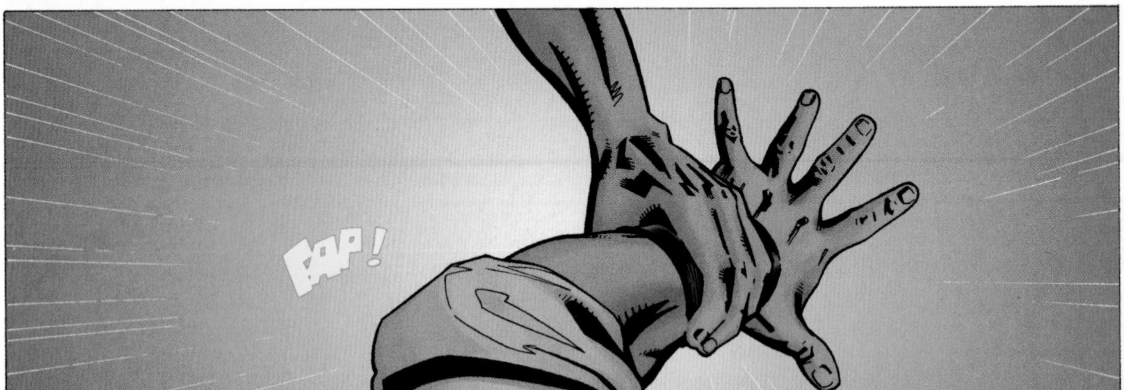
FAP!

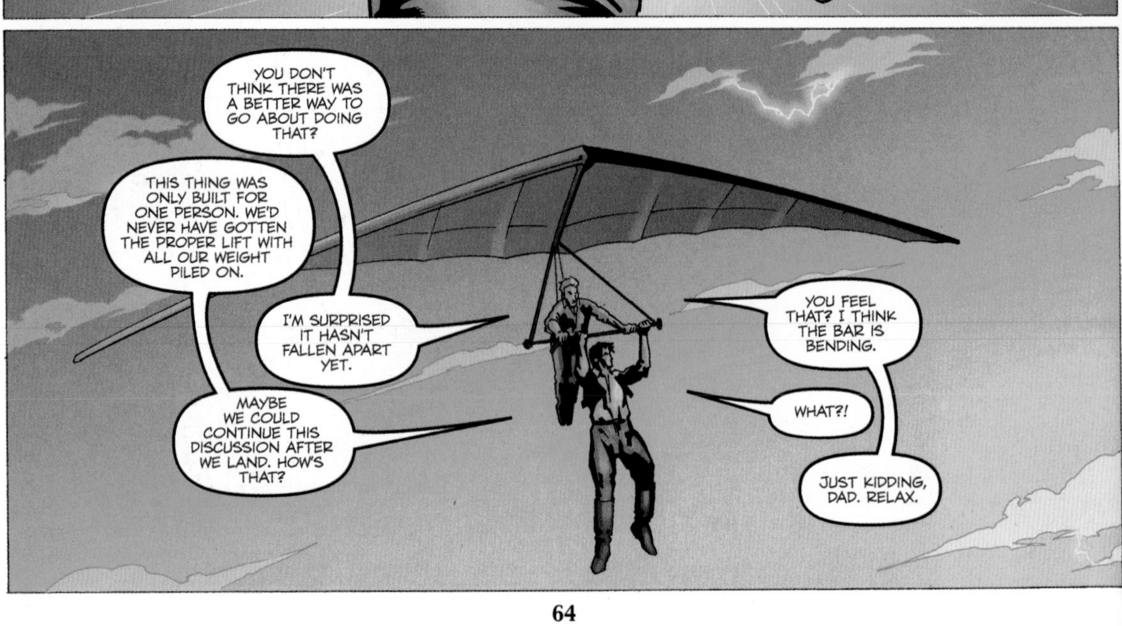
YOU DON'T THINK THERE WAS A BETTER WAY TO GO ABOUT DOING THAT?
THIS THING WAS ONLY BUILT FOR ONE PERSON. WE'D NEVER HAVE GOTTEN THE PROPER LIFT WITH ALL OUR WEIGHT PILED ON.
I'M SURPRISED IT HASN'T FALLEN APART YET.
MAYBE WE COULD CONTINUE THIS DISCUSSION AFTER WE LAND. HOW'S THAT?
YOU FEEL THAT? I THINK THE BAR IS BENDING.
WHAT?!
JUST KIDDING, DAD. RELAX.

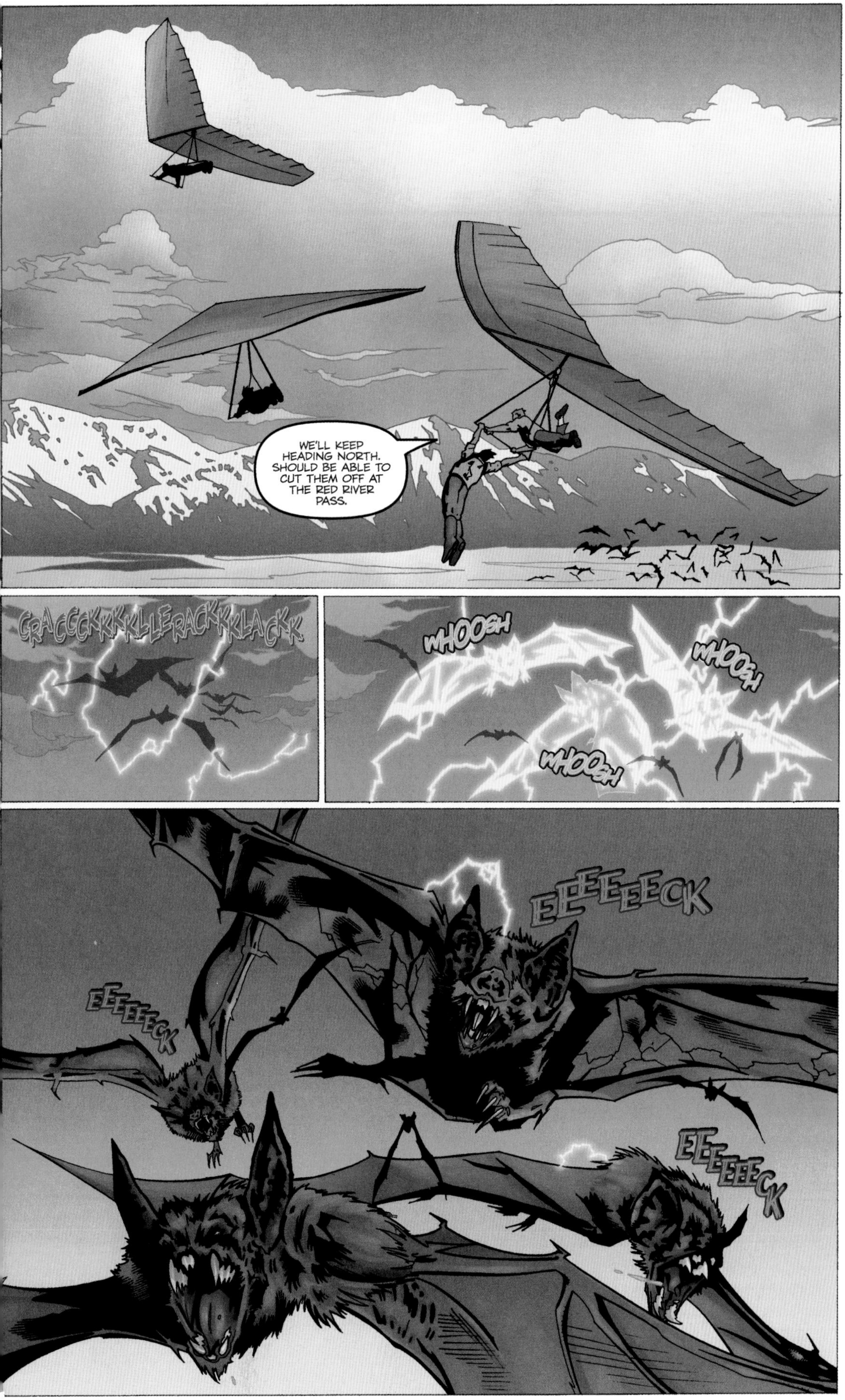
WE'LL KEEP HEADING NORTH. SHOULD BE ABLE TO CUT THEM OFF AT THE RED RIVER PASS.
CRACCCKKKKLLERACKKKLACKK
WHOOSH
WHOOSH
WHOOSH
EEEEEECK
EEEEEECK
EEEEEECK

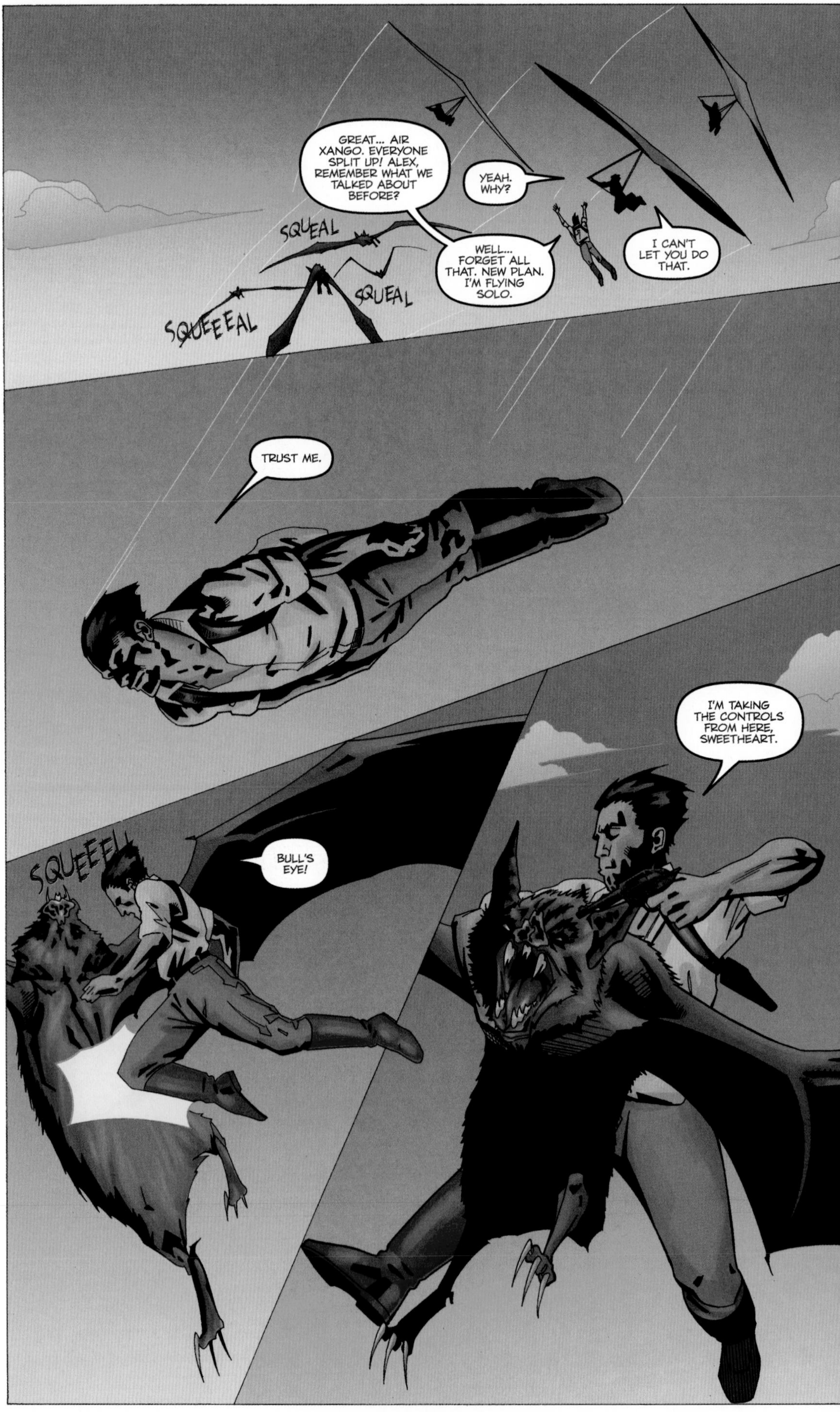
GREAT... AIR XANGO. EVERYONE SPLIT UP! ALEX, REMEMBER WHAT WE TALKED ABOUT BEFORE?
YEAH. WHY?
WELL... FORGET ALL THAT. NEW PLAN. I'M FLYING SOLO.
I CAN'T LET YOU DO THAT.
SQUEAL
SQUEAL
SQUEEEAL
TRUST ME.
SQUEEEL
BULL'S EYE!
I'M TAKING THE CONTROLS FROM HERE, SWEETHEART.

BLAM
BLAM
BLAM

SQUEEEAL
EEEE

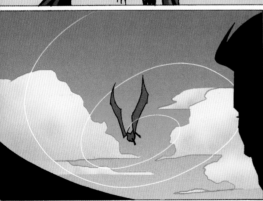

EASY DOES IT. GUESS THEY DON'T MAKE 'EM LIKE THEY USED TO, DO THEY, GIRL?

CLICK
CLICK
CLICK

GREAT. LIKE I DIDN'T SEE THAT COMIN'. BET THEY DON'T HAVE A PARACHUTE ONBOARD, EITHER.

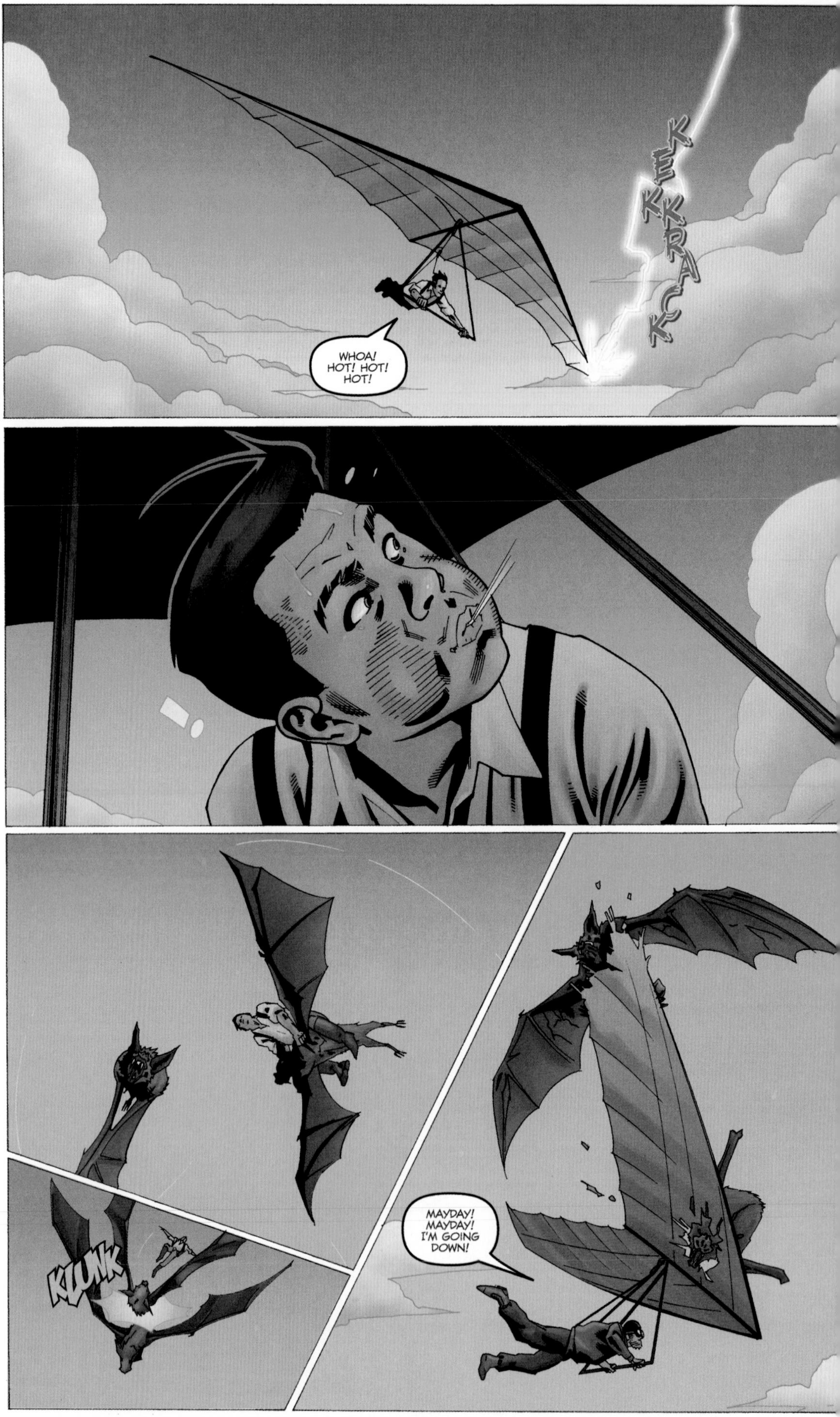
KEKKRACK
WHOA! HOT! HOT! HOT!
!
KLUNK
MAYDAY! MAYDAY! I'M GOING DOWN!

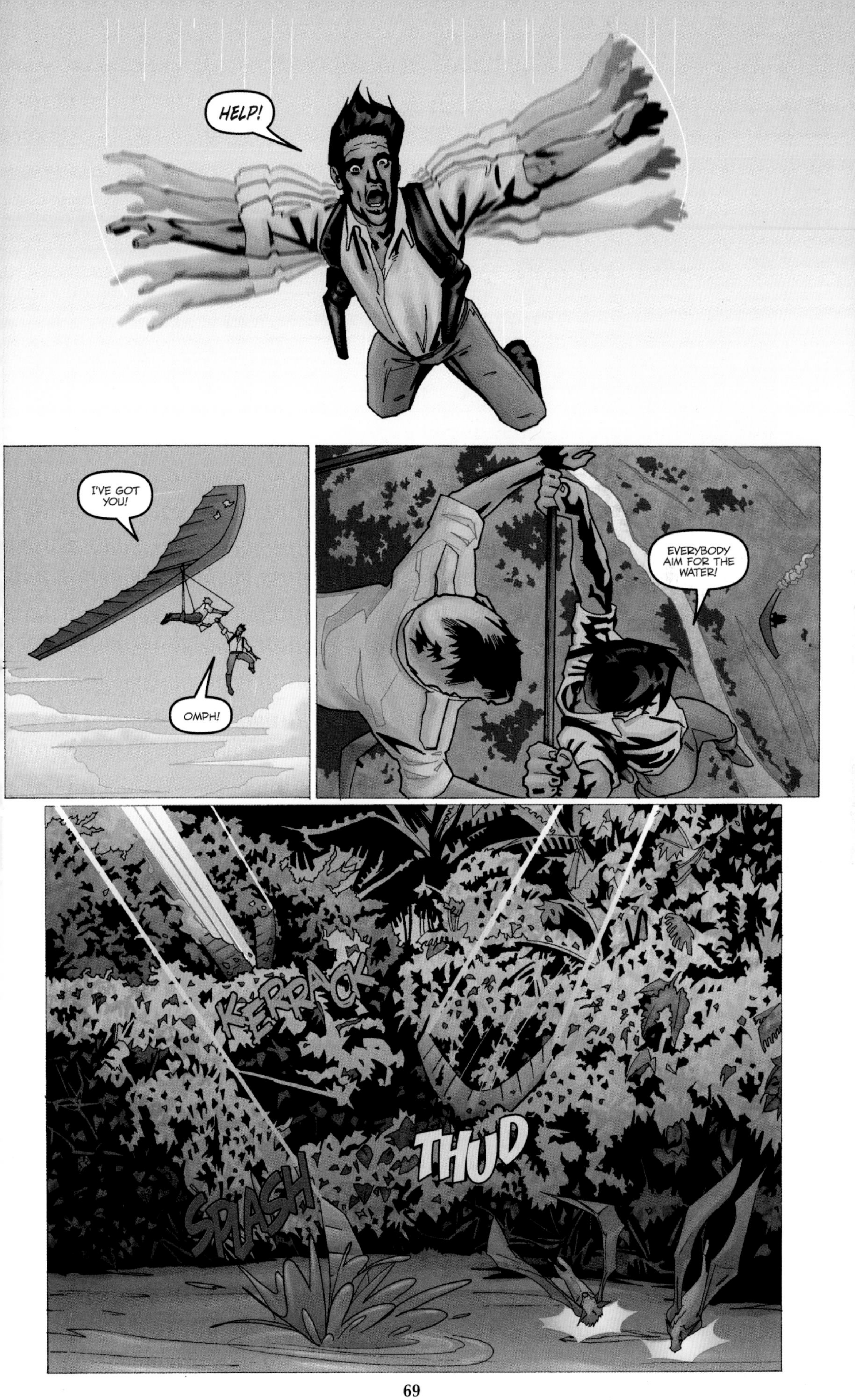
HELP!
I'VE GOT YOU!
OMPH!
EVERYBODY AIM FOR THE WATER!
KERRACK
THUD
SPLASH

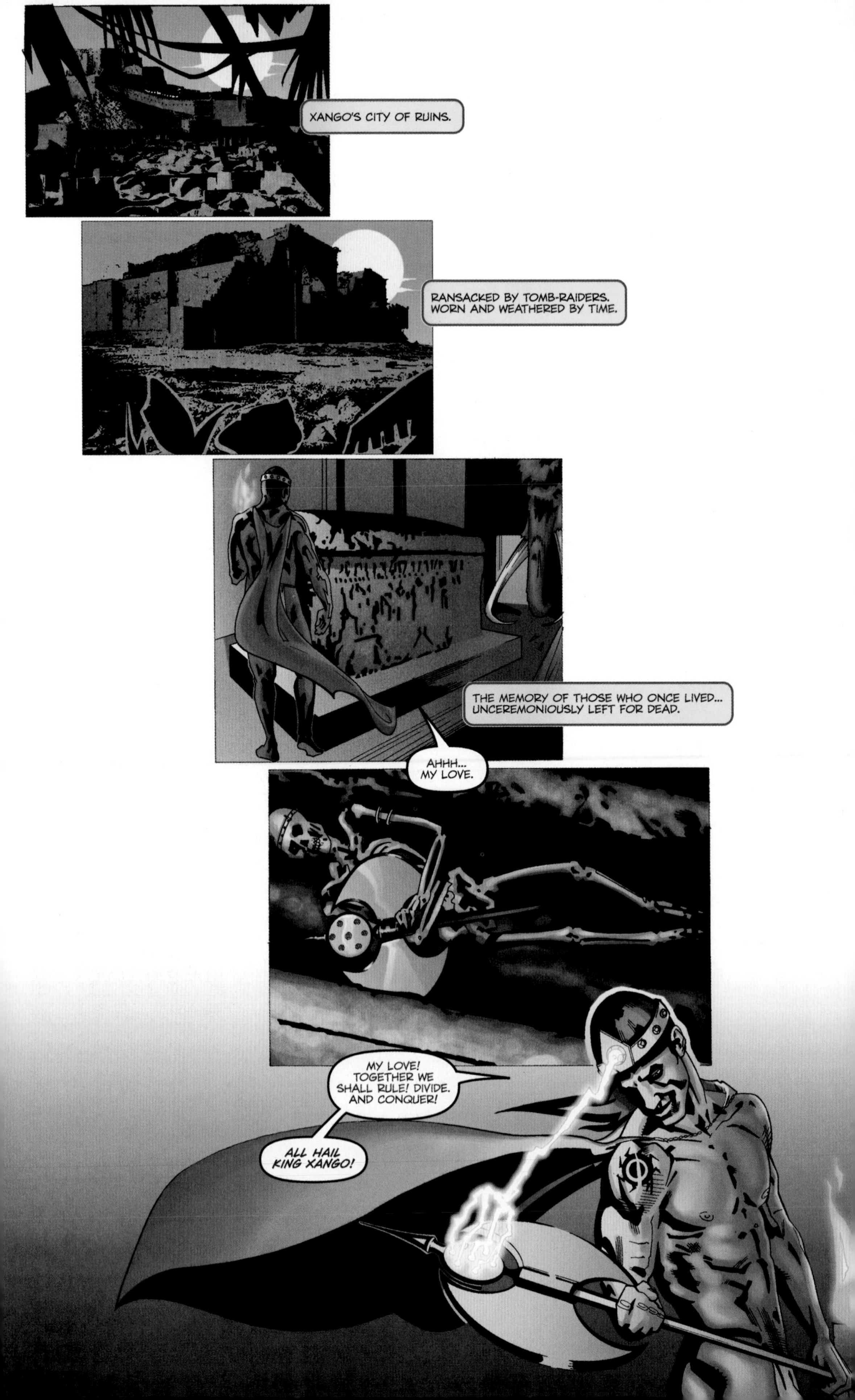
XANGO'S CITY OF RUINS.
RANSACKED BY TOMB-RAIDERS. WORN AND WEATHERED BY TIME.
THE MEMORY OF THOSE WHO ONCE LIVED... UNCEREMONIOUSLY LEFT FOR DEAD.
AHHH... MY LOVE.
MY LOVE! TOGETHER WE SHALL RULE! DIVIDE. AND CONQUER!
ALL HAIL KING XANGO!

CHAPTER FOUR

THE ALTAR OF THE GOD OF THUNDER.

OUR TRIBE IS STRONG. OUR SPECIES... STILL ENDANGERED, BUT NOT FOR LONG. WE ARE NO LONGER CAGED BY FATE.

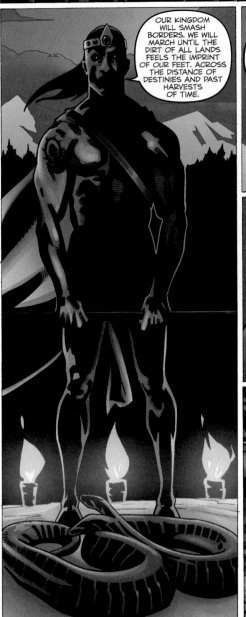

OUR KINGDOM WILL SMASH BORDERS. WE WILL MARCH UNTIL THE DIRT OF ALL LANDS FEELS THE IMPRINT OF OUR FEET. ACROSS THE DISTANCE OF DESTINIES AND PAST HARVESTS OF TIME.

WE SHALL FOLLOW THE PATH OF THE SUN AND HALT ONLY ONCE THE LAND HAS BECOME FAMILIAR AGAIN AND THE TIDE SINGS THE NAME "XANGO."

MY CROWN... MY AX... EXTENSIONS TO THE IMMORTALS. IT REACHES OUT TO THE GODS AND I SHALL REIN THEM IN.

HAIL KING XANGO!

HAIL KING XANGO!

71

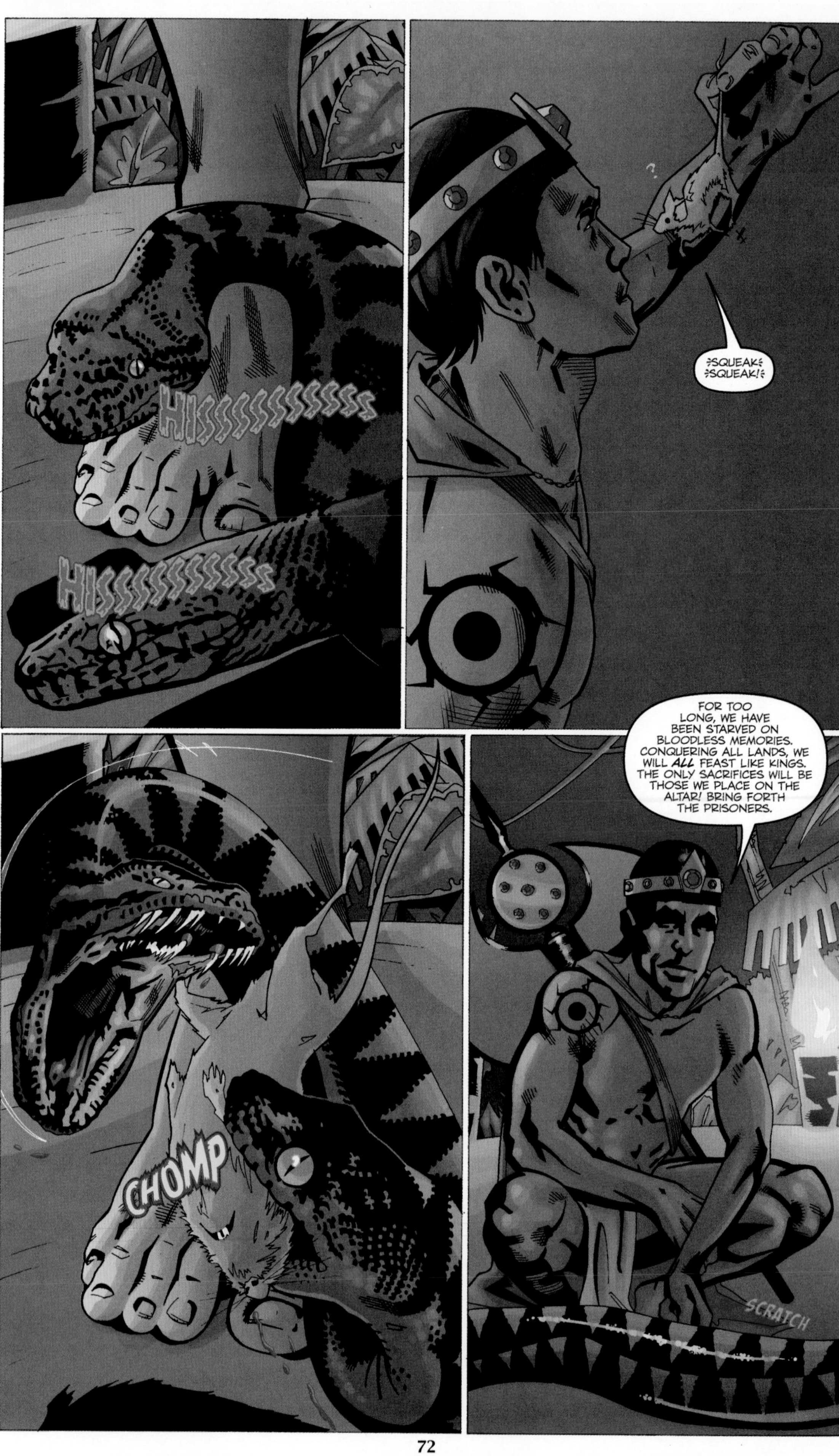
HISSSSSSSSSSS
HISSSSSSSSSSS
SQUEAK SQUEAK!
FOR TOO LONG, WE HAVE BEEN STARVED ON BLOODLESS MEMORIES. CONQUERING ALL LANDS, WE WILL ALL FEAST LIKE KINGS. THE ONLY SACRIFICES WILL BE THOSE WE PLACE ON THE ALTAR! BRING FORTH THE PRISONERS.
CHOMP
SCRATCH

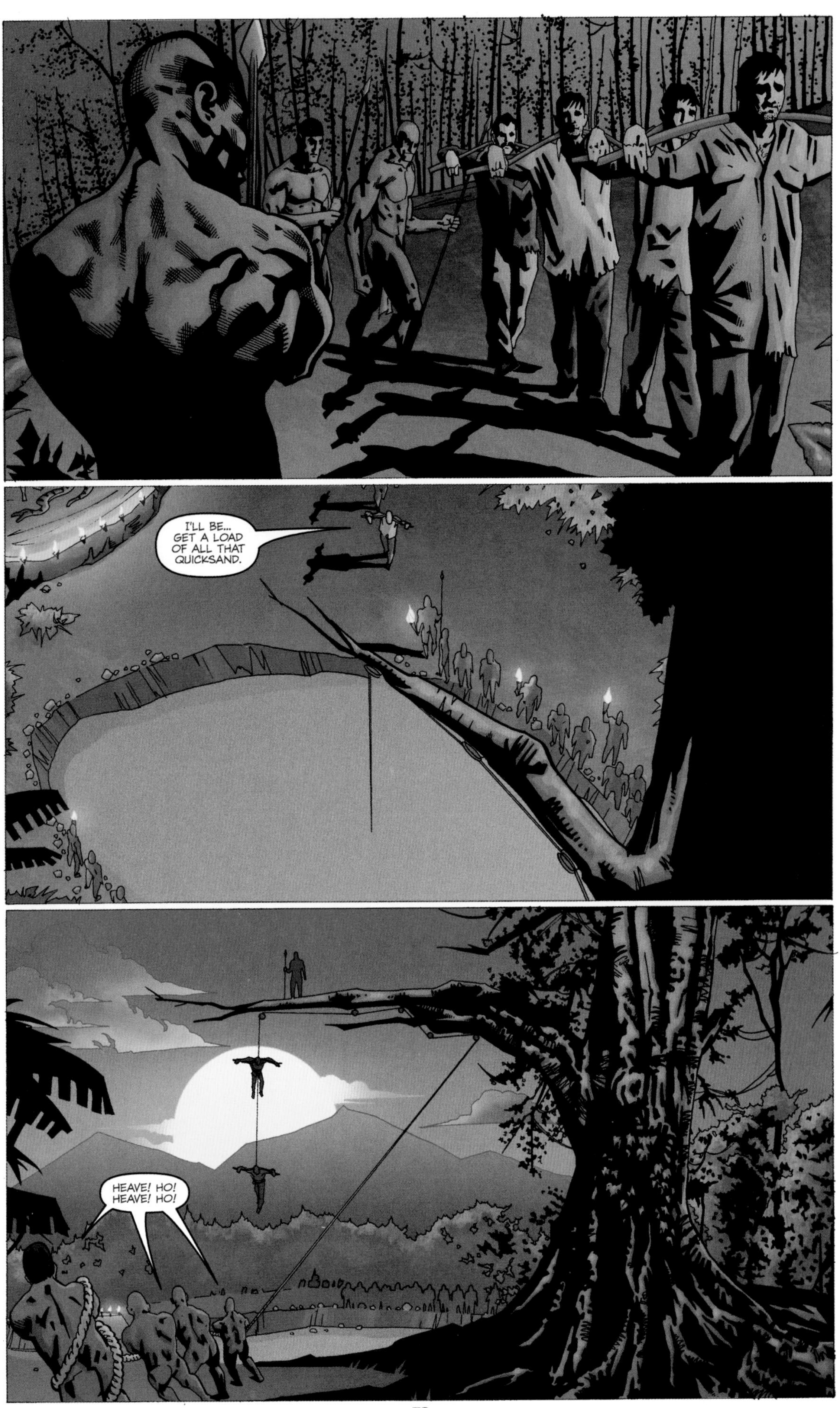
I'LL BE... GET A LOAD OF ALL THAT QUICKSAND.
HEAVE! HO! HEAVE! HO!

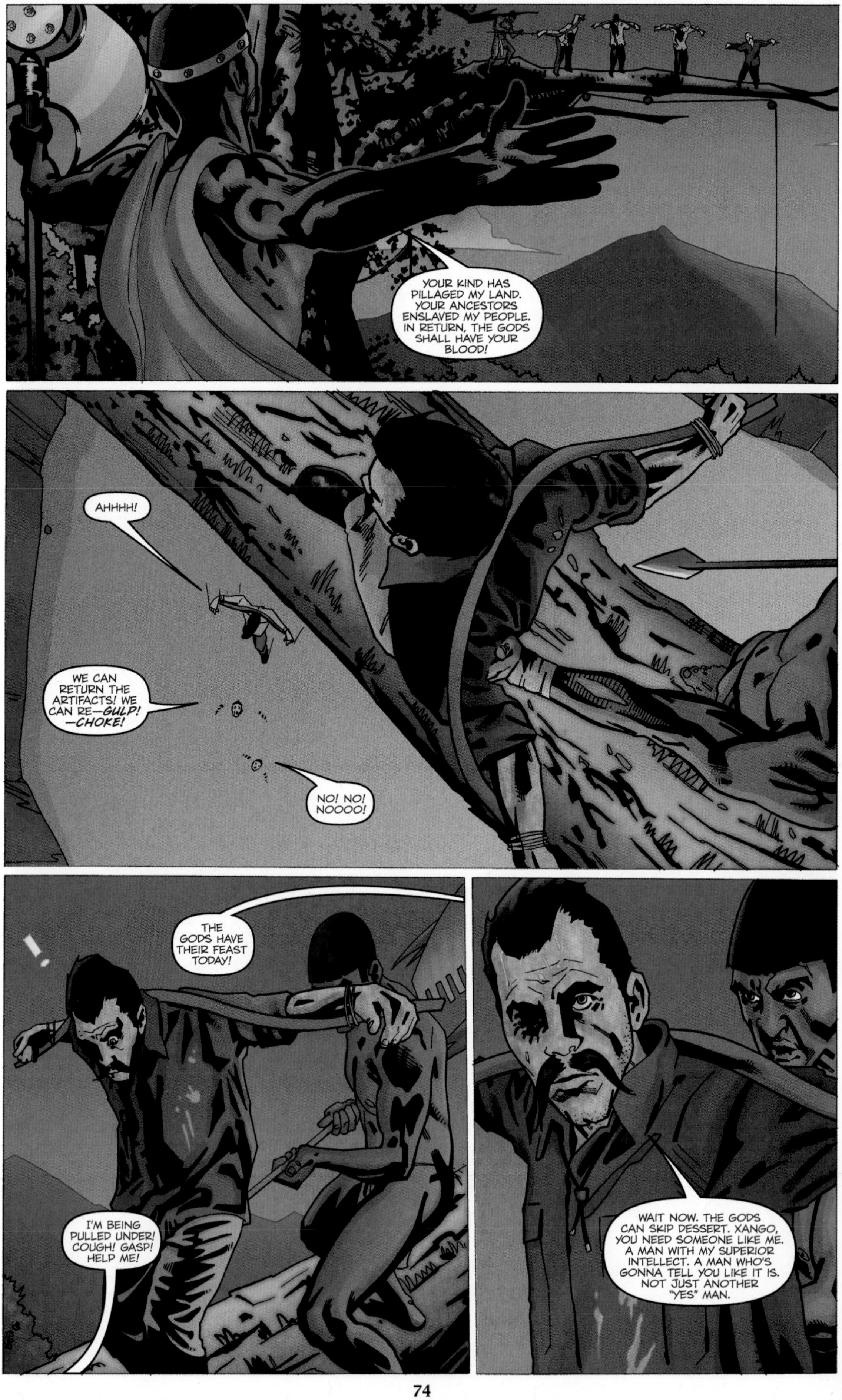
YOUR KIND HAS PILLAGED MY LAND. YOUR ANCESTORS ENSLAVED MY PEOPLE. IN RETURN, THE GODS SHALL HAVE YOUR BLOOD!
AHHHH!
WE CAN RETURN THE ARTIFACTS! WE CAN RE—*GULP!* —*CHOKE!*
NO! NO! NOOOO!
THE GODS HAVE THEIR FEAST TODAY!
I'M BEING PULLED UNDER! COUGH! GASP! HELP ME!
WAIT NOW. THE GODS CAN SKIP DESSERT. XANGO, YOU NEED SOMEONE LIKE ME. A MAN WITH MY SUPERIOR INTELLECT. A MAN WHO'S GONNA TELL YOU LIKE IT IS. NOT JUST ANOTHER "YES" MAN.

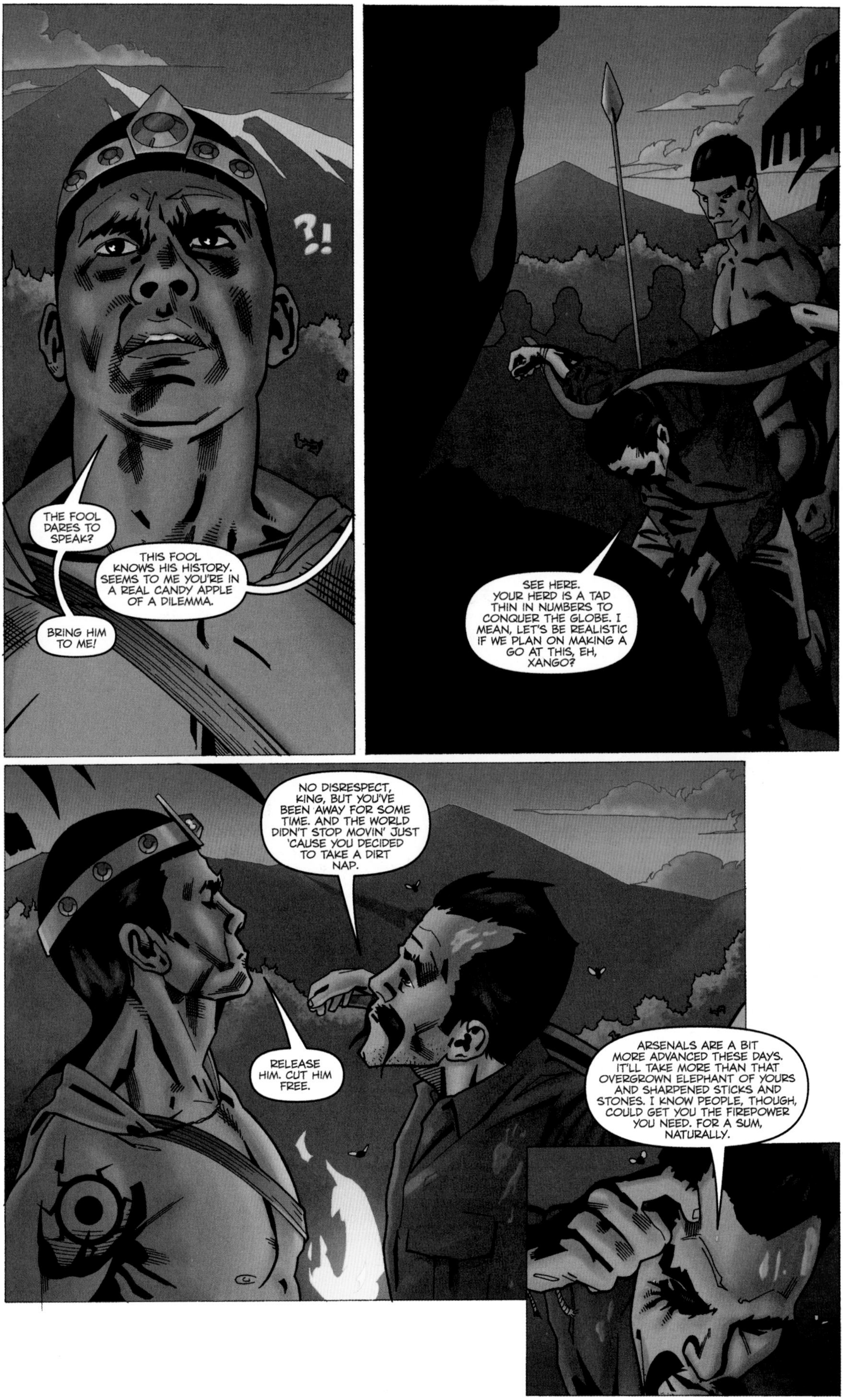
?!
THE FOOL DARES TO SPEAK?
THIS FOOL KNOWS HIS HISTORY. SEEMS TO ME YOU'RE IN A REAL CANDY APPLE OF A DILEMMA.
BRING HIM TO ME!
SEE HERE. YOUR HERD IS A TAD THIN IN NUMBERS TO CONQUER THE GLOBE. I MEAN, LET'S BE REALISTIC IF WE PLAN ON MAKING A GO AT THIS, EH, XANGO?
NO DISRESPECT, KING, BUT YOU'VE BEEN AWAY FOR SOME TIME. AND THE WORLD DIDN'T STOP MOVIN' JUST 'CAUSE YOU DECIDED TO TAKE A DIRT NAP.
RELEASE HIM. CUT HIM FREE.
ARSENALS ARE A BIT MORE ADVANCED THESE DAYS. IT'LL TAKE MORE THAN THAT OVERGROWN ELEPHANT OF YOURS AND SHARPENED STICKS AND STONES. I KNOW PEOPLE, THOUGH, COULD GET YOU THE FIREPOWER YOU NEED. FOR A SUM, NATURALLY.

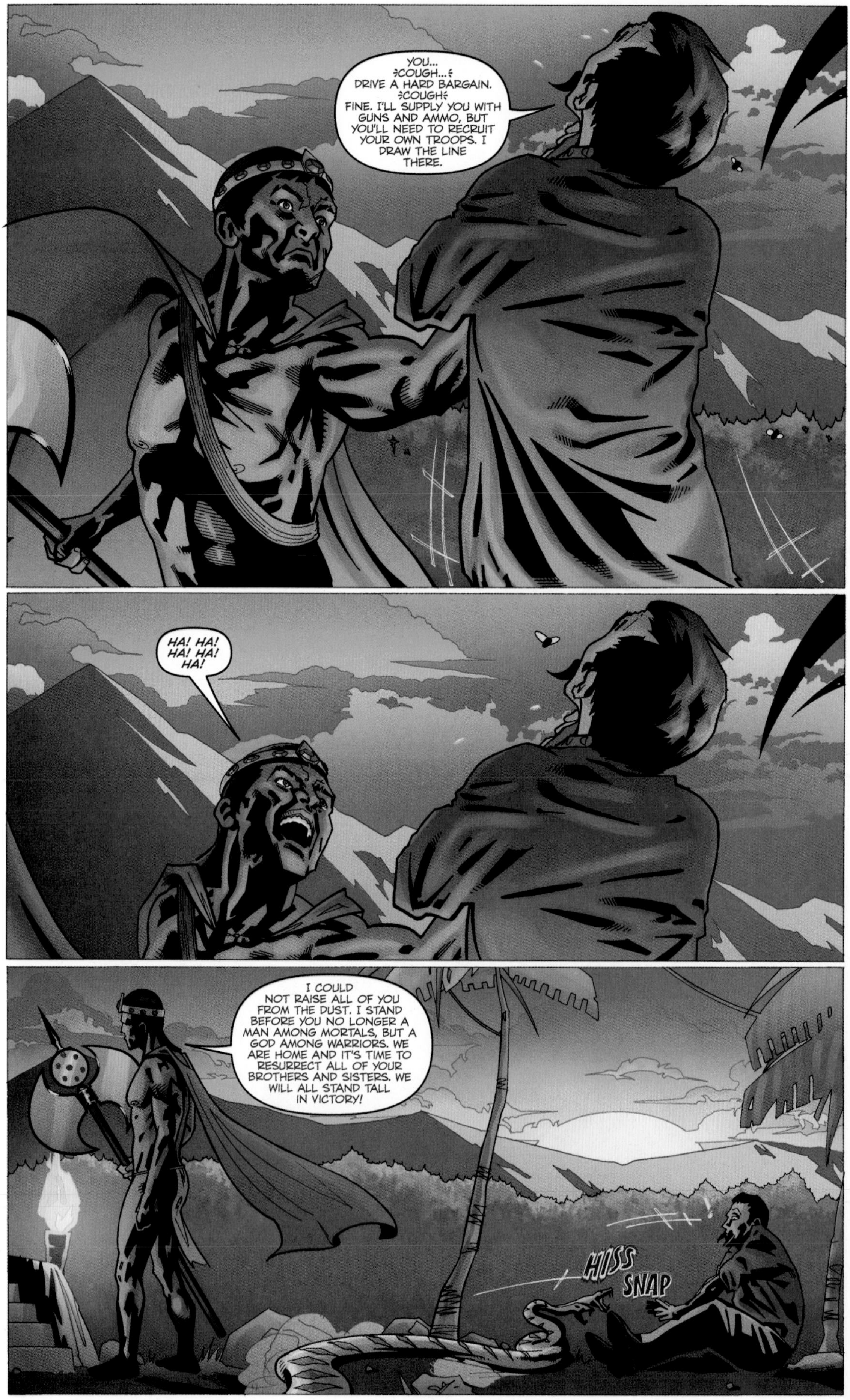
YOU... COUGH... DRIVE A HARD BARGAIN. COUGH FINE. I'LL SUPPLY YOU WITH GUNS AND AMMO, BUT YOU'LL NEED TO RECRUIT YOUR OWN TROOPS. I DRAW THE LINE THERE.
HA! HA! HA! HA! HA!
I COULD NOT RAISE ALL OF YOU FROM THE DUST. I STAND BEFORE YOU NO LONGER A MAN AMONG MORTALS, BUT A GOD AMONG WARRIORS. WE ARE HOME AND IT'S TIME TO RESURRECT ALL OF YOUR BROTHERS AND SISTERS. WE WILL ALL STAND TALL IN VICTORY!
HISS
SNAP

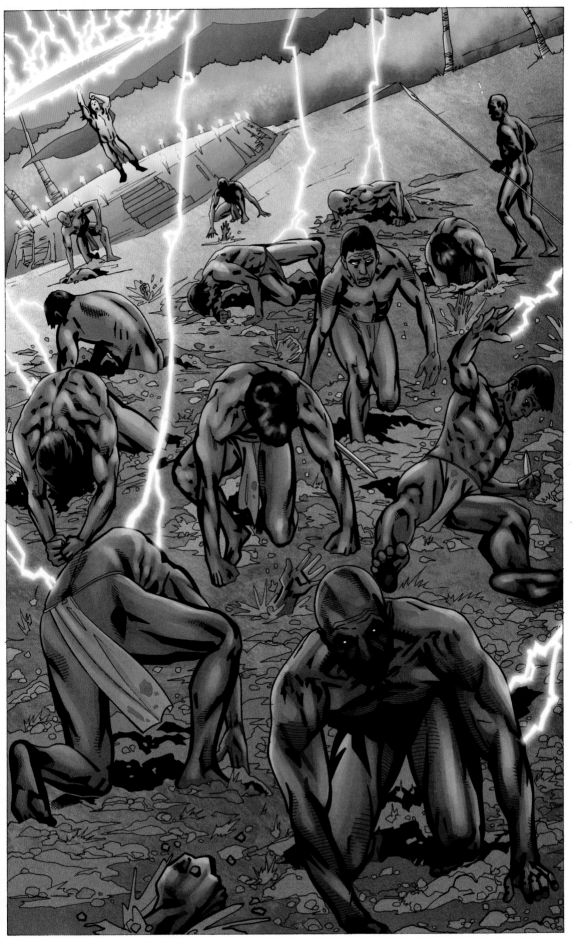

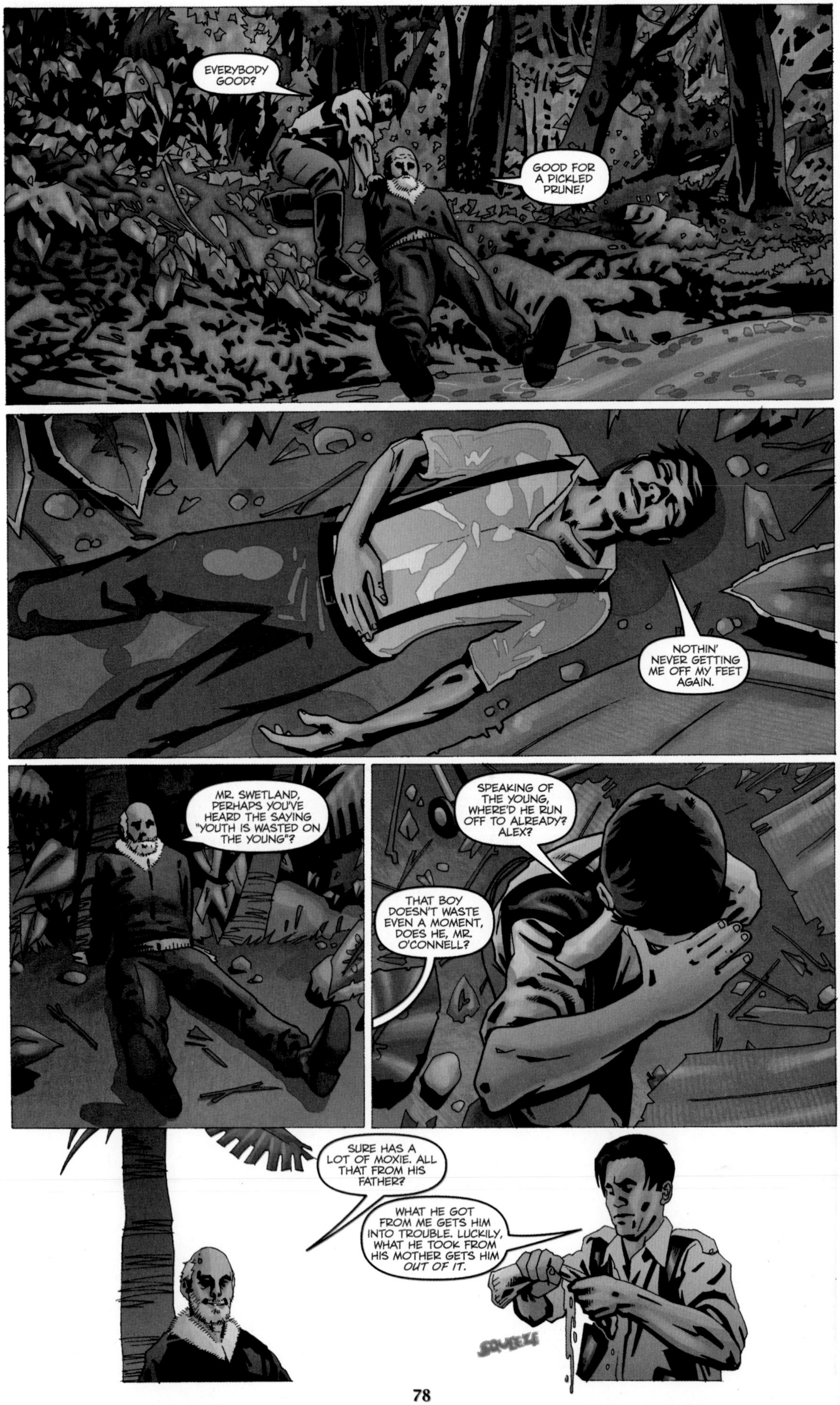
EVERYBODY GOOD?
GOOD FOR A PICKLED PRUNE!
NOTHIN' NEVER GETTING ME OFF MY FEET AGAIN.
MR. SWETLAND, PERHAPS YOU'VE HEARD THE SAYING "YOUTH IS WASTED ON THE YOUNG"?
SPEAKING OF THE YOUNG, WHERE'D HE RUN OFF TO ALREADY? ALEX?
THAT BOY DOESN'T WASTE EVEN A MOMENT, DOES HE, MR. O'CONNELL?
SURE HAS A LOT OF MOXIE. ALL THAT FROM HIS FATHER?
WHAT HE GOT FROM ME GETS HIM INTO TROUBLE. LUCKILY, WHAT HE TOOK FROM HIS MOTHER GETS HIM *OUT OF IT.*
SQUEEZE

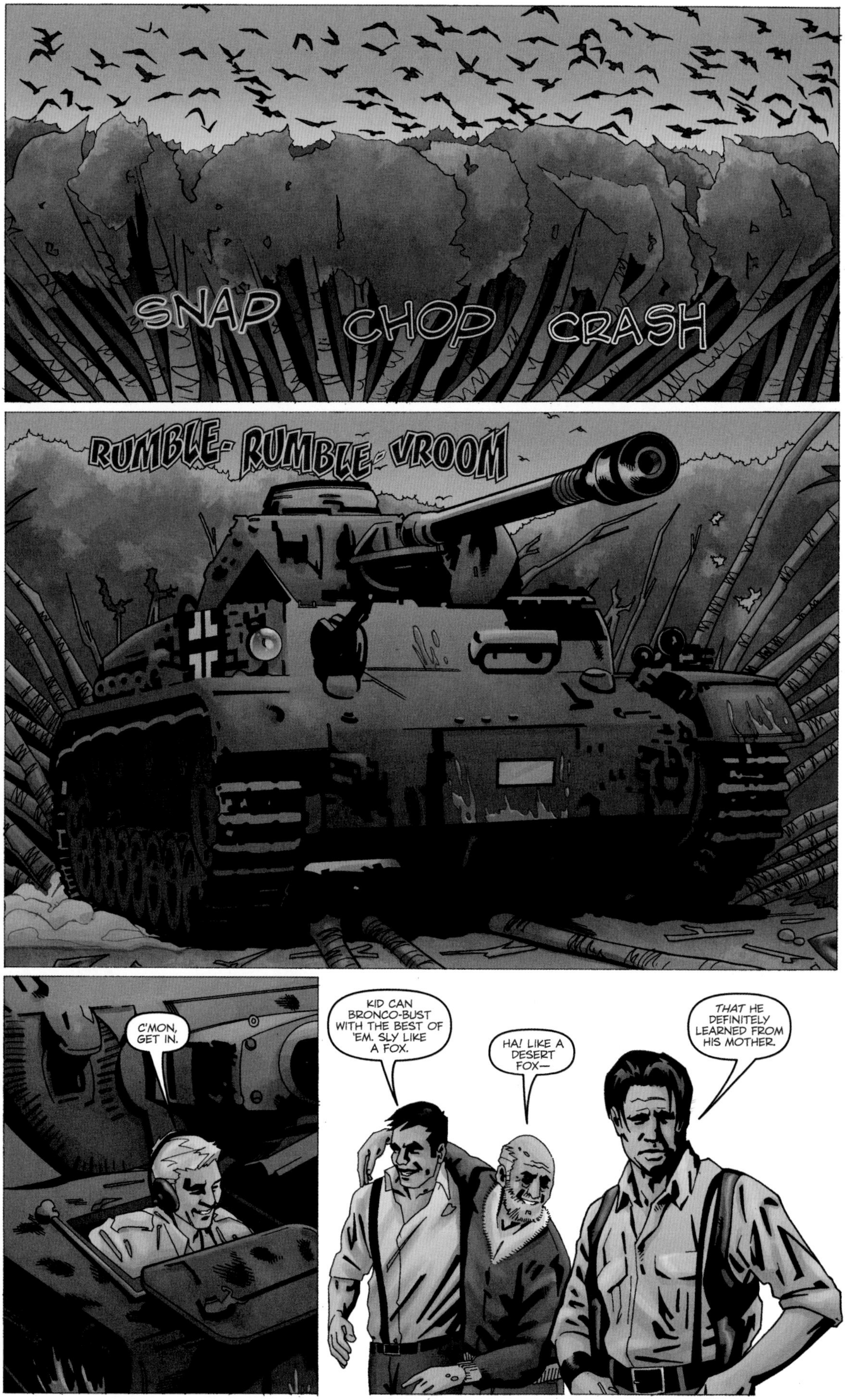
SNAP
CHOP
CRASH
RUMBLE-RUMBLE-VROOM
C'MON, GET IN.
KID CAN BRONCO-BUST WITH THE BEST OF 'EM. SLY LIKE A FOX.
HA! LIKE A DESERT FOX—
THAT HE DEFINITELY LEARNED FROM HIS MOTHER.

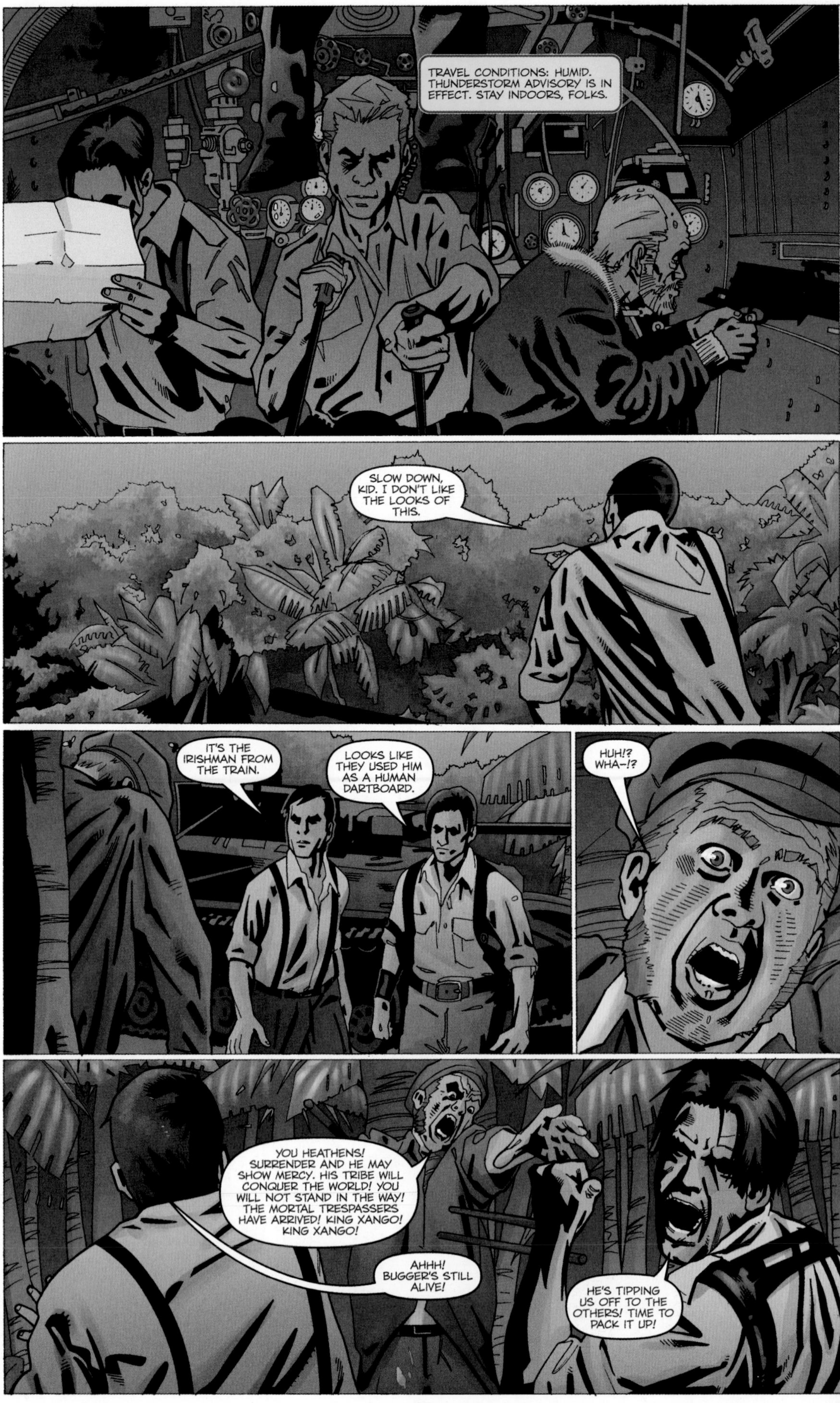
TRAVEL CONDITIONS: HUMID. THUNDERSTORM ADVISORY IS IN EFFECT. STAY INDOORS, FOLKS.
SLOW DOWN, KID. I DON'T LIKE THE LOOKS OF THIS.
IT'S THE IRISHMAN FROM THE TRAIN.
LOOKS LIKE THEY USED HIM AS A HUMAN DARTBOARD.
HUH!? WHA-!?
YOU HEATHENS! SURRENDER AND HE MAY SHOW MERCY. HIS TRIBE WILL CONQUER THE WORLD! YOU WILL NOT STAND IN THE WAY! THE MORTAL TRESPASSERS HAVE ARRIVED! KING XANGO! KING XANGO!
AHHH! BUGGER'S STILL ALIVE!
HE'S TIPPING US OFF TO THE OTHERS! TIME TO PACK IT UP!

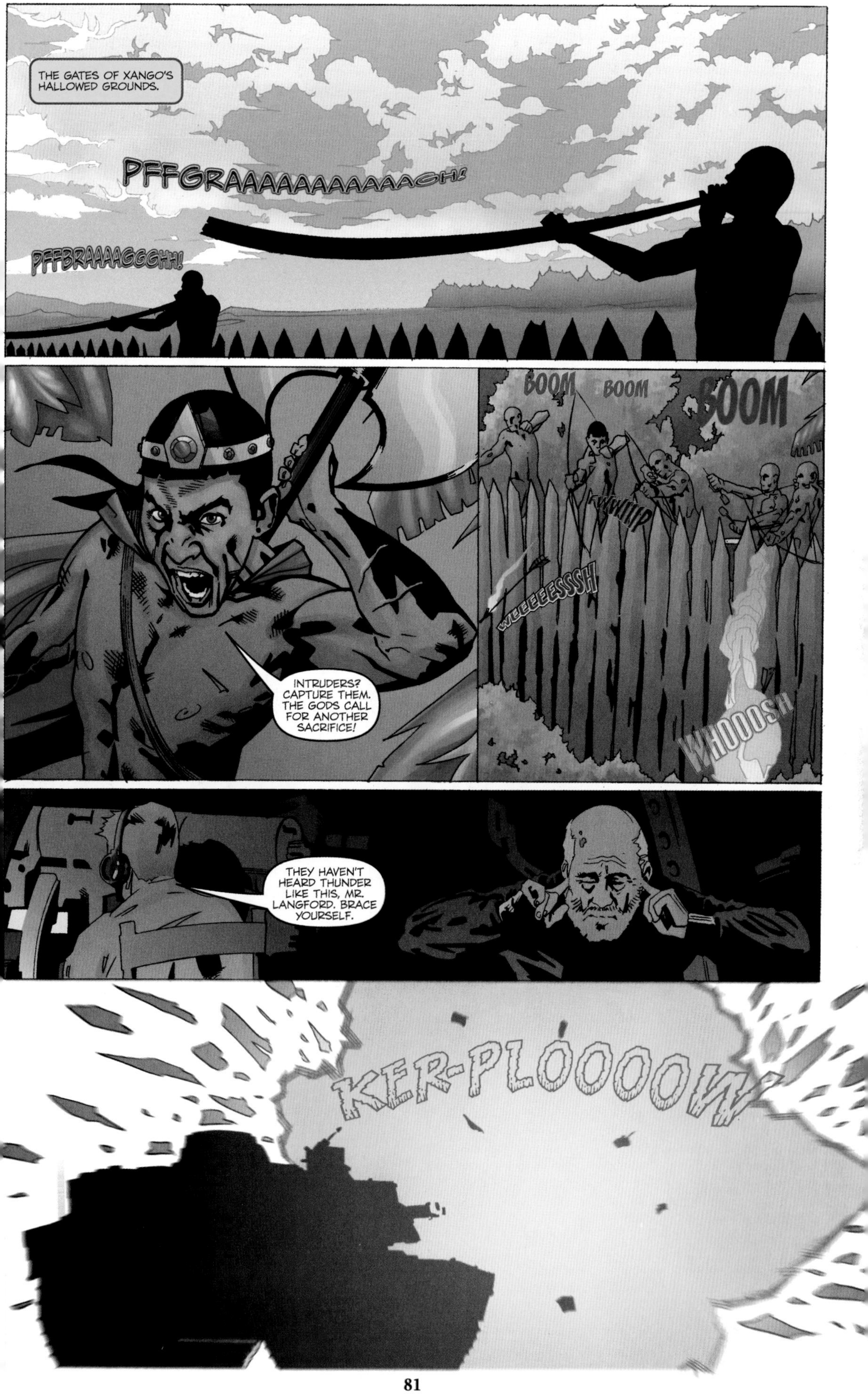
THE GATES OF XANGO'S HALLOWED GROUNDS.
PFFGRAAAAAAAAAAAAGH!
PFFBRAAAAGGGHH!
INTRUDERS? CAPTURE THEM. THE GODS CALL FOR ANOTHER SACRIFICE!
BOOM
BOOM
BOOM
WEEEEEESSSH
WHOOOSH
THEY HAVEN'T HEARD THUNDER LIKE THIS, MR. LANGFORD. BRACE YOURSELF.
KER-PLOOOOW

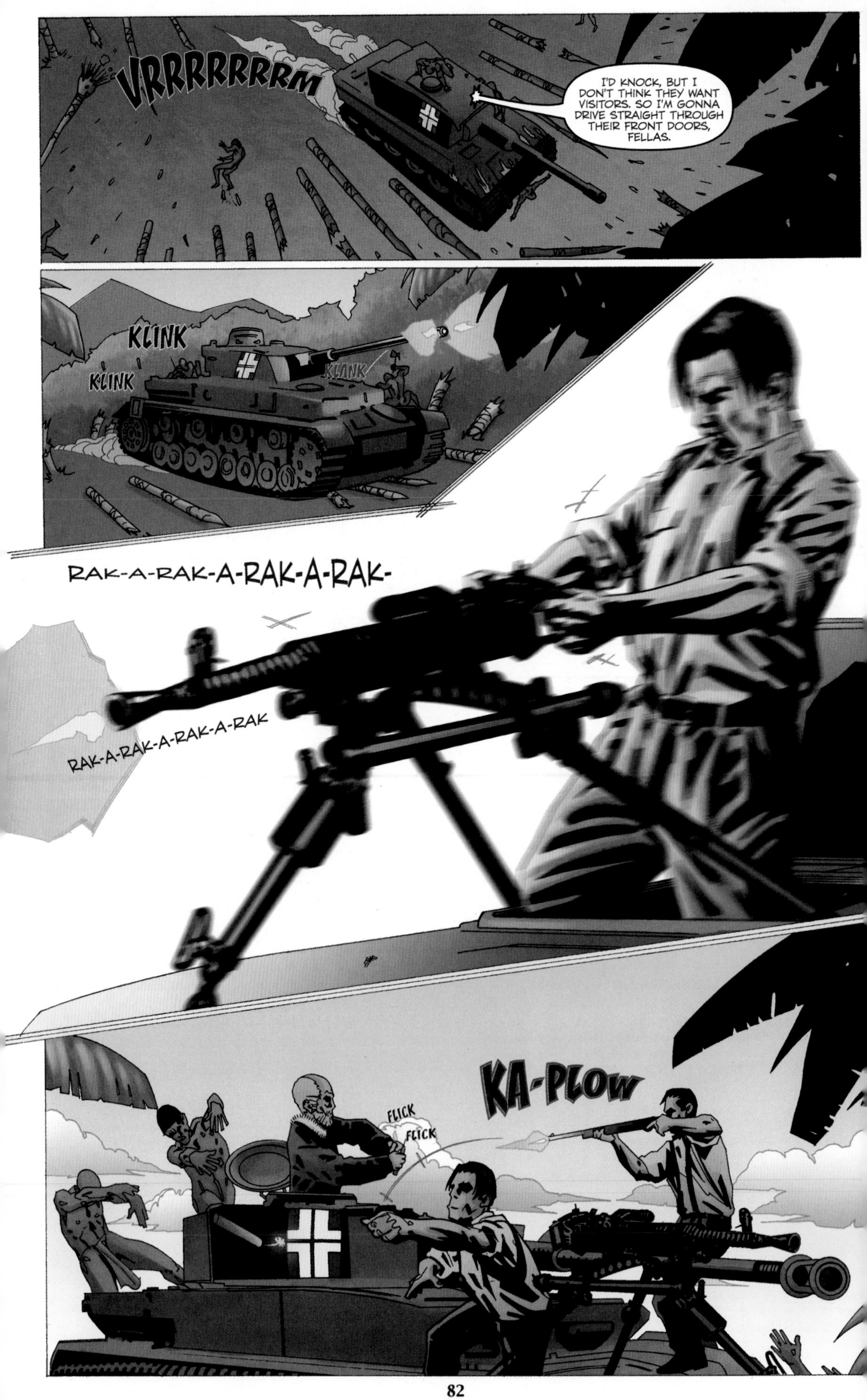
VRRRRRRRM
I'D KNOCK, BUT I DON'T THINK THEY WANT VISITORS. SO I'M GONNA DRIVE STRAIGHT THROUGH THEIR FRONT DOORS, FELLAS.
KLINK
KLINK
KLANK
RAK-A-RAK-A-RAK-A-RAK-
RAK-A-RAK-A-RAK-A-RAK
KA-PLOW
FLICK
FLICK

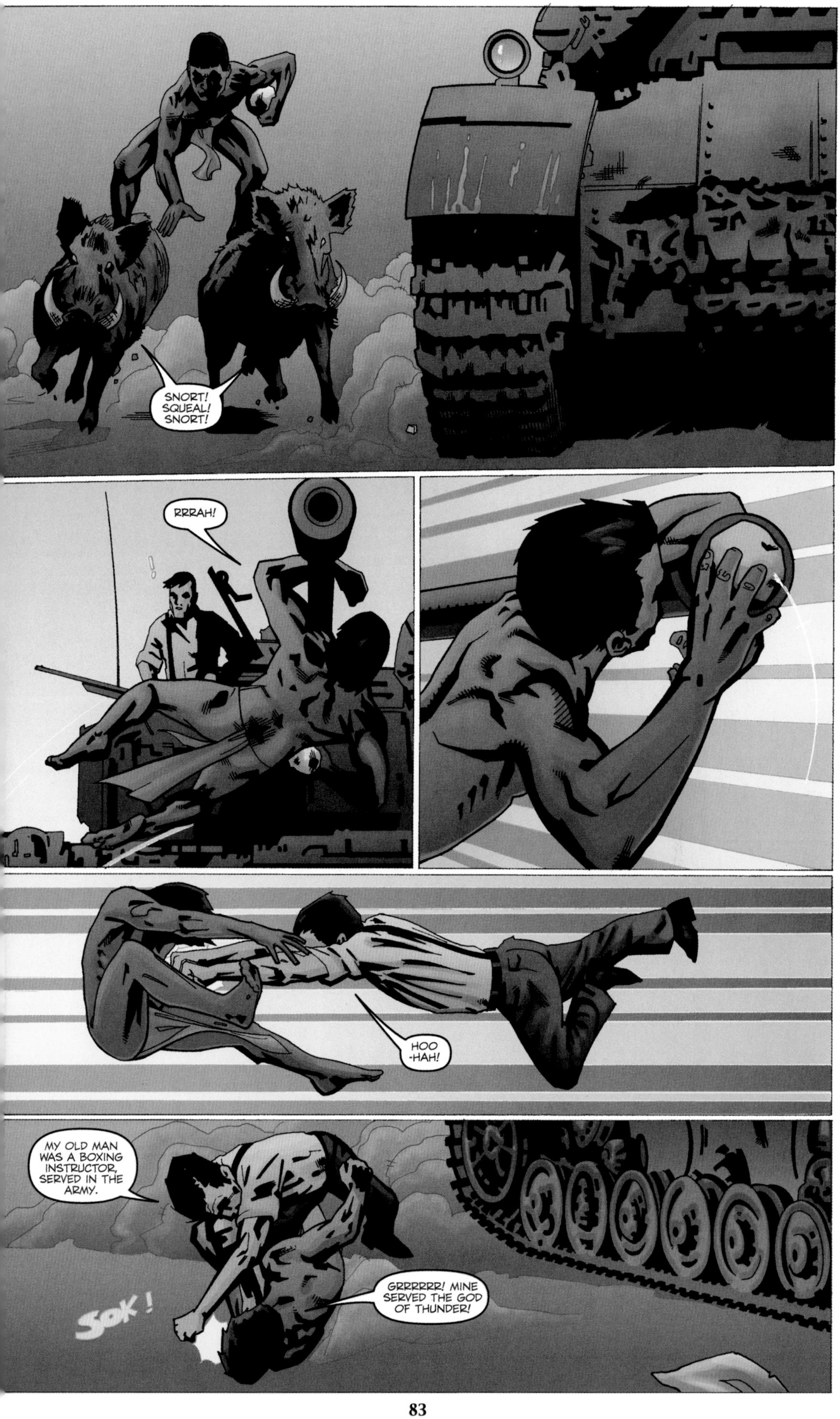
SNORT! SQUEAL! SNORT!
RRRAH!
!
HOO -HAH!
MY OLD MAN WAS A BOXING INSTRUCTOR, SERVED IN THE ARMY.
GRRRRRR! MINE SERVED THE GOD OF THUNDER!
SOK!

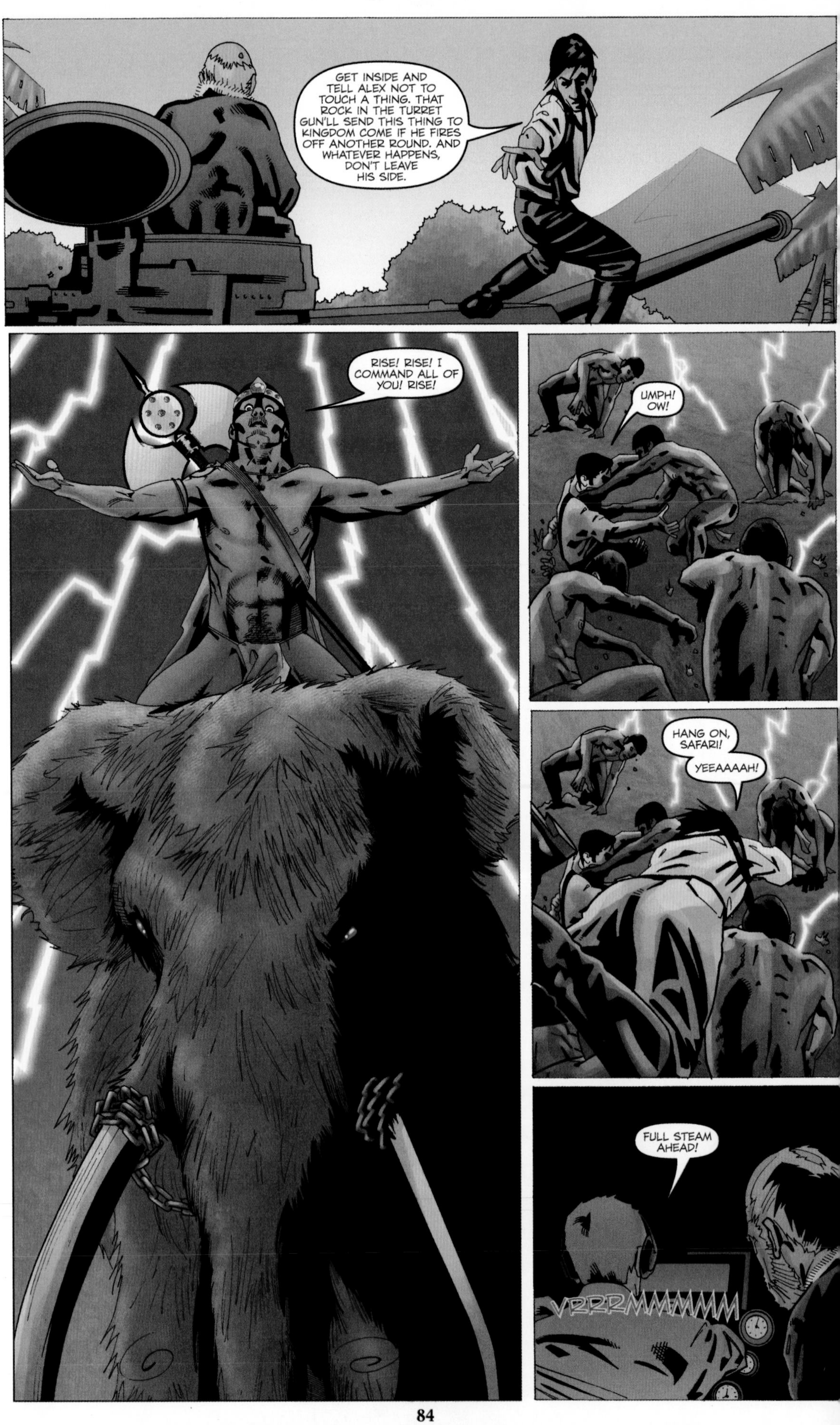
GET INSIDE AND TELL ALEX NOT TO TOUCH A THING. THAT ROCK IN THE TURRET GUN'LL SEND THIS THING TO KINGDOM COME IF HE FIRES OFF ANOTHER ROUND. AND WHATEVER HAPPENS, DON'T LEAVE HIS SIDE.
RISE! RISE! I COMMAND ALL OF YOU! RISE!
UMPH! OW!
HANG ON, SAFARI!
YEEAAAAH!
FULL STEAM AHEAD!
VRRRMMMMMM

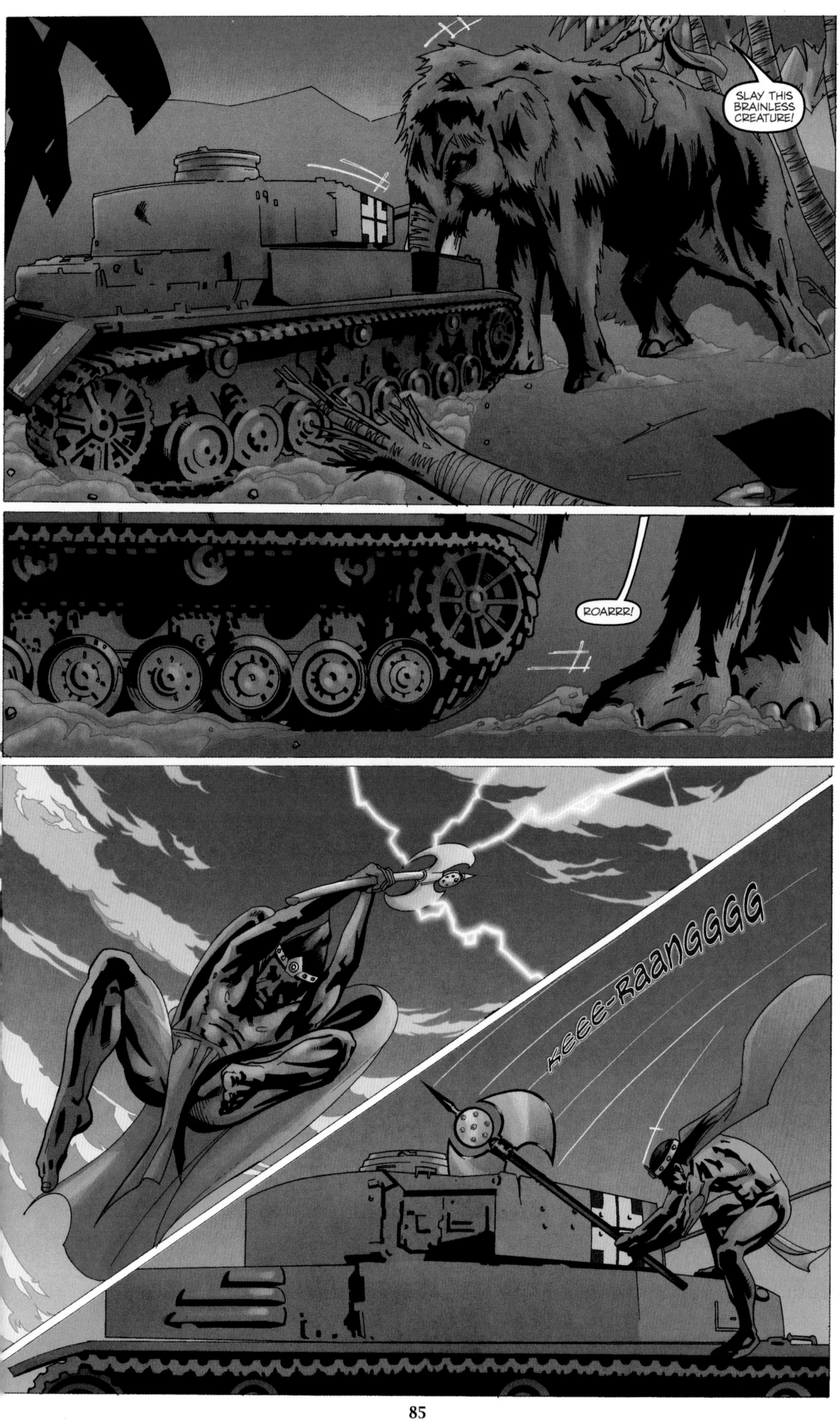
SLAY THIS BRAINLESS CREATURE!
ROARRR!
KEEE-RAANGGGG

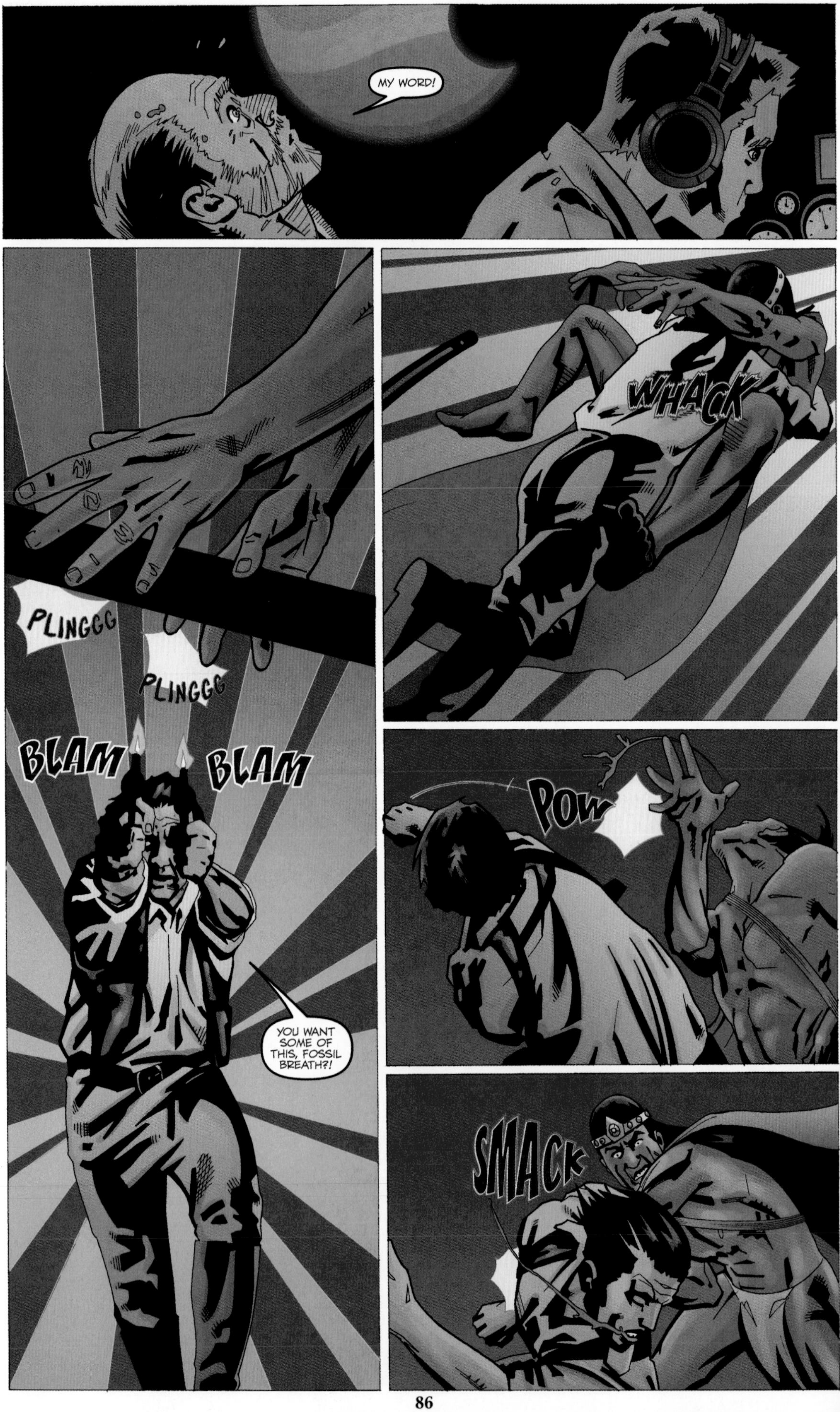
MY WORD!
WHACK
PLINGGG
PLINGGG
BLAM
BLAM
YOU WANT SOME OF THIS, FOSSIL BREATH?!
POW
SMACK

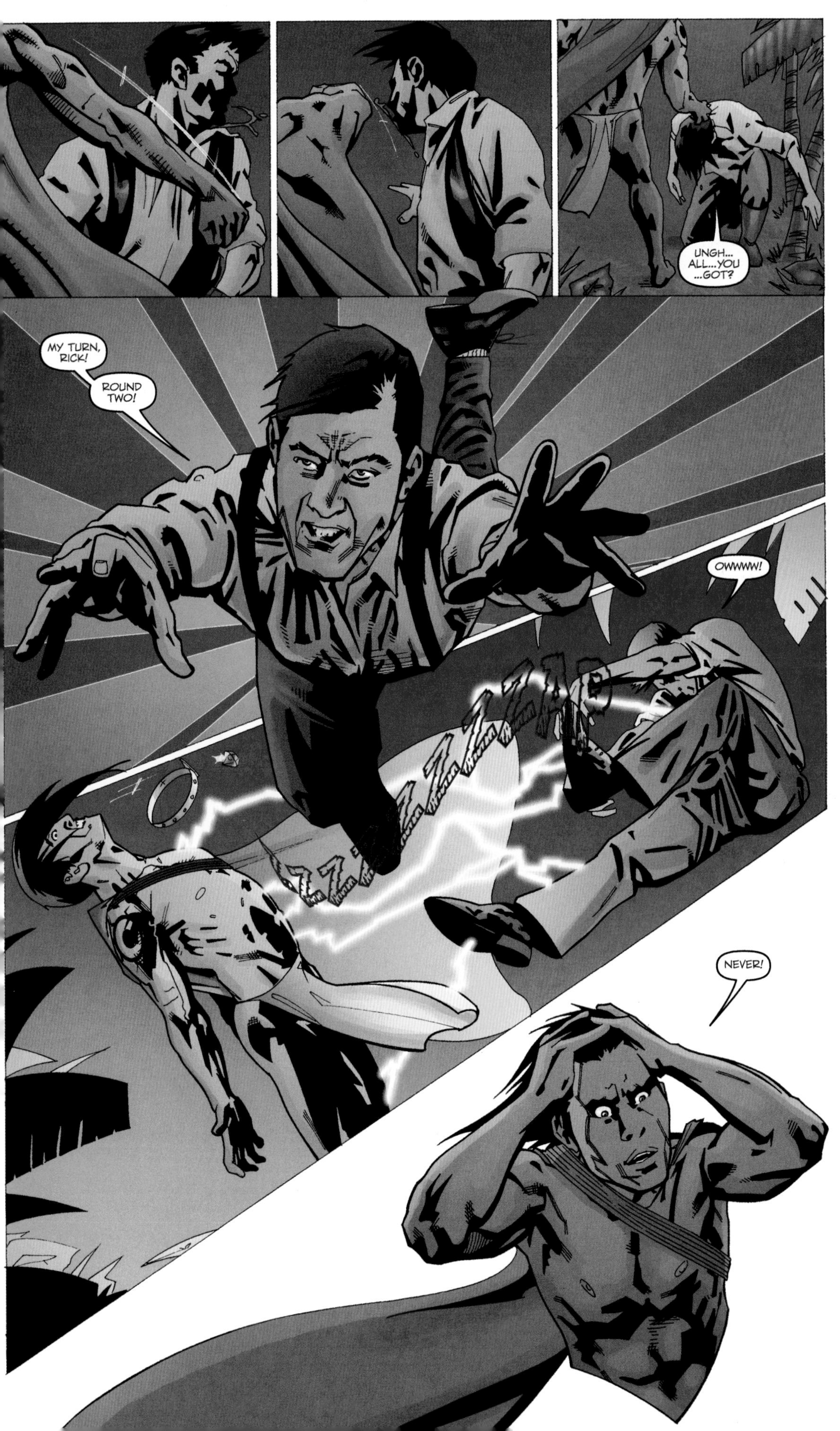
UNGH... ALL...YOU ...GOT?
MY TURN, RICK!
ROUND TWO!
OWWWW!
NEVER!

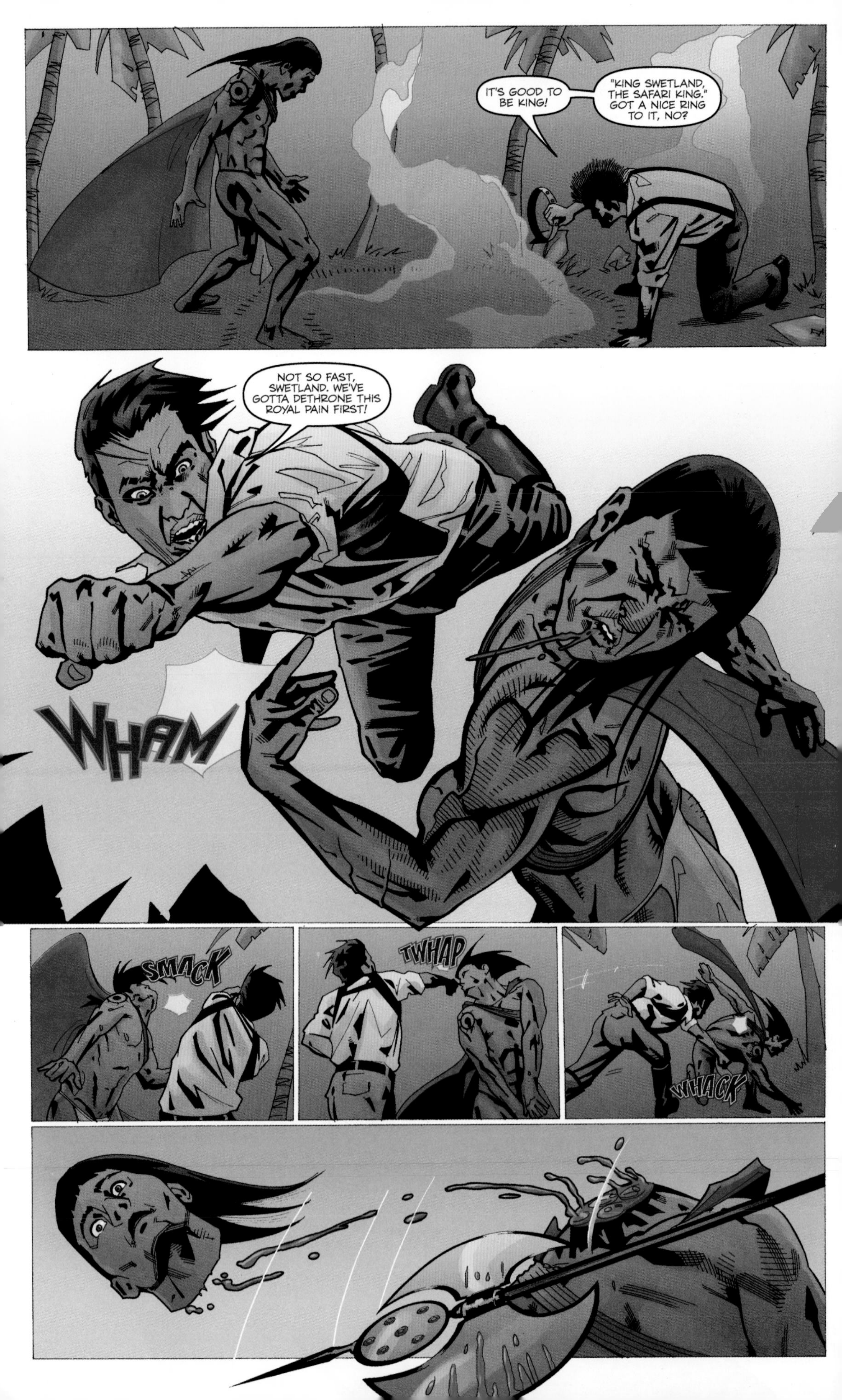
IT'S GOOD TO BE KING!
"KING SWETLAND, THE SAFARI KING." GOT A NICE RING TO IT, NO?
NOT SO FAST, SWETLAND. WE'VE GOTTA DETHRONE THIS ROYAL PAIN FIRST!
WHAM
SMACK
TWHAP
WHACK

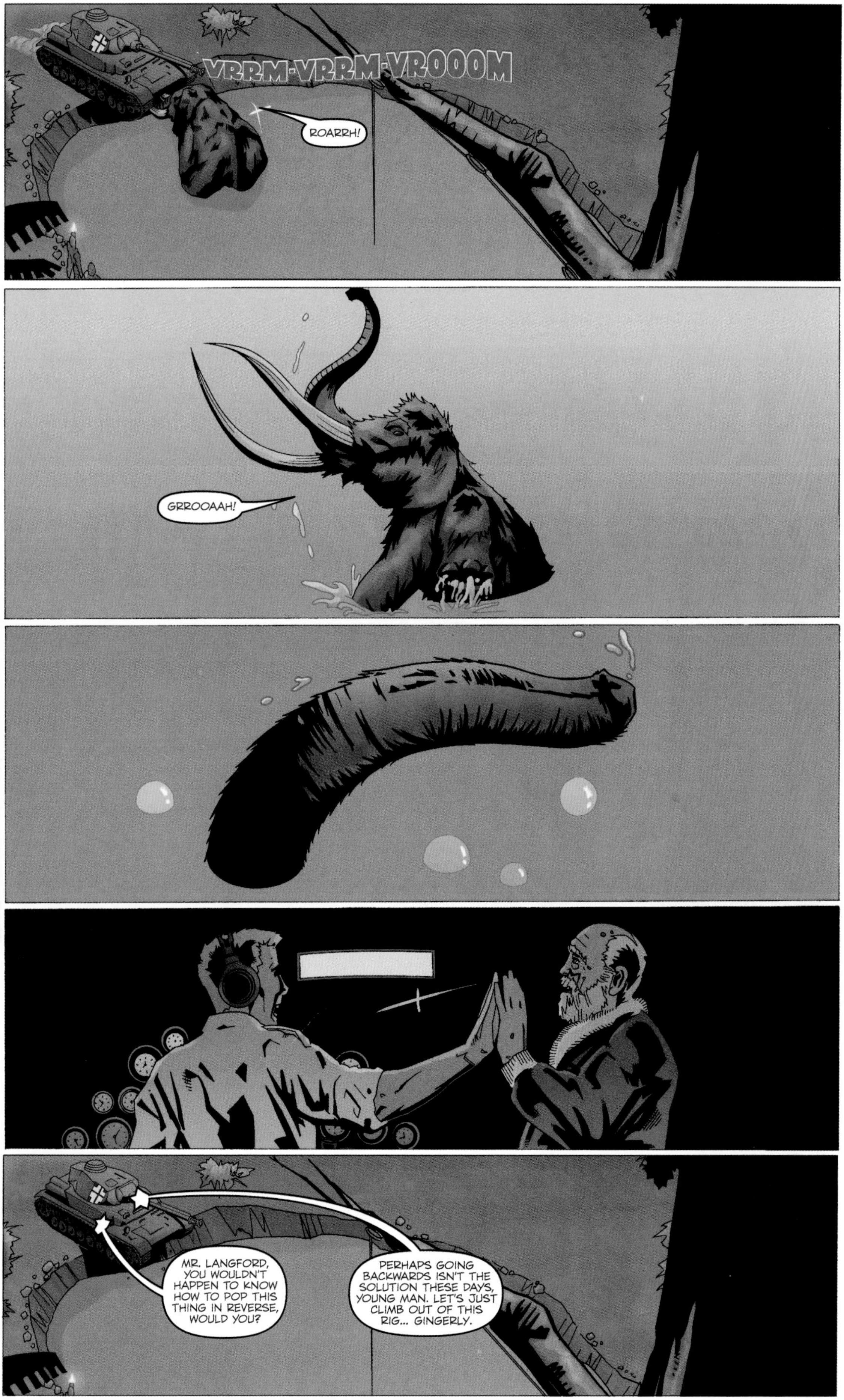
VRRM-VRRM-VROOOM
ROARRH!
GRROOAAH!
MR. LANGFORD, YOU WOULDN'T HAPPEN TO KNOW HOW TO POP THIS THING IN REVERSE, WOULD YOU?
PERHAPS GOING BACKWARDS ISN'T THE SOLUTION THESE DAYS, YOUNG MAN. LET'S JUST CLIMB OUT OF THIS RIG... GINGERLY.

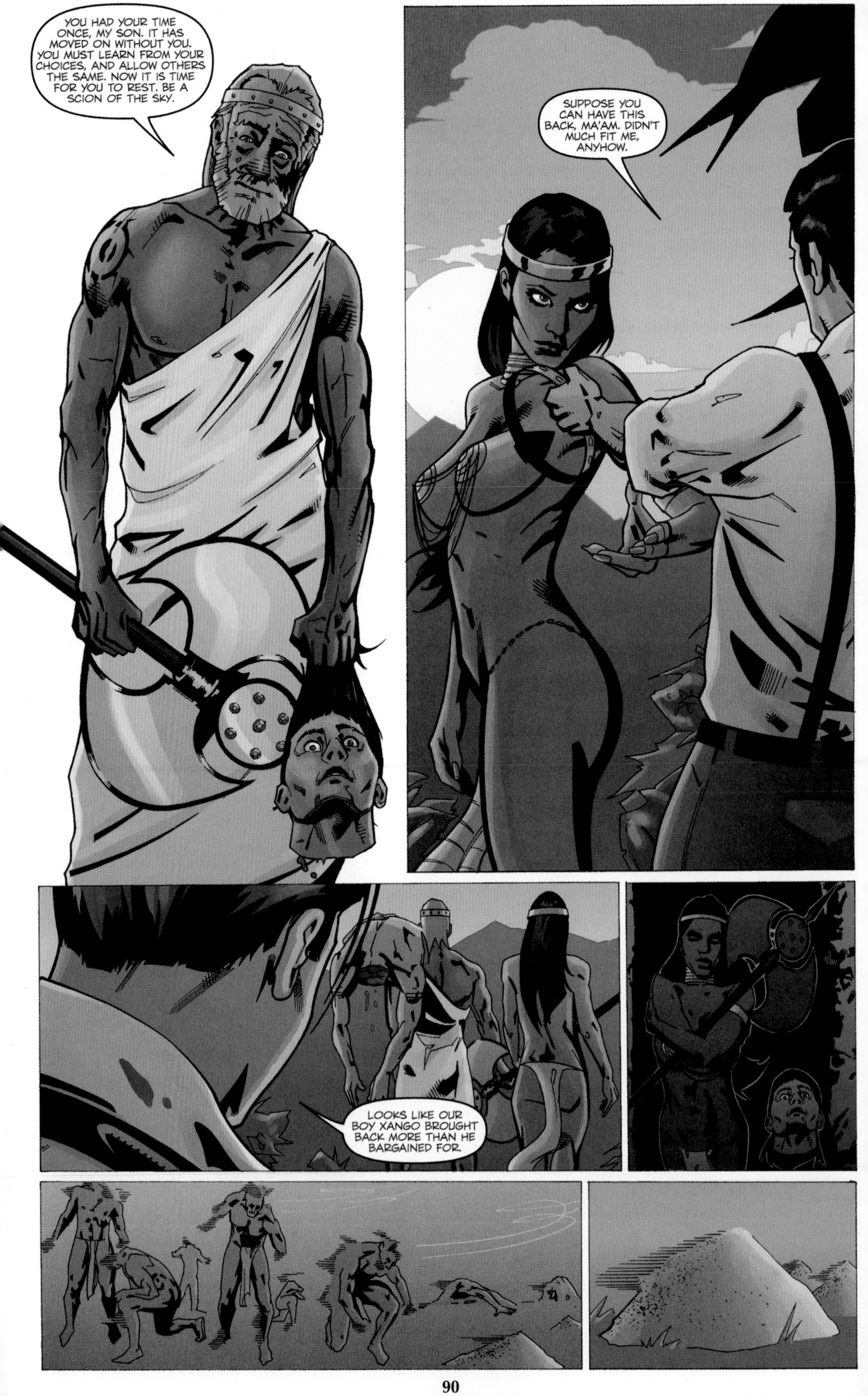
YOU HAD YOUR TIME ONCE, MY SON. IT HAS MOVED ON WITHOUT YOU. YOU MUST LEARN FROM YOUR CHOICES, AND ALLOW OTHERS THE SAME. NOW IT IS TIME FOR YOU TO REST. BE A SCION OF THE SKY.
SUPPOSE YOU CAN HAVE THIS BACK, MA'AM. DIDN'T MUCH FIT ME, ANYHOW.
LOOKS LIKE OUR BOY XANGO BROUGHT BACK MORE THAN HE BARGAINED FOR.

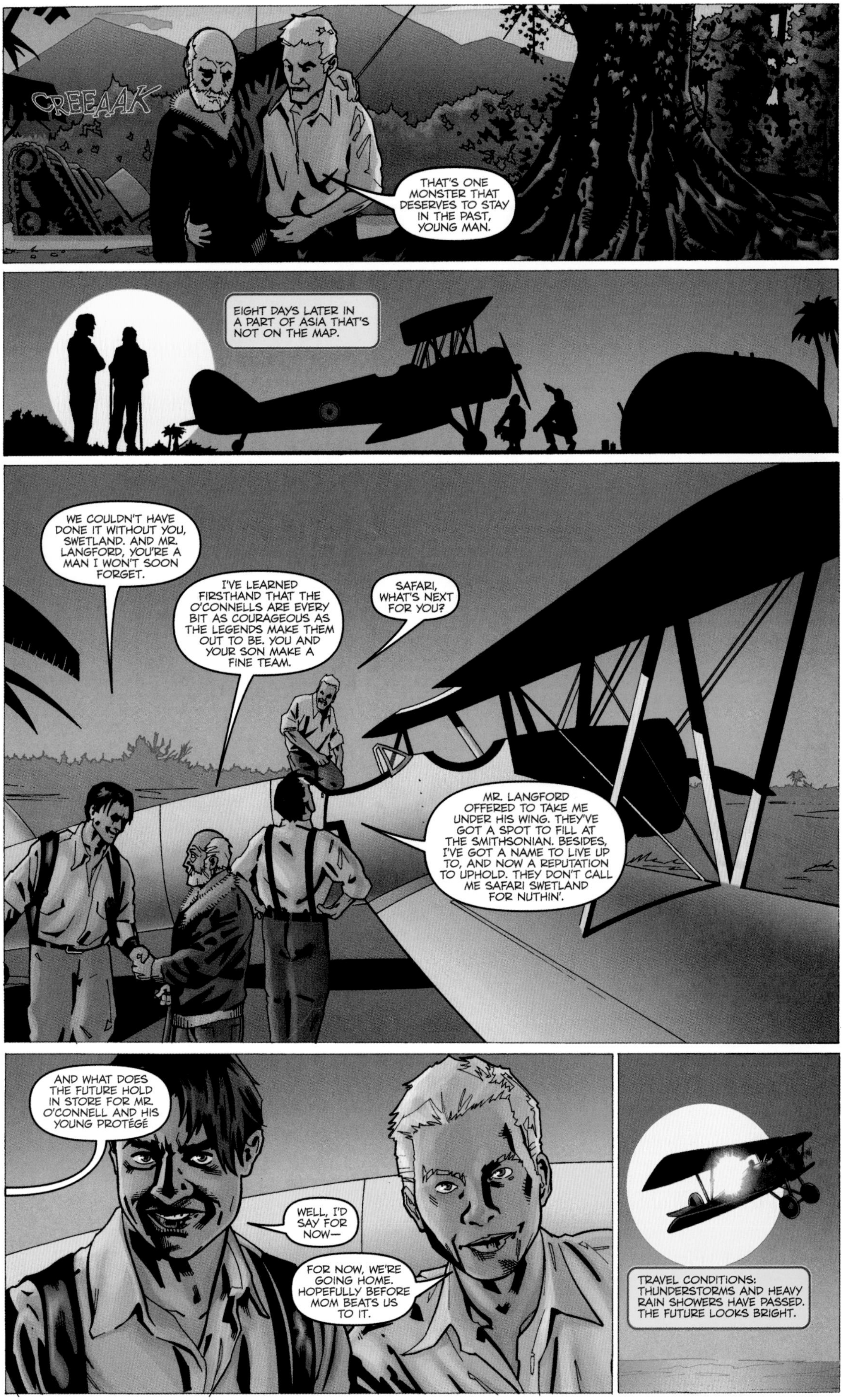
CREEAAK
THAT'S ONE MONSTER THAT DESERVES TO STAY IN THE PAST, YOUNG MAN.
EIGHT DAYS LATER IN A PART OF ASIA THAT'S NOT ON THE MAP.
WE COULDN'T HAVE DONE IT WITHOUT YOU, SWETLAND. AND MR. LANGFORD, YOU'RE A MAN I WON'T SOON FORGET.
I'VE LEARNED FIRSTHAND THAT THE O'CONNELLS ARE EVERY BIT AS COURAGEOUS AS THE LEGENDS MAKE THEM OUT TO BE. YOU AND YOUR SON MAKE A FINE TEAM.
SAFARI, WHAT'S NEXT FOR YOU?
MR. LANGFORD OFFERED TO TAKE ME UNDER HIS WING. THEY'VE GOT A SPOT TO FILL AT THE SMITHSONIAN. BESIDES, I'VE GOT A NAME TO LIVE UP TO, AND NOW A REPUTATION TO UPHOLD. THEY DON'T CALL ME SAFARI SWETLAND FOR NUTHIN'.
AND WHAT DOES THE FUTURE HOLD IN STORE FOR MR. O'CONNELL AND HIS YOUNG PROTÉGÉ
WELL, I'D SAY FOR NOW—
FOR NOW, WE'RE GOING HOME. HOPEFULLY BEFORE MOM BEATS US TO IT.
TRAVEL CONDITIONS: THUNDERSTORMS AND HEAVY RAIN SHOWERS HAVE PASSED. THE FUTURE LOOKS BRIGHT.

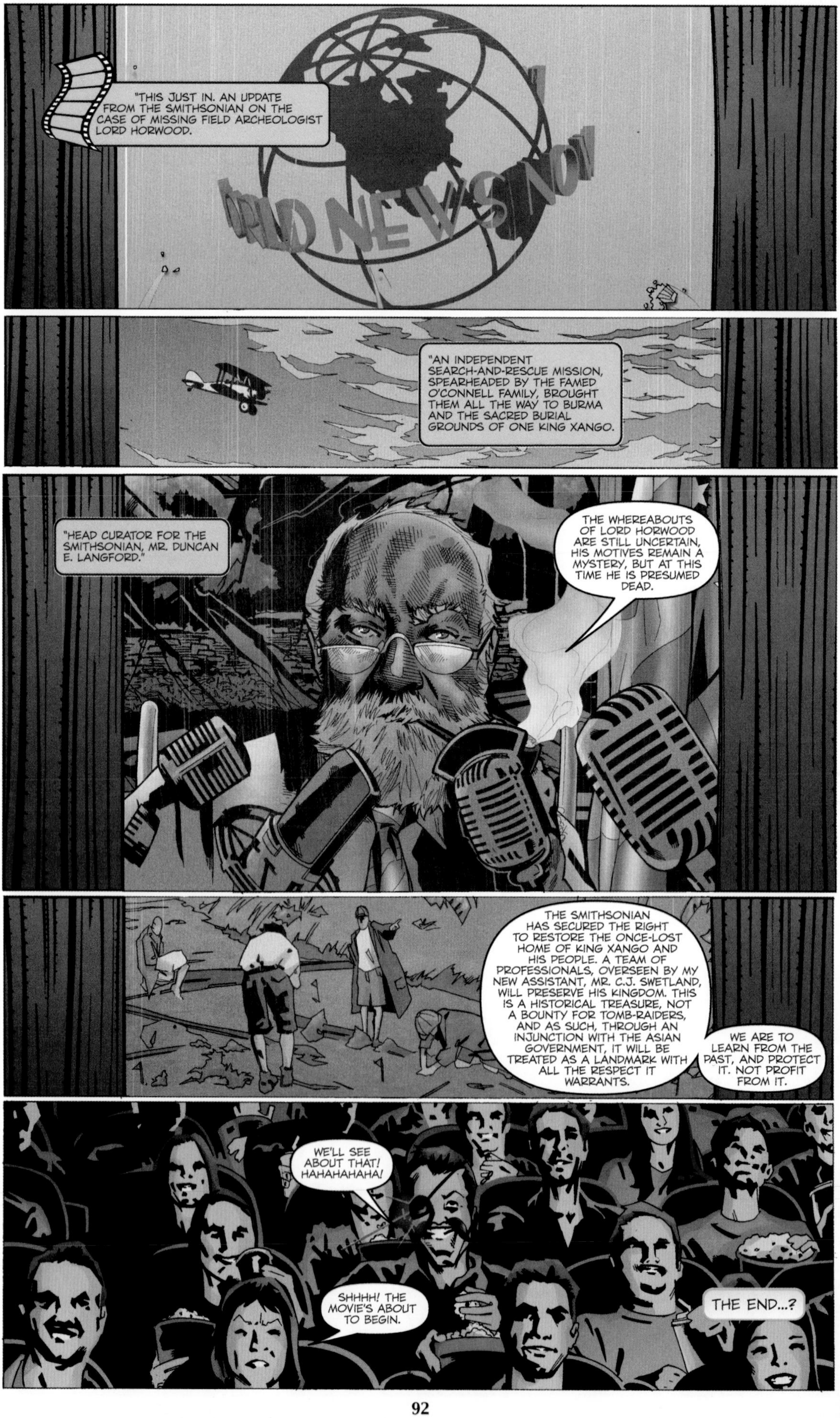
"THIS JUST IN. AN UPDATE FROM THE SMITHSONIAN ON THE CASE OF MISSING FIELD ARCHEOLOGIST LORD HORWOOD.
WORLD NEWS NOW
"AN INDEPENDENT SEARCH-AND-RESCUE MISSION, SPEARHEADED BY THE FAMED O'CONNELL FAMILY, BROUGHT THEM ALL THE WAY TO BURMA AND THE SACRED BURIAL GROUNDS OF ONE KING XANGO.
"HEAD CURATOR FOR THE SMITHSONIAN, MR. DUNCAN E. LANGFORD."
THE WHEREABOUTS OF LORD HORWOOD ARE STILL UNCERTAIN, HIS MOTIVES REMAIN A MYSTERY, BUT AT THIS TIME HE IS PRESUMED DEAD.
THE SMITHSONIAN HAS SECURED THE RIGHT TO RESTORE THE ONCE-LOST HOME OF KING XANGO AND HIS PEOPLE. A TEAM OF PROFESSIONALS, OVERSEEN BY MY NEW ASSISTANT, MR. C.J. SWETLAND, WILL PRESERVE HIS KINGDOM. THIS IS A HISTORICAL TREASURE, NOT A BOUNTY FOR TOMB-RAIDERS, AND AS SUCH, THROUGH AN INJUNCTION WITH THE ASIAN GOVERNMENT, IT WILL BE TREATED AS A LANDMARK WITH ALL THE RESPECT IT WARRANTS.
WE ARE TO LEARN FROM THE PAST, AND PROTECT IT. NOT PROFIT FROM IT.
WE'LL SEE ABOUT THAT! HAHAHAHAHA!
SHHHH! THE MOVIE'S ABOUT TO BEGIN.
THE END...?

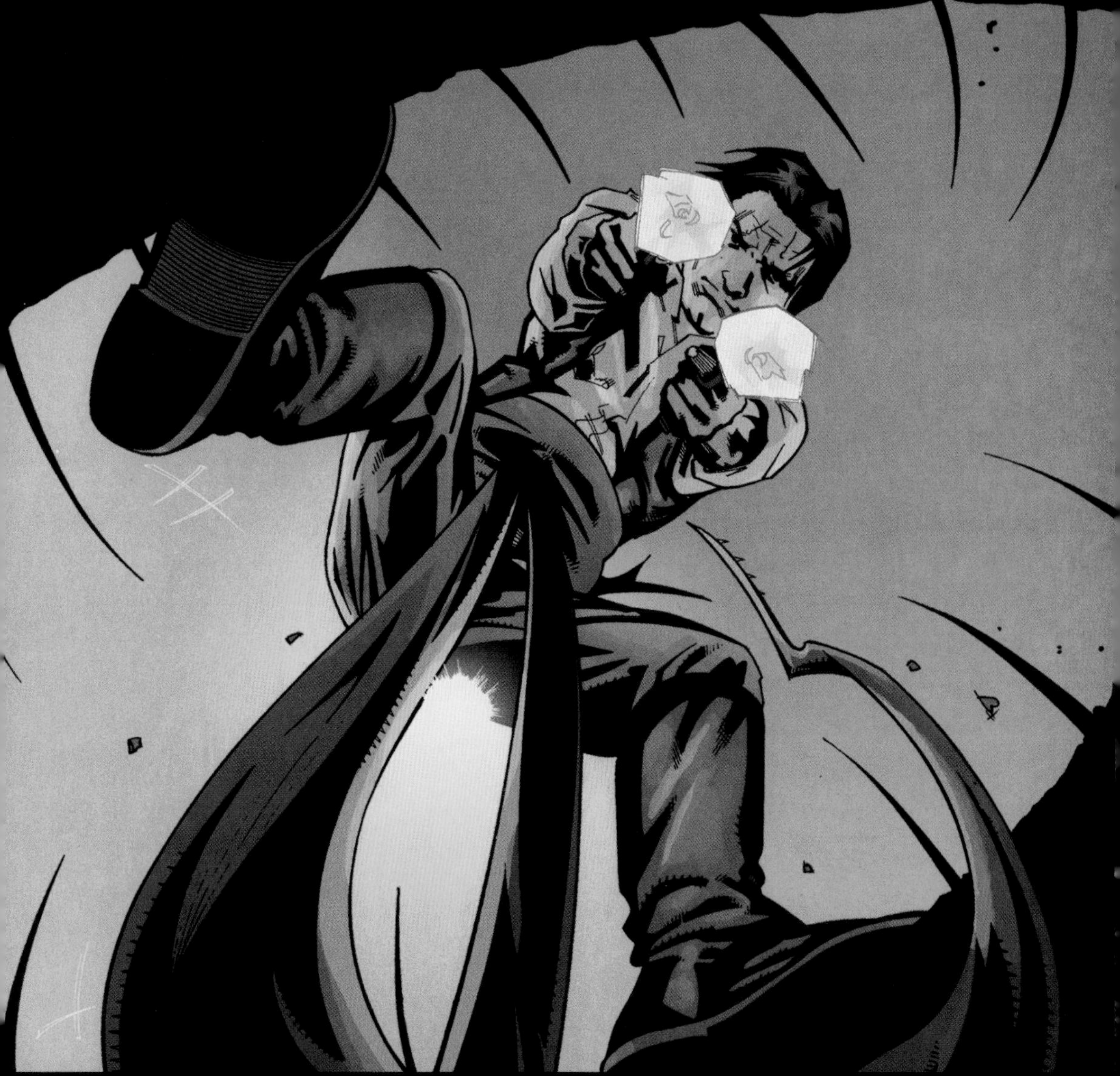

IMAGE GALLERY

ART BY STEPHEN MOONEY
COLORS BY LISA JACKSON

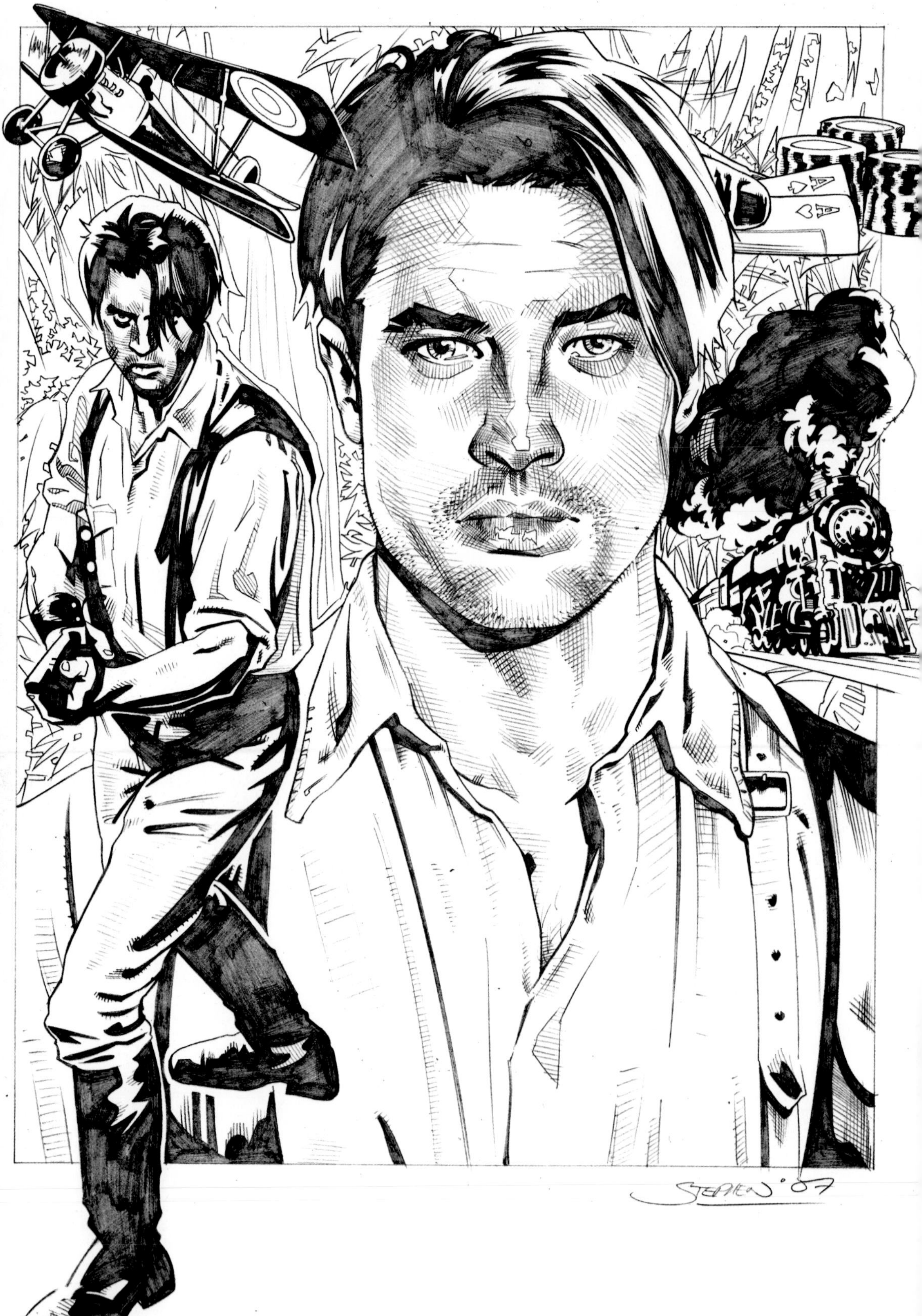
STEPHEN '07

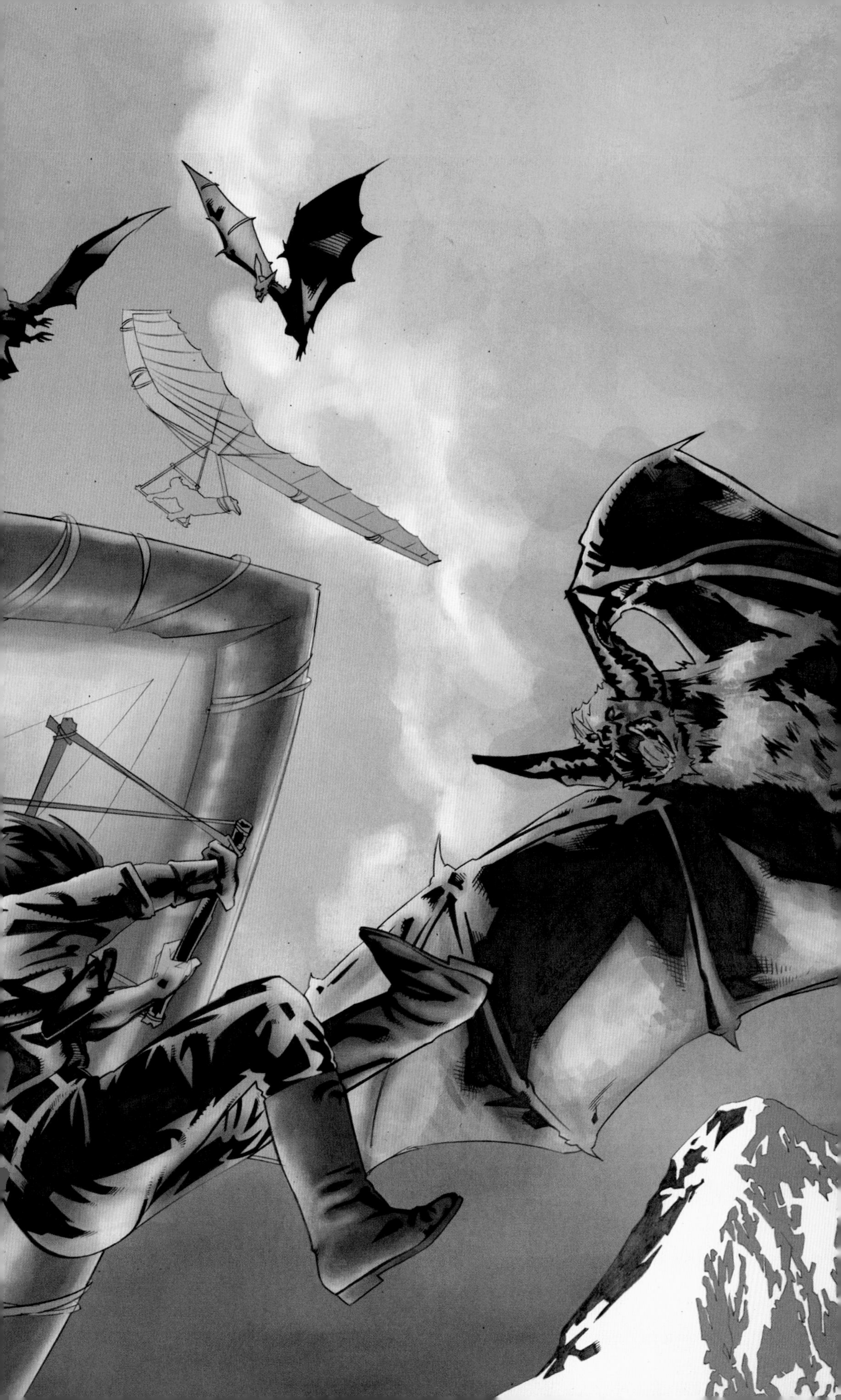

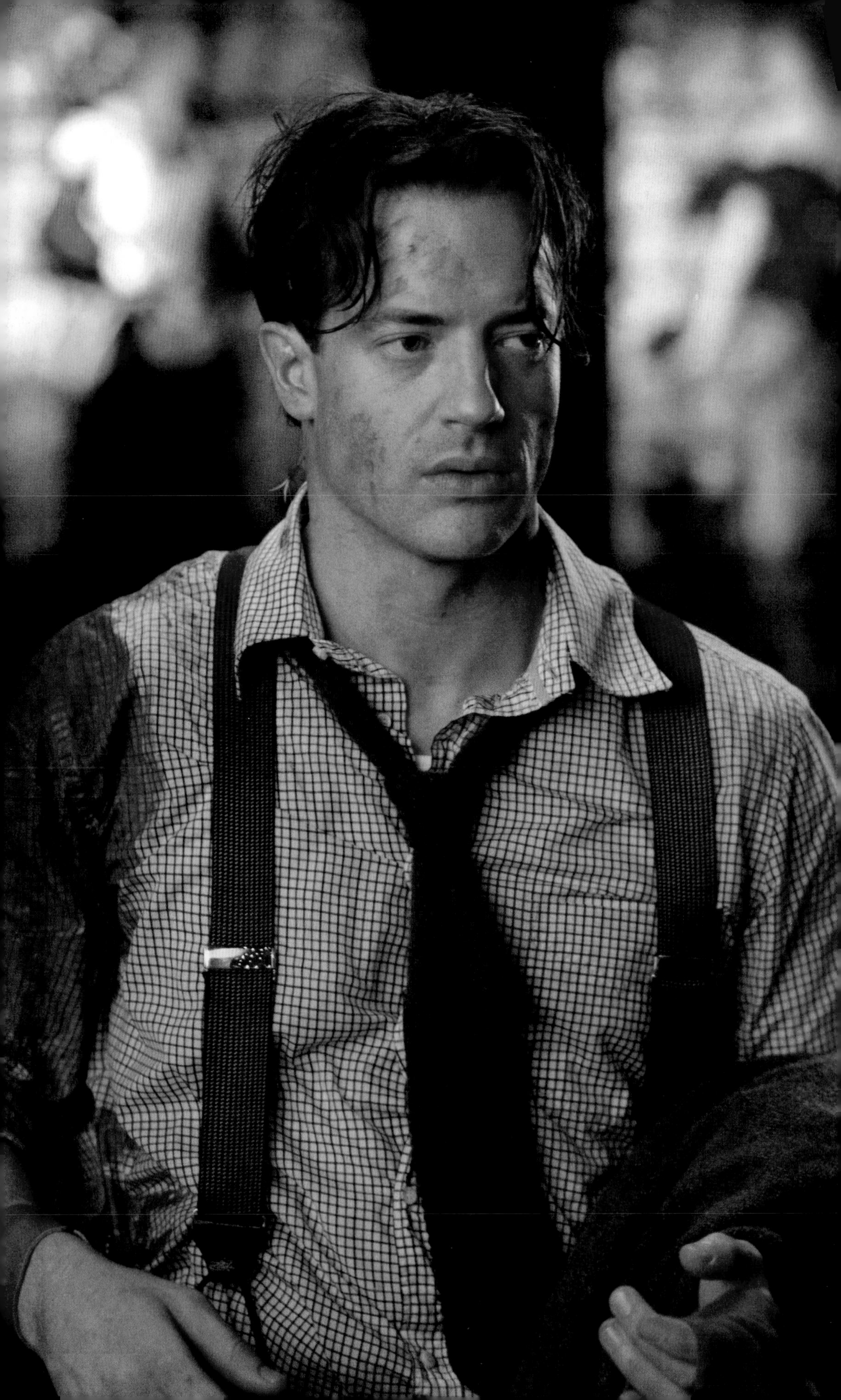

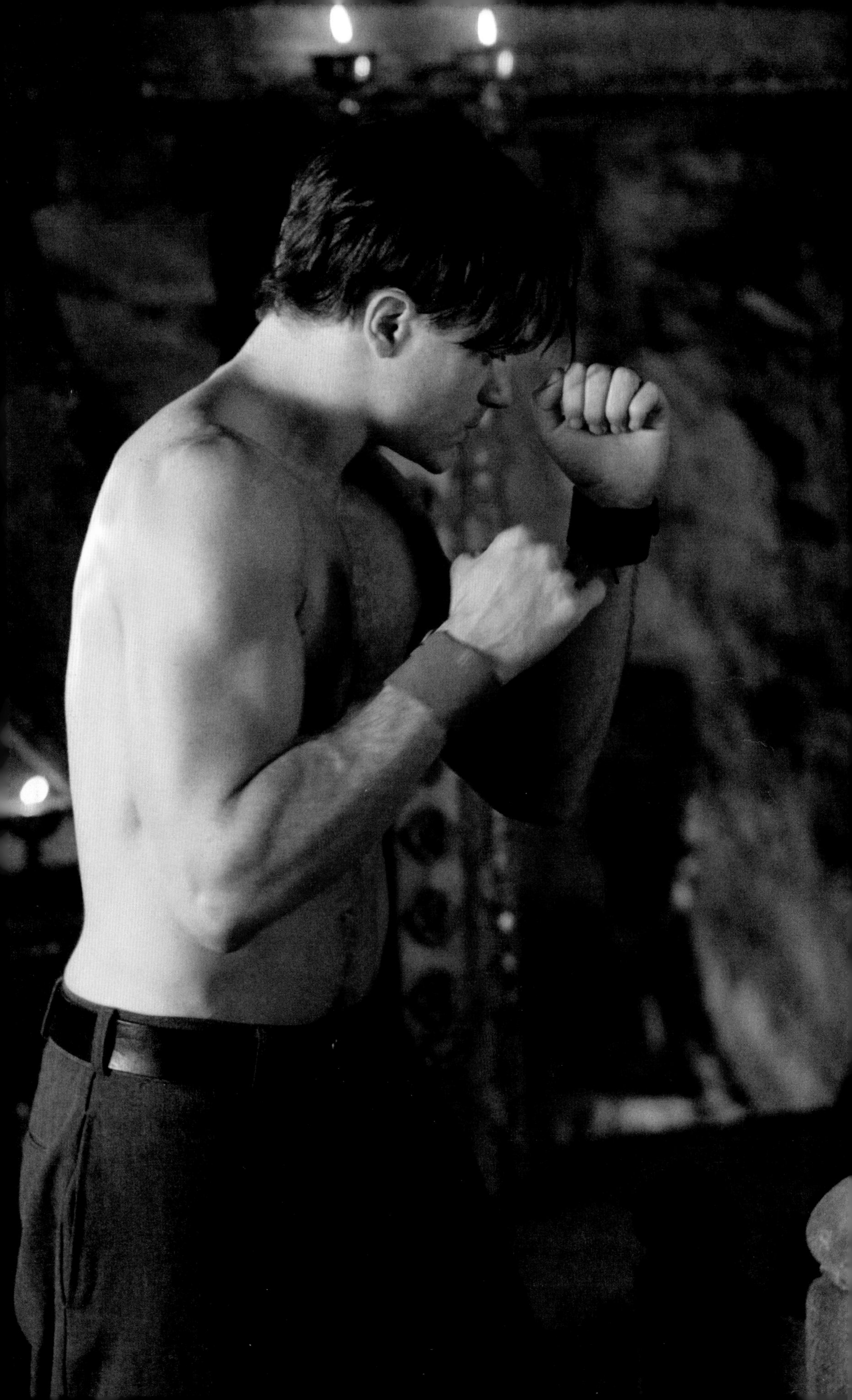

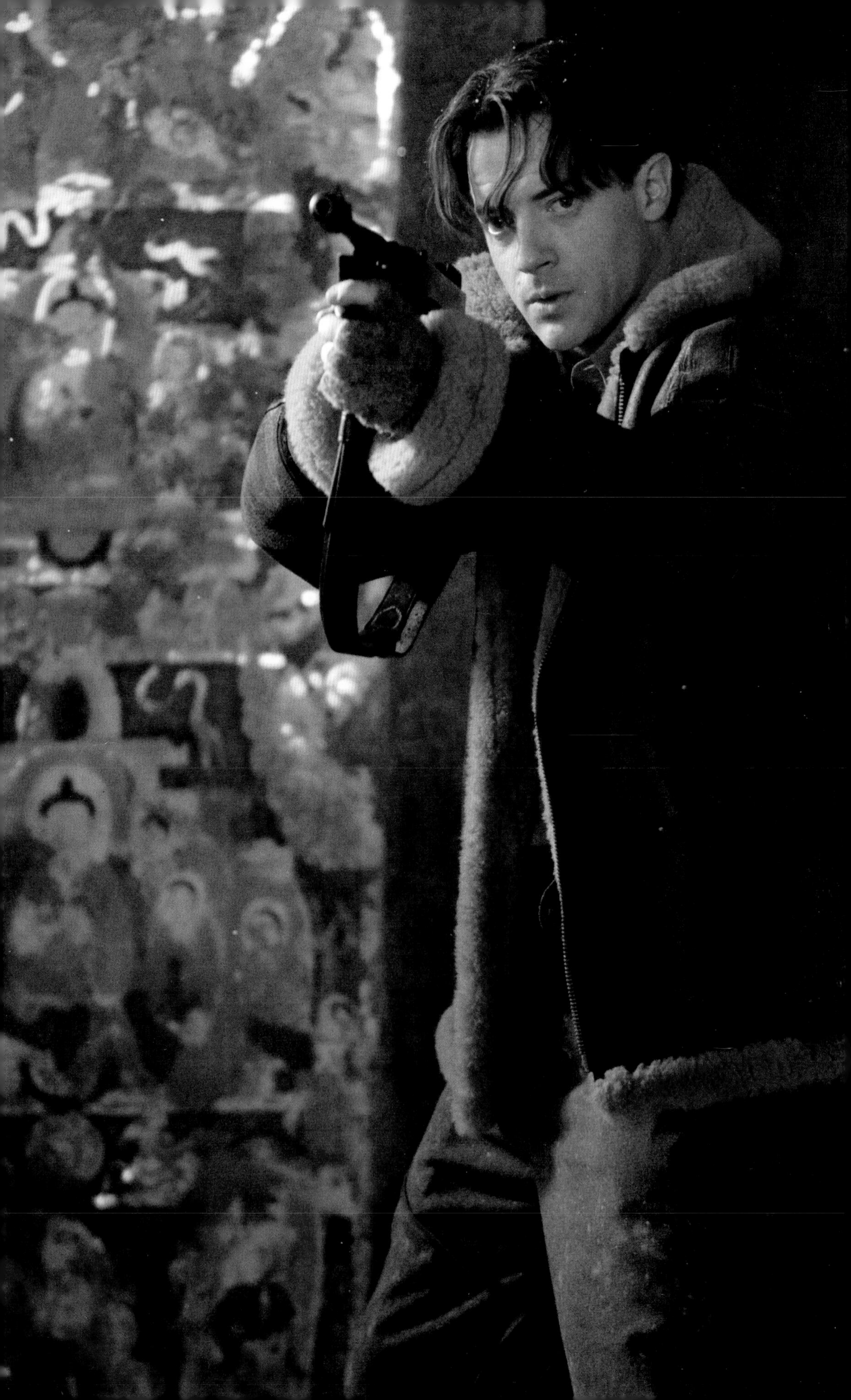